Siegel's
EVIDENCE

Essay and Multiple-Choice Questions and Answers

By

BRIAN N. SIEGEL

J.D., Columbia Law School

Siegel's Series

Published by

Siegel's Evidence, 3rd Edition (1996)
Emanuel Publishing Corp. • 1865 Palmer Avenue • Larchmont, NY 10538

About the Author

Professor Brian N. Siegel received his *Juris Doctorate* from Columbia Law School, where he was designated a Harlan Fiske Stone Scholar for academic excellence. He is the author of *How to Succeed in Law School* and numerous works pertaining to preparation for the California Bar examination. Professor Siegel has taught as a member of the adjunct faculty at Pepperdine School of Law and Whittier College School of Law, as well as for the UCLA Extension Program.

Acknowledgment

The authors gratefully acknowledge the assistance of the California Committee of Bar Examiners which provided access to questions upon which many of the essay questions in this book are based.

Introduction

Although your grades are a significant factor in obtaining a summer internship or permanent position at a law firm, no formalized preparation for finals is offered at most law schools. Students, for the most part, are expected to fend for themselves in learning the exam-taking process. Ironically, law school exams ordinarily bear little correspondence to the teaching methods used by professors during the school year. They require you to spend most of your time briefing cases. Although many claim this is "great preparation" for issue-spotting on exams, it really isn't. Because you focus on one principle of law at a time, you don't get practice in relating one issue to another or in developing a picture of the entire course. When exams finally come, you're forced to make an abrupt 180-degree turn. Suddenly, you are asked to recognize, define and discuss a variety of issues buried within a single multi-issue fact pattern. In most schools, you are then asked to select among a number of possible answers, all of which look inviting but only one of which is right.

The comprehensive course outline you've created so diligently and with such pain, means little if you're unable to apply its contents on your final exams. There is a vast difference between reading opinions in which the legal principles are clearly stated, and applying those same principles to hypothetical exams and multiple choice questions.

The purpose of this book is to help you bridge the gap between memorizing a rule of law and **_understanding how to use it_** in the context of an exam. After an initial overview describing the exam writing process, you will be presented with a large number of hypotheticals which test your ability to write analytical essays and to pick the right answers to multiple-choice questions. ***Do them — all of them!*** Then review the suggested answers which follow. You'll find that the key to superior grades lies in applying your knowledge through questions and answers, not rote memory.

In the sample answers (both to the essays and to the multiple choice), you will notice references to *Emanuel* on *Evidence*. The reference tells you where in the outline to find the relevant discussion. Thus, a reference to "Ch. 2–VI(A)(3)(d)" means Chapter 2, section (Roman numeral) VI, capital letter A within that section, number 3, paragraph d. This notation is perhaps less convenient than page numbers, but it helps us keep the reference constant from one edition of a book to the next.

GOOD LUCK !

Table of Contents

Preparing Effectively for Essay Examinations

Essay Questions

Essay Answers

Multiple Choice Questions

Answers to Multiple Choice Questions

Tables and Index

Preparing Effectively for Essay Examinations[1]

To achieve superior scores on essay exams, a student must (i) learn and understand "blackletter" principles and rules of law for each subject, and (ii) analyze how those principles of law arise within a test fact pattern. One of the most common misconceptions about law school is that you must memorize each word on every page of your casebooks or outlines to do well on exams. The reality is that you can commit an entire casebook to memory and still do poorly on an exam. Reviewing hundreds of student answers has shown us that most students can recite the rules. The ones who do **best** on exams understand how problems (issues) stem from the rules which they have memorized and how to communicate their analysis of these issues to the grader. The following pages cover what you need to know to achieve superior scores on your law school essay exams.

The "ERC" Process

To study effectively for law school exams you must be able to *"ERC"* (*E*lementize, *R*ecognize, and *C*onceptualize) each legal principle listed in the table of contents of your casebooks and course outlines. *Elementizing* means reducing the legal theories and rules you learn, down to a concise, straightforward statement of their essential elements. Without a knowledge of these precise elements, it is not possible to anticipate all of the potential issues which can arise under them.

For example, if you are asked, "what is self-defense?", it is *not* sufficient to say, "self-defense is permitted when, if someone is about to hit you, you can prevent him from doing it." This layperson description would leave a grader wondering if you had actually attended law school. An accurate elementization of the self-defense principle would be something like this: "Where one reasonably believes she is in imminent danger of an offensive touching, she may assert whatever force she reasonably believes necessary under the circumstances to prevent the offensive touching from occurring." This formulation correctly shows that there are four separate, distinct elements which must be satisfied for this defense to be successfully asserted: (i) the actor must have a *reasonable belief* that (ii) the touching which he seeks to prevent is *offensive*, (iii) the offensive touching is *imminent*, and (iv) the actor must use no greater force than she *reasonably believes is necessary under the circumstances* to prevent the offensive touching from occurring.

---

1. To illustrate the principles of effective exam preparation, we have used examples from Torts and Constitutional Law. However, these principles apply to all subjects. One of the most difficult tasks faced by law students is learning how to apply principles from one area of the law to another. We leave it to you, the reader, to think of comparable examples for the subject-matter of this book.

Recognizing means perceiving or anticipating which words within a legal principle are likely to be the source of issues, and how those issues are likely to arise within a hypothetical fact pattern. With respect to the self-defense concept, there are four ***potential*** issues. Did the actor reasonably believe that the person against whom the defense is being asserted was about to make an offensive contact upon her? Was the contact imminent? Would the contact have been offensive? Did the actor use only such force as she reasonably believed was necessary to prevent the imminent, offensive touching?

Conceptualizing means imagining situations in which each of the elements of a rule of law have given rise to factual issues. ***Unless a student can illustrate to herself an application of each element of a rule of law, she does not truly understand the legal principles behind the rule!*** In our opinion, the inability to conjure up hypothetical problems involving particular rules of law foretells a likelihood that issues involving those rules will be missed on an exam. It is therefore ***crucial*** to (i) ***recognize*** that issues result from the interaction of facts with the appropriate words defining a rule of law; and ii) develop the ability to ***conceptualize*** fact patterns involving each of the words contained in the rule

For example, an illustration of the "reasonable belief" portion of the self-defense principle in tort law might be the following:

> One evening, A and B had an argument at a bar. A screamed at B, "I'm going to get a knife and stab you!" A then ran out of the bar. B, who was armed with a concealed pistol, left the bar about 15 minutes later. As B was walking home, he suddenly heard running footsteps coming up from behind him. B drew his pistol, turned and shot the person advancing toward him (who was only about ten feet away when the shooting occurred). When B walked over to his victim, he recognized that the person he had killed was not A (but was instead another individual who had simply decided to take an evening jog). There would certainly be an issue whether B had a reasonable belief that the person who was running behind him was A. In the subsequent wrongful-death action, the victim's estate would certainly contend that the earlier threat by A was not enough to give B a reasonable belief that the person running behind him was A. B could certainly contend in rebuttal that given the prior altercation at the bar, A's threat, the darkness, and the fact that the incident occurred within a time frame soon after A's threat, his belief that A was about to attack him was "reasonable."

An illustration of how use of the word "imminent" might generate an issue is the following:

> X and Y had been feuding for some time. One afternoon, X suddenly attacked Y with a hunting knife. However, Y was able to wrest the knife away From X. At that point X retreated about four feet away from Y and screamed: "You were lucky this time, but next time I'll have a gun and you'll be finished." Y, having good reason to believe that X would subsequently carry out his threats (after all,

X had just attempted to kill Y), immediately thrust the knife into X's chest, killing him. While Y certainly had a reasonable belief that X would attempt to kill him the ***next time*** the two met, Y would probably ***not*** be able to successfully assert the self-defense privilege since the "imminency" element was absent.

A fact pattern illustrating the actor's right to use only that force which is reasonably necessary under the circumstances might be following:

D rolled up a newspaper and was about to strike E on the shoulder with it. As D pulled back his arm for the purpose of delivering the blow, E drew a knife and plunged it into D's chest. While E had every reason to believe that D was about to deliver an offensive impact on him, E probably could not successfully assert the self-defense privilege because the force he utilized in response was greater than reasonably necessary under the circumstances to prevent the impact. E could simply have deflected D's prospective blow or punched D away. The use of a knife constituted a degree of force by E which was ***not*** reasonable, given the minor injury which he would have suffered from the newspaper's impact.

"Mental gymnastics" such as these must be played with every element of every rule you learn.

Issue-Spotting

One of the keys to doing well on an essay examination is issue-spotting. In fact, issue spotting is ***the*** most important skill you will learn in law school. If you recognize all of the legal issues, you can always find an applicable rule of law (if there is any) by researching the issues. However, if you fail to perceive an issue, you may very well misadvise your client about the likelihood of success or failure. It is important to remember that (1) an issue is a question to be decided by the judge or jury; and (2) a question is "in issue" when it can be disputed or argued about at trial. The bottom line is that if ***you don't spot an issue, you can't discuss it***.

The key to issue-spotting is to approach a problem in the same way as an attorney would. Let's assume you're a lawyer and someone enters your office with a legal problem. He will recite the facts to you and give you any documents that may be pertinent. He will then want to know if he can sue (or be sued, if your client seeks to avoid liability). To answer your client's question intelligently, you will have to decide the following: (1) what theories can possibly be asserted by your client; (2) what defense or defenses can possibly be raised to these theories; (3) what issues may arise if these theories and defenses are asserted; (4) what arguments can each side make to persuade the factfinder to resolve the issue in his favor; and (5) finally, what will the ***likely*** outcome of each issue be. ***All the issues which can possibly arise at trial should be discussed in your answer.***

How to Discuss an Issue

Keep in mind that *rules of law are the guides to issues* (i.e., an issue arises where there is a question whether the facts do, or do not, satisfy an element of a rule); a rule of law *cannot dispose of an issue* unless the rule can reasonably be *applied to the facts.*

A good way to learn how to discuss an issue is to start with the following mini-hypothetical and the two student responses which follow it.

Mini-Hypothetical

A and B were involved in making a movie which was being filmed at a bar. The script called for A to appear to throw a bottle (which was actually a rubber prop) at B. The fluorescent lighting at the bar had been altered, the subdued blue lights being replaced with rather bright white lights. The cameraperson had stationed herself just to the left of the swinging doors which served as the main entrance to the bar. As the scene was unfolding, C, a regular patron of the bar, unwittingly walked into it. The guard who was stationed immediately out-side the bar, had momentarily left his post to visit the restroom. As C pushed the barroom doors inward, the left door panel knocked the camera to the ground with a resounding crash. The first (and only) thing which C saw, how-ever, was A (who was about 5 feet from C) getting ready to throw the bottle at B, who was at the other end of the bar (about 15 feet from A). Without hesita-tion, C pushed A to the ground and punched him in the face. Plastic surgery was required to restore A's profile to its Hollywood-handsome pre-altercation form.

Discuss A's right against C.

Pertinent Principles of Law:

1. Under the rule defining the prevention-of-crime privilege, if one sees that someone is about to commit what she reasonably believes to be a felony or misdemeanor involving a breach of the peace, she may exercise whatever degree of force is reasonably necessary under the circumstances to prevent that person from committing the crime.

2. Under the defense-of-others privilege, where one reasonably believes that someone is about to cause an offensive contact upon a third party, she may use whatever force is reasonably necessary under the circumstances to prevent the contact. Some jurisdictions, however, limit this privilege to situations in which the actor and the third party are related.

First Student Answer

"Did C commit an assault and battery upon A?

"An assault occurs where the defendant intentionally causes the plaintiff to be reasonably in apprehension of an imminent, offensive touching. The facts state that C punched A to the ground. Thus, a battery would have occurred at this point. We are also told that C punched A in the face. It is reasonable to assume that A saw the punch being thrown at him, and therefore A felt in imminent danger of an offensive touching. Based upon the facts, C is liable for an assault and battery upon A.

"Were C's actions justifiable under the defense-of-others privilege?

"C could successfully assert the defense of others and prevention of crime privileges. When C opened the bar doors, A appeared to be throwing the bottle at B. Although the "bottle" was actually a prop, C had no way of knowing this fact. Also, it was necessary for C to punch A in the face to assure that A could not get back up, retrieve the bottle, and again throw it at B. While the plastic surgery required by A is unfortunate, C could not be successfully charged with assault and battery."

Second Student Answer

"Assault and Battery:

"C committed an assault (causing A to be reasonably in apprehension of an imminent, offensive contact) when A saw C's punch about to hit him, and battery (causing an offensive contact upon A) when he (i) C knocked A to the ground, and (ii) C punched A.

"Defense-of-Others/Prevention-of-Crime Defenses:

"C would undoubtedly assert the privileges of defense-of-others (where defendant reasonably believed the plaintiff was about to make an offensive contact upon a third party, he was entitled to use whatever force was reasonably necessary to prevent the contact); and prevention-of-crime defense (where one reasonably believes another is about to commit a felony or misdemeanor involving a breach of the peace, he may exercise whatever force is reasonably necessary to prevent that person from committing a crime).

"A could contend that C was not reasonable in believing that A was about to cause harm to B because the enhanced lighting at the bar and camera crash should have indicated to C, a regular customer, that a movie was being filmed. However, C could probably successfully contend in rebuttal that his belief was reasonable in light of the facts that (i) he had not seen the camera when he attacked A, and (ii) instantaneous action was required (he did not have time to notice the enhanced lighting around the bar).

"A might also contend that the justification was forfeited because the degree of force used by C was not reasonable, since C did not have to punch A in the face after A had already been pushed to the ground (i.e., the danger to B was no longer present). However, C could argue in rebuttal that it was necessary to knockout A (an individual with apparently violent propensities) while the opportunity existed, rather than risk a drawn-out scuffle in which A might prevail. The facts do not indicate how big A and C were; but assuming C was not significantly larger than A, C's contention will probably be successful. If, however, C was significantly larger than A, the punch may have been excessive (since C could presumably have simply held A down)."

Critique

Let's examine the First Student Answer first. It mistakenly phrases as an "issue" the assault and battery committed by C upon A. While the actions creating these torts must be mentioned in the facts to provide a foundation for a discussion of the applicable privileges, there was no need to discuss them further because they were not the issue the examiners were testing for.

The structure of the initial paragraph of First Student Answer is also incorrect. After an assault is defined in the first sentence, the second sentence abruptly describes the facts necessary to constitute the commission of a battery. The third sentence then sets forth the elements of a battery. The fourth sentence completes the discussion of assault by describing the facts pertaining to that tort. The two-sentence break between the original mention of assault and the facts which constitute this tort is confusing; the facts which call for the application of a rule should be mentioned *immediately* after the rule is stated.

A more serious error, however, occurs in the second paragraph of the First Student Answer. While there is an allusion to the correct principle of law (prevention of crime), the **rule is not defined**. As a consequence, the grader can only guess why the student thinks the facts set forth in the subsequent sentences are significant. A grader reading this answer could not be certain that the student recognized that the issues revolved around the **reasonable belief** and **necessary force** elements of the prevention-of-crime privilege. Superior exam-writing requires that the pertinent facts be **tied** directly and clearly to the operative rule.

The Second Student Answer is very much better than the First Answer. It disposes of C's assault and battery upon A in a few words (yet tells the grader that the writer knows these torts are present). More importantly, the grader can easily see the issues which would arise if the prevention-of crime-privilege were asserted (i.e., "whether C's belief that A was about to commit a crime against B was reasonable" and "whether C used unnecessary force in punching A after A had been knocked to the ground"). Finally, it also utilizes all the facts by indicating how each attorney would assert those facts which are most advantageous to her client.

Structuring Your Answer

Graders will give high marks to a clearly-written, well-structured answer. Each issue you discuss should follow a specific and consistent structure which a grader can easily follow.

The Second Student Answer above basically utilizes the *I-R-A-A-O format* with respect to each issue. In this format, the *I* stands for the word *Issue,* the *R* for *Rule of law,* the initial *A* for the words *one side's Argument,* the second *A* for *the other party's rebuttal Argument,* and the *O* for your *Opinion as to how the issue would be resolved.* The *I-R-A-A-O* format emphasizes the importance of (1) discussing *both* sides of an issue, and (2) communicating to the grader that where an issue arises, an attorney can only advise her client as to the *probable* decision on that issue.

A somewhat different format for analyzing each issue is the *I-R-A-C format.* The "I" stands for "Issue;" the "R" for "Rule of law;" the "A" for "Application of the facts to the rule of law;" and the "C" for "Conclusion." I-R-A-C is a legitimate approach to the discussion of a particular issue, within the time constraints imposed by the question. The *I-R-A-C format* must be applied to each issue; it is not the solution to an entire exam answer. If there are six issues in a question, for example, you should offer six separate, independent *I-R-A-C* analyses.

We believe that the *I-R-A-C* approach is preferable to the *I-R-A-A-O* formula. However, either can be used to analyze and organize essay exam answers. Whatever format you choose, however, you should be consistent throughout the exam and remember the following rules:

First, *analyze all of the relevant facts.* Facts have significance in a particular case *only as they come under the applicable rules of law.* The facts presented must be analyzed and examined to see if they do or do not satisfy one element or another of the applicable rules, and the essential facts and rules must be stated and argued in your analysis.

Second, you must communicate to the grader the *precise rule of law* controlling the facts. In their eagerness to commence their arguments, students sometimes fail to state the applicable rule of law first. Remember, the "*R*" in either format stands for "Rule of Law." Defining the rule of law ***before*** an analysis of the facts is essential in order to allow the grader to follow your reasoning.

Third, it is important to treat ***each side of an issue with equal detail.*** If a hypothetical describes how an elderly man was killed when he ventured upon the land of a huge power company to obtain a better view of a nuclear reactor, your sympathies might understandably fall on the side of the old man. The grader will nevertheless expect you to see and make every possible argument for the other side. Don't permit your personal viewpoint to affect your answer! A good lawyer never does! When discussing an issue, always state the arguments for each side.

Finally, don't forget to ***state your opinion or conclusion*** on each issue. Keep in mind, however, that your opinion or conclusion is probably the ***least*** important part of an exam answer. Why? Because your professor knows that no attorney can tell her client exactly how a judge or jury will decide a particular issue. By definition, an issue is a legal dispute which can go either way. An attorney, therefore, can offer her client only her best opinion about the likelihood of victory or defeat on an issue. Since the decision on any issue lies with the judge or jury, no attorney can ever be absolutely certain of the resolution.

Discuss All Possible Issues

As we've noted, a student should draw ***some*** type of conclusion or opinion for each issue raised. Whatever your conclusion on a particular issue, it is essential to anticipate and discuss ***all of the issues*** which would arise if the question were actually tried in court.

Let's assume that a negligence hypothetical involves issues pertaining to duty, breach of duty, proximate causation and contributory negligence. If the defendant prevails on any one of these issues, he will avoid liability. Nevertheless, even if you feel strongly that the defendant owed no duty to the plaintiff, you ***must*** go on to discuss all of the other potential issues as well (breach of duty, proximate causation and contributory negligence). If you were to terminate your answer after a discussion of the duty problem only, you'd receive an inferior grade.

Why should you have to discuss every possible potential issue if you are relatively certain that the outcome of a particular issue would be dispositive of the entire case? Because at the commencement of litigation, neither party can be ***absolutely positive*** about which issues he will win at trial. We can state with confidence that every attorney with some degree of experience has won issues he thought he would lose, and has lost issues on which he thought victory was assured. Since one can never be absolutely certain how a factual issue will be resolved by the factfinder, a good attorney (and exam-writer) will consider *all* possible issues.

To understand the importance of discussing all of the potential issues, you should reflect on what you will do during the actual practice of law. If you represent the defendant, for example, it is your job to raise every possible defense. If there are five potential defenses, and your pleadings only rely on three of them (because you're sure you will win on all three), and the plaintiff is somehow successful on all three issues, your client may well sue you for malpractice. Your client's contention would be that you should be liable because if you had only raised the two additional issues, you might have prevailed on at least one of them, and therefore liability would have been avoided. It is an attorney's duty to raise *all* legitimate issues. A similar philosophy should be followed when taking essay exams.

What exactly do you say when you've resolved the initial issue in favor of the defendant, and discussion of any additional issues would seem to be moot? The answer is simple. You simply begin the discussion of the next potential issue with something like, "Assuming, however, the plaintiff prevailed on the foregoing issue, the next issue would be…" The grader will understand and appreciate what you have done.

The corollary to the importance of raising all potential issues is that you should avoid discussion of obvious non-issues. Raising non-issues is detrimental in three ways: first, you waste a lot of precious time; second, you usually receive absolutely no points for discussing a point which the grader deems extraneous; third, it suggests to the grader that you lack the ability to distinguish the significant from the irrelevant. The best guideline for avoiding the discussion of a non-issue is to ask yourself, "would I, as an attorney, feel comfortable about raising that particular issue or objection in front of a judge"?

Delineate the Transition From One Issue to the Next

It's a good idea to make it easy for the grader to see the issues which you've found. One way to accomplish this is to cover no more than one issue per paragraph. Another way is to underline each issue statement. Provided time permits, both techniques are recommended. The essay answers in this book contain numerous illustrations of these suggestions.

One frequent student error is to write a two-paragraph answer in which all of the arguments for one side are made in the initial paragraph, and all of the rebuttal arguments by the other side are made in the next paragraph. This is *a bad idea*. It obliges the grader to reconstruct the exam answer in his mind several times to determine whether all possible issues have been discussed by both sides. It will also cause you to state the same rule of law more than once. A better-organized answer presents a given argument by one side and follows that immediately in the same paragraph with the other side's rebuttal to that argument.

Understanding the "Call" of a Question

The statements *at the end of* an essay question or of the fact pattern in a multiple-choice question is sometimes referred to as the "call" of the question. It usually asks you to do something specific like "discuss," "discuss the rights of the parties," "what are X's rights?" "advise X," "the best grounds on which to find the statute unconstitutional are:," "D can be convicted of:," "how should the estate be distributed," etc. The call of the question should be read carefully because it tells you exactly what you're expected to do. If a question asks, "what are X's rights against Y?" or "X is liable to Y for:..." you don't have to spend a lot of time on Y's rights against Z. You will usually receive absolutely no credit for discussing facts that are not required by the question. On the other hand, if the call of an essay question is simply "discuss" or "discuss the rights of the parties" then *all* foreseeable issues must be covered by your answer.

Students are often led astray by an essay question's call. For example, if you are asked for "X's rights against Y" or to "advise X", you may think you may limit yourself to X's viewpoint with respect to the issues. This is *not correct*! You cannot resolve one party's rights against another party without considering the issues which might arise (and the arguments which the other side would assert) if litigation occurred. In short, although the call of the question may appear to focus on one of the parties to the litigation, a superior answer will cover all the issues and arguments which that person might *encounter* (not just the arguments she would *make*) in attempting to pursue her rights against the other side.

The Importance of Analyzing the Question Carefully Before Writing

The overriding *time pressure* of an essay exam is probably a major reason why many students fail to analyze a question carefully before writing. Five minutes into the allocated time for a particular question, you may notice that the person next to you is writing furiously. This thought then flashes through your mind, "Oh, my goodness, he's putting down more words on the paper than I am, and therefore he's bound to get a better grade." It can be stated *unequivocally* that there is no necessary correlation between the number of words on your exam paper and the grade you'll receive. Students who begin their answer after only five minutes of analysis have probably seen only the most obvious issues, and missed many, if not most, of the subtle ones. They are also likely to be less well organized.

Opinions differ as to how much time you should spend analyzing and outlining a question before you actually write the answer. We believe that you should spend at least 12-18 minutes analyzing, organizing, and outlining a one-hour question before writing your answer. This will usually provide sufficient time to analyze and organize the question thoroughly *and* enough time to write a relatively complete answer. Remember that each word of the question must be scrutinized to determine if it (i) suggests an issue under the operative rules of law, or (ii) can be used in making an argument for the resolution of an issue. Since you can't receive points for an issue you don't spot, it is usually wise to read a question *twice* before starting your outline.

When to Make an Assumption

The instructions on an exam may tell you to *"assume"* facts which are necessary to the answer. Even where these instructions are *not* specifically given, you may be obliged to make certain assumptions with respect to missing facts in order to write a thorough answer. Assumptions should be made when you, as the attorney for one of the parties described in the question, would be obliged to solicit additional information from your client. On the other hand, assumptions should *never be used to change or alter the question.* Don't ever write something like "if the facts in the question were ..., instead of ..., then ... would result." If you do this, you are wasting time on facts which are extraneous to the problem before you. Professors want you to deal with *their* fact patterns, not your own.

Students sometimes try to "write around" information they think is missing. They assume that their professor has failed to include every piece of data necessary for a thorough answer. This is generally *wrong.* The professor may have omitted some facts deliberately to see if the student *can figure out what to do* under the circumstances. In some instances, the professor may have omitted them inadvertently (even law professors are sometimes human).

The way to deal with the omission of essential information is to describe (i) what fact (or facts) are missing, and (ii) why that information is important. As an example, go back to the "movie shoot" hypothetical we discussed above. In that fact pattern, there was no mention of the relative strength of A and C. This fact could be extremely important. If C weighed 240 pounds and was built like a professional football linebacker, while A tipped the scales at a mere 160 pounds, punching A in the face after he had been pushed to the ground would probably constitute unnecessary force (thereby causing C to forfeit the prevention-of-crime privilege). If the physiques of the parties were reversed, however, C's punch to A's face would probably constitute reasonable behavior. Under the facts, C had to deal the *"knockout"* blow while the opportunity presented itself. The last sentences of the Second Student Answer above show that the student

understood these subtleties and correctly stated the essential missing facts and
assumptions.

Assumptions should be made in a manner which keeps the other issues open
(i.e., necessitates discussion of all other possible issues). Don't assume facts
which would virtually dispose of the entire hypothetical in a few sentences. For
example, suppose that A called B a "convicted felon" (a statement which is
inherently defamatory, *i.e.*, a defamatory statement is one which tends to subject
the plaintiff to hatred, contempt or ridicule). If A's statement is true, he has a
complete defense to B's action for defamation. If the facts don't tell whether A's
statement was true or not, it would ***not*** be wise to write something like, "We'll
assume that A's statement about B is accurate, and therefore B cannot
successfully sue A for defamation." So facile an approach would rarely be
appreciated by the grader. The proper way to handle this situation would be to
state, "if we assume that A's statement about B is not correct, A can not raise the
defense of truth." You've communicated to the grader that you recognize the
need to assume an essential fact and that you've assumed it in such a way as to
enable you to proceed to discuss all other potential issues.

Case Names

A law student is ordinarily ***not*** expected to recall case names on an exam. The
professor knows that you have read several hundred cases for each course, and
that you would have to be a memory expert to have all of the names at your
fingertips. If you confront a fact pattern which seems similar to a case which you
have reviewed (but you cannot recall the name of it), just write something like,
"One case held that ..." or "It has been held that ..." In this manner, you have
informed the grader that you are relying on a case which contained a fact pattern
similar to the question at issue.

The only exception to this rule is in the case of a landmark decision. Landmark
opinions are usually those which change or alter established law.[2] These cases are
usually easy to identify, because you will probably have spent an entire class
period discussing each of them. *Palsgraf v. Long Island Rail Road* is a prime
example of a landmark case in Torts. In these special cases, you may be expected
to remember the case by name, as well the proposition of law which it stands for.
However, this represents a very limited exception to the general rule which
counsels against wasting precious time trying to memorize case names.

---

2. The only subject to which this does not apply is Constitutional Law, since here virtually
every case you study satisfies this definition. Students studying Constitutional Law should try
to associate case names with holdings and reproduce them in their exam answers.

How To Handle Time Pressures

What do you do when there are five minutes left in the exam and you have only written down two-thirds of your answer? One thing *not* to do is write something like, "No time left!" or "Not enough time!" This gets you nothing but the satisfaction of knowing you have communicated your personal frustrations to the grader. Another thing *not* to do is insert the outline you may have made on scrap paper into the exam booklet. Professors rarely will look at these items.

First of all, it is not necessarily a bad thing to be pressed for time. The person who finishes five minutes early has very possibly missed some important issues. The more proficient you become in knowing what is expected of you on an exam, the greater the difficulty you may experience in staying within the time limits. Second, remember that (at least to some extent) you're graded against your classmates' answers and they're under exactly the same time pressure as you. In short, don't panic if you can't write the "perfect" answer in the allotted time. Nobody does!

The best hedge against misuse of time is to *review as many old exams as possible*. These exercises will give you a familiarity with the process of organizing and writing an exam answer, which, in turn, should result in an enhanced ability to stay within the time boundaries. If you nevertheless find that you have about 15 minutes of writing to do and five minutes to do it in, write a paragraph which summarizes the remaining issues or arguments you would discuss if time permitted. As long as you've indicated that you're aware of the remaining legal issues, you'll probably receive some credit for them. Your analytical and argumentative skills will already be apparent to the grader by virtue of the issues that you have previously discussed.

Write Legibly

Make sure your answer is legible. Students should *not* assume that their professors will be willing to take their papers to the local pharmacist to have them deciphered. Remember, your professor may have 75-150 separate exam answers to grade. If your answer is difficult to read, you will rarely be given the benefit of the doubt. On the other hand, a legible, well-organized paper creates a very positive mental impact upon the grader.

Many schools allow students to type their exams. If you're an adequate typist, you may want to seriously consider typing. Typing has two major advantages. First, it should help assure that your words will be readable (unless, of course, there are numerous typos). Second, it should enable you to put a lot more words onto the paper than if your answer had been handwritten. Most professors prefer a typed answer to a written one.

There are, however, a few disadvantages to typing. For one thing, all the typists are usually in a single room. If the clatter of other typewriters will make it difficult for you to concentrate, typing is probably **not** wise. To offset this problem, some students wear earplugs during the exam. Secondly, typing sometimes makes it difficult to change or add to an earlier portion of your answer. You may have to withdraw your paper from the carriage and insert another. Try typing out a few practice exams before you decide to type your exam. If you do type, be sure to leave at least one blank line between typewritten lines, so that handwritten changes and insertions in your answers can be made easily.

If you decide against typing, your answer will probably be written in a "bluebook" (a booklet of plain, lined, white paper which has a light blue cover and back). It is usually a good idea to write only on the odd numbered pages (i.e., 1, 3, 5, etc.). You may also want to leave a blank line between each written line. Doing these things will usually make the answer easier to read. If you discover that you have left out a word or phrase, you can insert it into the proper place by means of a caret sign ("^"). If you feel that you've omitted an entire issue, you can write it on the facing blank page. A symbol reference can be used to indicate where the additional portion of the answer should be inserted. While it's not ideal to have your answer take on the appearance of a road map, a symbol reference to an adjoining page is much better than trying to squeeze six lines into one, and will help the grader to discover where the same symbol appears in another part of your answer.

The Importance of Reviewing Prior Exams

As we've mentioned, it is ***extremely important to review old exams.*** The transition from blackletter law to essay exam can be a difficult experience if the process has not been practiced. Although this book provides a large number of essay and multiple-choice questions, ***don't stop here***! Most law schools have recent tests on file in the library, by course. We strongly suggest that you make a copy of every old exam you can obtain (especially those given by your professors) at the beginning of each semester. The demand for these documents usually increases dramatically as "finals time" draws closer.

The exams for each course should be scrutinized ***throughout the semester.*** They should be reviewed as you complete each chapter in your casebook. Generally, the order of exam questions follows the sequence of the materials in your casebook. Thus, the first question on a law school test may involve the initial three chapters of the casebook; the second question may pertain to the fourth and fifth chapters, etc. In any event, ***don't wait*** until the semester is nearly over to begin reviewing old exams.

Keep in mind that no one is born with the ability to analyze questions and write superior answers to law school exams. Like any skill, it is developed and perfected only through application. If you don't take the time to analyze numerous examinations from prior years, this evolutionary process just won't occur. Don't just **think about** the answers to past exam questions; take the time to **write the answers down**. It's also wise to look back at an answer a day or two after you've written it. You will invariably see (i) ways in which the organization could have been improved, and (ii) arguments you missed.

As you practice spotting issues on past exams, you will see how rules of law become the sources of issues on finals. As we've already noted, if you don't **understand** how rules of law translate into issues, you won't be able to achieve superior grades on your exams. Reviewing exams from prior years should also reveal that certain issues tend to be lumped together in the same question. For instance, where a fact pattern involves a false statement made by one person about another, three potential theories of liability are often present — defamation, invasion of privacy (false, public light) and intentional infliction of severe emotional distress. You will need to see if any or all of these apply to the facts.

Finally, one of the best means of evaluating if you understand a course (or a particular area within a subject) is to attempt to create a hypothetical exam for that topic. Your exam should contain as many issues as possible. If you can write an issue-packed exam, you probably know that particular area of law. If you can't, then you probably haven't yet acquired an adequate understanding of how the principles of law in that subject can spawn issues.

As Always, a Caveat

The suggestions and advice offered in this book represent the product of many years of experience in the field of legal education. We are confident that the techniques and concepts described in these pages will help you prepare for, and succeed, at your exams. Nevertheless, particular professors sometimes have a preference for exam-writing techniques which are not stressed in this work. Some instructors expect at least a nominal reference to the **prima facie** elements of all pertinent legal theories (even though one or more of those principles is **not** placed into issue). Other professors want their students to emphasize public policy considerations in the arguments they make on a particular issue. Because this book is intended for nationwide consumption, these individualized preferences have **not** been stressed. The best way to find out whether your professor has a penchant for a particular writing approach is to ask her to provide you with a model answer to a previous exam. If an item is not available, speak to upperclass students who received a superior grade in that professor's class.

One final point. While the rules of law stated in the answers to the questions in this book have been drawn from commonly used sources (i.e., casebooks, hornbooks, etc.), it is still conceivable that they may be slightly at odds with those taught by your professor. In instances where a conflict exists between our formulation of a legal principle and the one which is taught by your professor, *follow the latter!* Since your grades are determined by your professors, their views should always supersede the views contained in this book.

Essay Exam Questions

Question 1

Dan was tried for theft and burglary of the home of Mr. and Mrs. Charles in Central City. The crimes had been committed during the early morning hours of April 17. Dan's defense was that he had been 200 miles away at the time. Mrs. Charles testified to the losses, described the scene, and identified a half-eaten piece of cheese found in the kitchen following the burglary.

The court admitted the following evidence offered by the prosecution:

The testimony of Mr. Charles that while he and Mrs. Charles were sitting in a park a week following the burglary, Dan walked by and Mrs. Charles screamed, "You stole that jacket from our house," whereupon Dan ran away without saying a word.

The testimony of Yank, a dentist, that, based upon a comparison of legally obtained impressions of Dan's teeth and a cast of the piece of cheese identified by Mrs. Charles, the bite in the cheese was made by Dan's teeth.

The court then admitted the following evidence offered by the defense:

The testimony of Bob that on April 16, Dan told Bob that he wanted to use Bob's mountain cabin, which was 200 miles from Central City, for the next two days; that Bob consented and gave Dan the key to the cabin; that on April 18, Dan returned the key and said that the stove had exploded when the stove pipe was struck by lightning during the early morning hours of April 17; and that when he visited the cabin on the evening of April 18, the stove was as Dan had described.

The prosecution then offered, and the court admitted, Able's testimony that Bob had told him that Bob had not seen Dan during the entire month of April.

Assuming that all appropriate objections were timely made, did the court err in admitting the testimony of Mr. Charles, Yank, Bob and Able? Discuss.

Question 2

Payne sued Don alleging an oral contract to paint Don's portrait for $4,000. Don denied making the contract. The following evidence was offered by the plaintiff:

(A) Witt testified that on May 1 he heard Payne offer to paint Don's portrait for $4,000 and heard Don say he'd let Payne know within a few days.

(B) Maida, Don's maid, testified that Don's wife was a lawyer, and that while eavesdropping at Don's bedroom door on the evening of May 2, she heard Don tell his wife: "Since oral agreements are valid, I'm going to call Payne and tell him to go ahead with the portrait."

(C) Belle testified that she personally operated an answering service which handled phone calls for several artists, including Payne, and remembered receiving a call for Payne on May 3. She testified that she did not recognize the voice and could not now remember the name of the caller or the message, but remembered that she had accurately recorded the caller's name and message immediately in her "Telephone Log." After she identified the Log, an entry in it ("May 3, Mr. Don called Payne, said he accepted Payne's offer to paint Don's portrait for $4,000") was admitted into evidence.

(D) Belle abruptly died of a heart attack before cross-examination. The judge refused to strike her testimony and denied a defense motion to exclude the Telephone Log from evidence.

Assume that all appropriate objections to the foregoing evidence were made by Don. Discuss the admissibility of the evidence in (A), (B) and (C), and the ruling in (D).

Question 3

P received injuries in an automobile accident involving two vehicles driven by D and X. The cars collided at an intersection, causing the vehicle driven by D to strike P, a pedestrian. P brings suit against D for $15,000.

1. At the trial, P called Dr. Jones, who testified that P was brought to his office by D shortly after the accident, and that D said: "I'll pay this man's bill."

2. P testified that prior to trial there had been extensive settlement negotiations between the parties and that D had offered to pay $5,000 in full settlement of P's claim. P also testified that during these negotiations, D had said to him on one occasion: "I might have gone through the light a little late."

3. Mrs. D, D's wife, was called as a witness by P. She testified that one evening during dinner, and while the butler was present, D said to her: "I'm afraid that I'm at fault in that collision with X."

4. Bystander is called as a witness for D. Bystander testifies that, shortly after the accident, he heard X say: "I'm dying, I'm dying. The accident was all my fault. I'm glad I have insurance." Other evidence disclosed that X, although injured, was not in serious condition. However, X died shortly thereafter en route to the hospital when the ambulance into which he had been placed struck a tree.

Discuss the admissibility of the above items of evidence, assuming that all appropriate objections have been made.

Question 4

Corp sued Dan for $12,463 alleged to be the unpaid balance due for merchandise supplied to Dan pursuant to a written contract. Dan's answer alleged that he had paid the contract price for all merchandise delivered.

At the trial before a jury the following occurred:

1. Alex, the Corp salesman who had negotiated that deal with Dan, identified the contract. One page was missing. After explaining that a file clerk had inadvertently burnt the missing page while lighting a cigarette, Alex was allowed to testify from memory to 27 stock item descriptions and prices which he said were on the missing page.

2. The court refused to allow Dan's lawyer, on cross-examination, to Question Alex about the details of contracts he had negotiated with other customers.

The contract was then received as evidence.

3. Corp was permitted to introduce into evidence a computer print-out which was identified by Corp's office manager as showing all deliveries made to Dan, all payments made on Dan's account and the unpaid balance. The office manager testified that, under his general supervision, clerks at Corp daily transferred the information from the previous day's receipts, invoices, credit slips and other documents to punch cards which were fed into the computer, where the information was electronically stored on magnetic tape, as the corporation's usual method of bookkeeping. The computer is programmed to print out billings and other business documents, including the print-out which he identified.

4. Prex, the president of Corp, was permitted to testify on direct examination that, at a settlement conference Corp offered to compromise its claim for $6,200 and Dan responded, "But my bookkeeper says we only owe you $5,500."

Assuming that in each instance all appropriate objections were timely made, did the trial judge commit any error? Discuss.

Question 5

Peter suffered a head injury when the car he was driving collided with a car owned by Moses and driven by Adams, Moses' chauffeur. Peter sued Moses, alleging that the accident was due to the negligence of Adams who was driving on business for Moses. Moses denied that Adams was negligent, and also alleged that at the time of the accident Adams was on his own business. He further asserted that the accident was due solely to Peter's negligence.

At trial, the following items of evidence were received on behalf of Peter, over Moses' objections:

(1) Testimony of Officer Jones that when he arrived at the scene 20 minutes after the accident occurred, Adams said to him, "I was going to the drug store on an errand for Moses when the accident happened."

(2) Testimony of Officer Jones that, in his opinion, Moses' vehicle was traveling at least 70 miles per hour. (Prior to this, Officer Jones testified that he had 15 years experience as a police officer; that he had not seen the accident in question, but that he had examined both cars on the day of the accident; and that he had investigated the skid marks of Moses' vehicle and the distance it traveled after the point of collision.)

(3) Testimony of Dr. Medic, that he first saw Peter the day before the trial; that he examined Peter solely to prepare himself to testify; and that during the examination, Peter complained to him of a severe headache from which he was then suffering and had suffered ever since the accident.

On cross-examination of Dr. Medic, Moses asked, over Peter's objection, "Doctor, how much are you being paid for testifying in this case?" The doctor answered, "$500."

Peter then called Walter, who, after being properly qualified, stated over Moses' objections that he knew the doctor's reputation for truth and veracity and that it was good.

On cross-examination, over Peter's objection, Walter was asked whether he had heard that two months prior to trial Dr. Medic had been indicted for falsification of his income tax returns and for concealment of assets in a bankruptcy proceeding. Walter answered that he had not heard that.

Assuming all appropriate reasons for admission and exclusion were timely presented by counsel, did the court rule correctly on the various objections? Discuss.

Question 6

P sued D Bus Co. to recover for brain injuries he allegedly received when struck by D's bus at noon on January 15 of the previous year, at Front and Elm Streets, in C city. D filed an answer alleging that P's injuries were caused by a fall at his office. At trial, the following issues arose:

(1) P testified that his head injuries had affected his memory so that he no longer remembered the accident. Counsel for P then called F, P's best friend, to testify that P had told him on January 14 of the previous year that he was meeting another friend for lunch at noon the next day, at Front and Elm. F also would testify that P had told him a week after the accident, before his memory began to fail, that the bus had struck him when it was driven onto the sidewalk to get past the right side of a car stopped in the street. Are F's statements admissible over objection?

(2) L testified for P, as an eyewitness. He stated that at the time of the accident he had been in C city on a short vacation and was staying at M Motel on the out-skirts. Thereafter, counsel for D offered evidence to show that L had been prosecuted a few months before for letting the air out of bus tires, and further, that L had resided in C city all his life and had never stayed at M Motel. Counsel for P objects to this evidence. Is he correct?

(3) In D's defense, counsel proposed to call X, an accountant who had known P for many years, to testify that P's memory problems and insane behavior were not caused by his injuries, but stemmed from anxiety over his business, which was failing. May X so testify over objection?

(4) Counsel for D also called Dr. Q, a brain specialist, who stated that he had examined P and that P's loss of memory and insane behavior were caused by worry and anxiety, not by any injury. On cross-examination, counsel for P showed Dr. Q a book and then read him its title, which indicated that it was a reference work on brain injuries. After Dr. Q admitted that he had heard of the book, counsel for P proposed to ask whether Dr. Q realized that the author had come to a conclusion directly contrary to Dr. Q's. The book was not offered or admitted into evidence. Should counsel for P be allowed to ask the questions over objection?

Question 7

Peter sued Dan for damages for breach of a written contract. Peter's attorney is Row. Dan's answer in the case denied that he ever signed or entered into any such contract.

At the trial, before a jury, Peter testified that after extensive negotiations, he and Dan executed a written contract. Peter identified a document, purportedly signed and acknowledged by Dan before a notary public, as the original of the contract which he and Dan had signed and acknowledged. That document was then offered in evidence by Row and was admitted.

Thereafter, the following took place:

(1) Abel was called as a witness by Dan. Abel testified without objection that he was a teller in the bank where Dan had his commercial account and that he had seen Dan's signature hundreds of times. Abel was then asked whether, in his opinion, the signature on the contract was Dan's and, over objection, was permitted to answer that it was not.

(2) On cross-examination, Abel was asked: "Is it not a fact that Peter is suing the bank that employs you?" Defendant's objection was sustained.

(3) Dan testified in his own behalf that the signature on the contract was not his. On cross-examination, Dan admitted attending a meeting in Row's office at which Peter showed him the original of the contract. On further cross-examination, Dan was asked: "Didn't Peter then say to you, 'You know that's your signature' and didn't you then smile and shrug your shoulders?" After objection by Dan's attorney, Dan was required to answer the question and his answer was "No, that never took place."

(4) In rebuttal, Row was sworn as a witness and, over objection, testified that Peter did say to Dan "You know that's your signature" and that Dan then smiled and shrugged his shoulders.

At the close of the trial, at Row's request and over Dan's objection the jury was instructed: "The signatures on a document bearing a certificate of acknowledgment are presumed to be genuine. You will therefore assume that the signature on the contract is that of Dan unless you are persuaded to the contrary by a preponderance of the evidence." The Evidence Code of the jurisdiction provides in part: "Presumptions affecting the burden of producing evidence: The signatures on a document bearing a certificate of acknowledgment are presumed to be genuine."

A. For each objection, what might properly have been the grounds of the objection, and how should the court have ruled? Discuss.

B. Should the court have given the requested instructions? Discuss.

Question 8

Pete sued Doe Film Company (Doe) for infringement of literary property rights, alleging that Doe had copied an original play of his and used it as the basis for a motion picture entitled "Twenty-Four Long Hours on the Trail."

1. At the trial before a jury, the following evidence, offered by Pete, was admitted over defendant's objections:

    (a) A carbon copy of a script, entitled "A Long Day's Journey," after Pete testified that it was a copy of a story he had written; that he had submitted the original script to Doe by mail; and that he had never gotten the original script back.

    (b) Pete's testimony that his story was worth $100,000.

    (c) A reel of motion picture film entitled "Twenty-Four Long Hours on the Trail," after a film critic for a New York newspaper testified that he had viewed a projection of the film on the reel; that it was the same motion picture he had seen projected for audiences in three cities; and that at those three screenings the film bore the statement: "Doe Film Company Production." The film was then viewed by the jury.

2. Outside the presence of the jury, Pete testified that Alex had held himself out to be a literary agent for Doe, and had told him, "Your story line is pretty good but Doe doesn't have to buy stories. We pick up ideas and have our own writers develop them." The president of Doe denied that Alex was, or ever had been, an agent or employee of Doe. Pete was then allowed by the court to repeat his testimony before the jury, but Doe's president was not permitted to testify before the jury.

3. Ed, one of the mailroom employees of Doe, was called by Doe and testified that he ordinarily opened mail sent to Doe, and then placed it into the "in" box of the appropriate addressee; but he had no recollection of ever seeing Pete's script. He was not allowed to testify that at the time Pete claimed to have mailed the script, it was Doe's invariable procedure to return all unsolicited mailed scripts immediately to the sender.

Discuss the propriety of the court's rulings. Assume all appropriate objections were timely made.

Question 9

P sued D for personal injuries. P claimed that D had negligently manufactured a wooden ladder which broke while being used by a man named Carpenter, causing Carpenter to fall upon P. Carpenter died as a result of the injuries received.

(1) A police officer was called as P's witness. He testified without objection that when he arrived at the scene, Carpenter, who could not move, was conscious, but appeared dazed; and that when the ambulance arrived, it backed over the ladder and broke it into several pieces. Over D's objection, the police officer was allowed to testify that at the scene of the accident he asked Carpenter what happened and Carpenter said, "The ladder broke and I fell. You don't think I'm going to die, do you?"

(2) P offered in evidence a certified copy of Carpenter's death certificate which stated, among other matters: "If caused by injury, describe how injury occurred: Rung of ladder broke and victim fell on head." The court sustained an objection thereto.

(3) P called Dr. Able. It was stipulated that he was an expert in the field of strength of materials and accident reconstruction. Over D's objection, Dr. Able was permitted to testify that based upon information obtained from the police report, wood fiber analysis reports from an independent laboratory, records of the company from which Carpenter rented the ladder, and his own inspection of the scene, it was his opinion that at least one of the breaks in the ladder pre-existed the ladder's being smashed by the ambulance.

(4) D called Hood as a witness. Hood refused to answer any questions about the falling of the ladder on the ground that his answers might tend to incriminate him. D then called Baker who testified, over P's objection, that Hood told him that he, Hood, had kicked the ladder out from under Carpenter.

(5) On cross-examination, Baker had difficulty remembering anything else that happened the day Hood made the statement to him, but the court sustained D's objection to the question, "How can you remember what Hood said so clearly when you can't remember anything else that happened that day?"

Assume that all appropriate objections were timely made. Were the court's rulings correct? Discuss.

Question 10

Paul and Dave were driving their respective cars when they collided at an intersection. In a suit brought by Paul to recover damages, Dave denied Paul's allegations, and also asserted that Paul was contributorily negligent. The critical issue was whether Dave had entered the intersection without stopping, in violation of a red traffic light. The trial court, over Dave's objection, permitted Paul to introduce the following evidence:

(1) Testimony of the clerk of the criminal court, in which Dave was charged with violating the red traffic signal at the time of the accident, that Dave had initially filed a plea of guilty; but that later, with the permission of the court, he had withdrawn that plea.

(2) Testimony of Oliver, in response to a question by P's attorney as to whether he saw the accident, and if so, what he saw; that he saw an accident, that Dave drove through the red light which was against him and that, "it was impossible for Paul to avoid the accident." The trial court, on motion by Dave, refused to strike the portion of Oliver's testimony in quotations.

(3) Testimony of White that Dave had confided in him that he had gone through the red light. On cross-examination of White, Dave's counsel asked only one question; namely, whether Paul was related to White?

(4) Later, in presenting his own case, over objection by Paul, Dave introduced the testimony of Brown who said that a week after the accident White told him that he was going to get even with Dave for barring his membership in the local Downtown club. Brown gave no further testimony on direct.

(5) Paul, over objection by Dave, asked Brown on cross-examination if he had seen the accident. Brown said he had, but had forgotten the details. Paul then, over objection by Dave, showed Brown a newspaper account of the accident and asked him if that refreshed his memory. Brown said it did, and then proceeded to describe the accident in a manner similar to Oliver's testimony (except for the statement in quotations).

Discuss the propriety of the court's rulings.

Question 11

Olson and Jones executed a burglary together. As they were leaving the building, the police arrived. A chase ensued and Jones was arrested. Jones told the police: "You never would have caught me if Olson had not been so slow in finishing the job." The police then found Olson at his home, told him he was suspected of the burglary, fully advised him of his rights and asked him where he had been earlier that evening. Olson replied that he had been to see the movie "Hellcat" at a downtown theater.

At Olson's trial for burglary, Wilson, the owner of the burglarized premises, was called as a witness. Olson objected to Wilson's competence to testify, charging that in a recent accident, Wilson had suffered brain injuries which had rendered him insane. The trial court ordered a psychiatric examination, to which both sides agreed. Following the examination, the psychiatrist testified (in the absence of the jury) that Wilson was not insane, but that he had suffered brain injuries and to some extent was unable to distinguish between his own independent recollection of events and what had been told him by others. The trial judge ruled that Wilson was competent as a witness, recalled the jury and offered both counsel opportunity to examine the psychiatrist concerning Wilson's reliability. Thereafter, Wilson testified that his premises had been burglarized.

At the trial, the following evidence was also offered by the prosecution:

(1) Officer Carlisle's testimony as to Jones' statement at the time of the latter's arrest;

(2) Olson's statement to the police, along with evidence that the movie "Hellcat" had closed two days prior to the day on which Olson was questioned;

(3) Testimony by a reporter who sat behind Olson, but whom Olson did not see, that during a recess after the offer of Jones' statement, she heard Olson say to his wife, "I should have known Jones would spill his guts";

(4) Testimony by a police officer that while searching Olson's house under a warrant authorizing the search, a map of the burglarized premises was found and seized by the police.

A. Discuss the propriety of the court's rulings on Wilson's testimony.

B. Assuming that all possible objections to the introduction of evidence items (1) through (4) were timely made, how should the trial judge have ruled? Discuss.

Question 12

Mary sued Acme Cosmetic Co. for injuries she was alleged to have suffered when her leg became infected as a result of using a hair remover manufactured by Acme known as Hairoff. At the trial Mary admitted on cross-examination that she was a drug addict and daily used heroin. She was not asked if she had ever gone to Dr. White and had ever told him that she suffered the leg infection by reason of falling on a rusty pitchfork.

Acme, on its case, offered the following items of evidence, to all of which Mary objected:

(1) Proof that it had sold over 800,000 tubes of Hairoff such as the one Mary complained of and that it had not received a single complaint except Mary's;

(2) Testimony of Dr. White that Mary came to him about her leg injury and told him she had gotten it infected by falling on a rusty pitchfork;

(3) Testimony of Dr. Spencer, a specialist in the care and treatment of narcotic addicts, to the effect that persons addicted to narcotics are untrustworthy and generally untruthful;

(4) Testimony establishing that during the past ten years Mary had brought seven suits against various cosmetic manufacturers claiming she had suffered injuries in using their cosmetics.

At the conclusion of the defendant's case, Mary offered the testimony of Louise, to which defendant objected, that Mary had frequently shown her infected leg to Louise and had told her it had become infected as a result of using Hairoff.

How should the court have ruled on the above objections assuming all appropriate reasons for admission or exclusion of the proffered evidence were made? Discuss.

Question 13

Peter sued Defenders Insurance Company for a loss which occurred in September of last year. Defenders' defense was that it had canceled the policy on August 15 of last year for non-payment of premium. Peter denied receiving any notice of cancellation (a requisite for cancellation to be effective).

At the trial, Abner, an underwriter for Defenders Insurance Company, was allowed to testify for Defenders over objection that he had prepared a notice of cancellation addressed to Peter and that it must have been mailed because it was the invariable practice of Defenders to mail notices of cancellation on the day they were initiated.

Baker, a postal inspector, was allowed to testify for Defenders over objection that in December of last year, while investigating the conduct of a letter carrier, he said to Peter, "You actually did receive that notice of cancellation, didn't you?", and Peter turned and walked away without answering.

Charlie, an underwriter for an insurance company which was in no way connected with Defenders, as a witness for Defenders, was not allowed to testify that his company had on three occasions canceled policies which Peter had with Charlie's company for non-payment of premiums.

After Peter's 5-year-old daughter, Debbie, told the judge, "People who do not tell the truth get spanked," she was allowed to testify for Peter over objection that on August 16th and 17th of last year, she got all the mail from the mailman and took it directly to her daddy.

Ethel, a neighbor of Peter, was allowed to testify for Peter over objection that the letter carrier who delivered mail to Peter's house, and who is now in prison in another state, told her that during the third week in August of last year, his back was hurting, and so he had destroyed several items of "junk" mail addressed to Peter and others.

Discuss the propriety of the court's rulings. Assume that all appropriate objections were timely made.

Question 14

You represent Don, the proprietor of a swimming pool supply business, against whom an apartment-house owner, Patterson, brought suit claiming injury to his respiratory system allegedly caused by Don's mislabelling a bottle of muriatic acid and selling it to Patterson as a chlorine compound.

At the trial, Patterson was allowed to testify, over your timely and appropriate objections, that he poured liquid from a bottle purchased from Don and labelled "SODIUM HYPOCHLORIDE, especially prepared by Don for use with any type of automatic pool filter dispenser," into the automatic dispenser on his swimming pool filter pump and was overcome by fumes; that when he recovered he destroyed the bottle; and that he later heard his friend Jack tell Don he ought to be run out of business for putting the chlorine label on muriatic acid, but Don simply ignored him. On cross-examination, Patterson admitted smoking two packs of cigarettes a day for over thirty years.

Dr. Walton, a specialist in internal medicine and environmental hygiene, was called by Patterson and allowed to testify, over your timely and appropriate objections, that Patterson has chronic bronchitis; that he, Dr. Walton, in his laboratory constructed a plastic reproduction of Patterson's pool filterhouse in which he poured muriatic acid into a metal receptacle containing a small amount of water and sodium hypochloride; that he measured the concentration of fumes which resulted; and that Patterson's chronic bronchitis could, and probably did, result from a similar exposure.

The court refused to allow you to cross-examine Dr. Walton about certain articles in the Wall Street Journal and Reader's Digest to the effect that cigarette smoking and air pollution are the principal causes of chronic bronchitis. The court also denied your motion that the jury be taken to the pool filterhouse under court supervision and be allowed to inspect it.

Judgment was for Patterson. What points would you make on appeal in regard to the rulings of the trial court? How would you expect the appellate court to rule on them? Discuss.

Question 15

Dave, a 32-year old man, was charged with a felony. He pleaded not guilty by reason of insanity. At trial the court admitted the following evidence over the prosecuting attorney's objections:

a. The testimony of Doctor Alienist, a duly qualified psychiatrist, that based upon her observations and what Dave told her during three psychiatric interviews, it was her opinion that Dave was unable to distinguish between right and wrong at the time of the alleged crime.

b. A portion of the hospital record concerning Dave's hospitalization while recovering from hernia surgery which contained a nurse's notation that "Patient refuses to void. Says he will not start the deluge until Noah finishes the ark." The record was received after the hospital's record librarian, who had no knowledge of the events recorded, identified the record and testified that it was the practice for nurses to make such entries promptly in the regular course of the hospital routine.

Dave did not testify, but his mother testified extensively about Dave's background and abnormal behavior. The court subsequently refused to receive the following rebuttal evidence offered by the prosecuting attorney:

c. The testimony of Dr. Bromide, Dave's family physician, that he had examined Dave for various physical ailments at least twice a year since Dave was a child, and that during these examinations Dave never behaved abnormally, and therefore he believed that Dave was normal.

d. The testimony of Doctor Cyko, a psychiatrist, that he had heard Dave's mother testify, and that on the basis of her testimony it was his opinion she had a psychopathic personality which made it impossible for her to distinguish truth from fantasy.

Assume that all appropriate objections were timely made. Were the court's rulings correct? Discuss.

Question 16

Dan is on trial for the murder of Flora. The prosecution contends that Dan and Flora were lovers and that when he discovered her involvement with another man, he intentionally pushed her from a pier into the ocean where she drowned. The theory of the defense is that Dan had jilted Flora and that in her despondency she had committed suicide by jumping off the pier.

(1) At the trial, the State offered the testimony of Nabor that the day after Flora's body was found, he witnessed a confrontation between Flora's father, Harvey, (who is now deceased) and Dan, during which Flora's father stated to Dan: "You killed my daughter. I saw what you did to her"; and that Dan made no reply.

(2) Also at the trial, the State offered the testimony of Jack, a jailer, that while Dan was in jail awaiting trial, he attempted to commit suicide.

(3) The defense called Rita, Flora's roommate, who testified that the day before Flora's death, she had inadvertently read a crumpled-up piece of paper in the wastebasket in their apartment, upon which Flora had written: "Dear Dan: I have nothing left to live for now that you have left me."

(4) Upon rebuttal, the State called Dr. Slade, a licensed psychologist, who testified that Flora had been undergoing therapy for over a year, that he was well acquainted with her psychological problems, and that based upon what Flora had related to him during therapy sessions, he was of the opinion that she was completely lacking in suicidal tendencies.

(5) Upon cross-examination, defense counsel asked Dr. Slade: "Doctor, on at last three separate occasions in the past two years, have you committed acts of shoplifting?" Over objection, Dr. Slade was ordered to answer the question. He stated: "No, that is not so." Defense counsel then asked: "How do you expect us to believe that, Doctor, when I have the investigation reports of the stores right here?" An objection to this question was sustained.

Discuss the admissibility of items (1), (2), (3) and (4), assuming that all appropriate objections were timely made. As to item (5), discuss the propriety of the court's rulings on the objection.

Question 17

Paul brought a personal injury action against Helico, a helicopter manufacturer. The injury occurred when Paul attempted to board a Model Z helicopter manufactured by Helico. As he approached the helicopter from the rear, he was struck by the rotating tail rotor.

Two days after the accident, Al, the pilot of the helicopter, told Sam, an investigator of the National Transportation Safety Board (Board), that immediately after Paul was struck by the tail rotor, Paul exclaimed: "It's not anyone's fault, I just wasn't paying attention, I goofed."

Paul's complaint alleged Helico was negligent because the tail rotor was not marked so as to be conspicuous when operating under normal daylight ground conditions as required by a regulation of the Federal Aviation Administration (FAA), and that Helico was strictly liable because the helicopter was defectively designed.

At the trial by jury, the following occurred:

(1) Paul testified that after his suit was brought an officer of Helico not only offered to settle the action, but also admitted during settlement negotiations that the company agreed with Paul that the helicopter was defectively designed.

(2) After the jury had viewed the helicopter involved in the accident, Paul called Professor Jason, a recognized expert in the areas of engineering, navigation, and the operation of aircraft. He testified that, based solely on his in-court examination of photographs of the Helico Model Z helicopter and photographs of other helicopters, in his expert opinion the tail rotors on Helico Model Z helicopters are not conspicuous when operating under normal daylight ground conditions as required by the FAA.

(3) When called by the defense, Al testified, after repeated attempts to refresh his recollection, that he could not remember what Paul said. The court then admitted Sam's testimony concerning what Al stated Paul had said.

Assuming that all appropriate objections were timely made, did the court properly admit the testimony of Paul, Jason, and Sam? Discuss.

Question 18

Tim was tried in a State A court for possession of 1/10 gram of heroin, a felony. The government's only witness was Officer Jenks, an undercover police officer. Jenks testified that after Tim arranged to sell drugs to Jenks, Tim, in company with Sue, met Jenks on September 13 of last year. Jenks also testified that Tim refused to make the sale, and that Jenks then arrested Tim, searched him, and found a substance which he believed to be heroin in Tim's jacket pocket.

(1) The prosecutor then offered as an exhibit a document entitled "Official State A Forensic Laboratory Report," which states that the unknown substance found in possession of Tim was tested and found to be heroin. The report concluded: "I certify that the above is a true and accurate statement of the findings of this state agency as made this date" and is signed by A. Smith, Executive Director and Custodian (seal).

(2) As its first witness, the defense called the defendant, Tim, who testified on direct that he was in possession only of powdered milk and that he was being framed by Jenks. On cross-examination, Tim was asked, "Isn't it true that, two years ago, on May 1, you were in possession of 1/2 gram of heroin?" Over defense objection, Tim was instructed by the court to answer, and said "Yes."

(3) As its second witness, the defense called Sue, who testified: that she had been dating the defendant for a year, that they had dined out prior to the offense on eight occasions, and that he always drank his coffee after having added powdered milk taken from a jacket pocket.

(4) Sue then testified: that Jenks once arrested her for prostitution and offered to release her on payment of a bribe; that, when she refused, Jenks said, "Just wait, I'll get you and all your friends."

(5) In rebuttal, the prosecution called Dr. Walt, M.D., who testified: that he had recently examined Tim, who complained of insomnia and anxiety; that during the private examination Tim stated he was a narcotics addict in need of money to supply his habit; and that Tim asked Dr. Walt if he would like to buy drugs.

Assume that all appropriate objections were timely made.

Were the items of evidence (1) through (5) properly admitted? Discuss.

In dealing with item (2), discuss only the cross-examination and ignore the defendant's privilege against self-incrimination.

Question 19

Bob was struck by an automobile owned by Owner and driven by Chauf, Owner's employee. After two weeks in a hospital, Bob died.

Chauf was convicted of involuntary vehicular manslaughter. He died in a prison knife fight one week after he was imprisoned.

Paula, Bob's wife, sued Owner for the wrongful death of Bob, alleging that Owner was liable, both under the doctrine of *respondeat superior* and because Owner was negligent in hiring Chauf.

At the trial by jury, the following occurred:

(1) Paula's first witness, Carl, a police officer, testified: that when he arrived on the scene immediately after the accident he asked Bob what had happened, but he does not remember what Bob said; however, he had immediately made a note of what Bob told him and incorporated it into his written report. Carl verified the accuracy of his report and read it aloud. The report stated that Bob told Carl that he, Bob, was crossing the street when a car crossed over the center line and hit him. Upon Paula's request, the report was introduced into evidence.

(2) Paula next called Flo, who testified: that she was on duty when Bob arrived at the hospital; that Bob complained of severe pain in his stomach and head; that Bob swore he would get even with the driver of the car that hit him; and that when asked what happened, Bob said he was hit by a speeding car driven by a drunken lunatic.

(3) Paula next called Earl, the warden of the prison where Chauf died, who identified a writing made by Chauf a few hours before Chauf's death. The writing commenced with the statement, "I believe I am about to die and I make this statement with no hope of recovery." The writing recited that Chauf was intoxicated and was driving about 80 m.p.h. in a 25 m.p.h. speed zone at the time of the accident. The writing was admitted into evidence.

(4) Paula next called Frank, who testified: that he had known Bob for thirty years; that he had seen Bob on many occasions cross the intersection where the accident occurred; and that Bob always waited for the green light and looked both ways before crossing the street.

(5) Paula called Owner as an adverse witness and asked Owner whether he had heard that Chauf had received five traffic citations over the last five years for driving under the influence of alcohol. Owner answered: "No, because Chauf never had a traffic citation."

Assume all appropriate objections were timely made. Were items of evidence (1) through (4) properly admitted and was the question and answer in item (5) proper? Discuss.

Question 20

Paul brought an action against Dexter Labs, based on strict liability in tort. Paul alleged that he had suffered permanent liver damage from using sleeping pills manufactured and marketed by Dexter. The answer to Paul's complaint denied that the pills did or could cause liver damage.

(1) At trial, Paul testified he took Dexter's pills and subsequently developed symptoms of liver damage. On cross-examination, the court sustained an objection to the question: "Isn't it a fact that this is the fifth time you sued a food or drug manufacturer?"

(2) Over defense objection, the court permitted the jury to view and hear a videotape recording of the deposition of Dr. Box, Paul's treating physician, consisting of Dr. Box's expert medical testimony supporting Paul's claim, and the cross-examination of Dr. Box by Dexter's attorney. A stenographic transcript of the deposition was available. Dr. Box refused to testify voluntarily at trial because Paul had refused to pay him a fee of $1,000 for each day of testimony in court. Dr. Box successfully avoided a subpoena requiring him to appear at trial. The only relevant statutory provisions require that, on a deposition, the testimony be taken stenographically and be transcribed, and permit such a deposition to "be used by any party for any purpose if the witness is deceased, out of the jurisdiction, or otherwise unavailable."

(3) Over defense objection, the court received into evidence the testimony of an officer of Dexter that after Paul filed suit, Dexter changed its sleeping pill formula to remove a chemical that tended to accumulate in the liver.

(4) Dr. Abel, a qualified expert, testified for the defense that nothing in the pills which Paul took could possibly have caused liver problems. Over defense objection, Paul's attorney was allowed to cross-examine Dr. Abel regarding the contents of a series of newspaper articles on the toxic effects of sleeping pills.

(5) The court sustained Paul's objection and refused to allow the defense to introduce the testimony of attorney Carl, to the effect that: Paul had previously consulted him concerning his claim against Dexter; Paul had told him that his liver was permanently damaged before Paul took the Dexter pills; and Carl had refused to represent Paul.

Assuming all appropriate objections were timely made, were the court's rulings correct? Discuss.

Question 21

Dick is brought to trial on an indictment charging him with larceny of a dangerous drug, a statutory offense. The prosecution's theory of the case, as revealed by its opening statement, is that Phil saw Dick enter Phil's Pharmacy, loiter about the prescription counter, reach behind the counter, grab two bottles, and flee by car. Phil called police officers who arrested Dick after a lengthy high-speed chase.

At the trial before a jury, the following events occur:

(a) The prosecution offers in evidence a properly authenticated transcript of testimony by Officer Oats given during a previous trial of Dick for reckless driving based on the high-speed chase from Phil's Pharmacy. Oats' testimony was that during the chase and while Dick's car was passing over a bridge, two objects were ejected from Dick's car into the river below. It is stipulated that Dick was represented by counsel at the earlier trial and that Oats is now deceased.

(b) The prosecution offers the testimony of Phil that the bottles seized by Dick were labeled "DLD," that the bottles were the original labeled containers received from the supplier, and that the bottles had not been opened.

(c) The prosecution requests the court to take judicial notice that "DLD" is a derivative of opium. The statute under which Dick is prosecuted does not list "DLD" as a "dangerous drug," but does define dangerous drugs to include "any derivative of opium." In support of its request, the prosecution offers for the court's inspection a standard pharmacological dictionary, which defines "DLD" as an opium derivative.

(d) The prosecution offers the testimony of Dick's divorced wife, Win, that during her marriage to Dick the latter frequently used narcotics, but attempted to conceal that fact from Win.

Assume all appropriate objections were timely made by Dick.

How should the court have ruled on each of the prosecution's offers and requests? Discuss.

Question 22

Plaintiffs as the parents and guardians *ad litem* of Peter, age 4, brought suit for damages against the parents of David, age 10, alleging that defendants had negligently entrusted David with an air rifle with which David had shot Peter in the eye, causing serious personal injury. Among other things, defendants denied that Peter's eye injury was inflicted by David.

At the trial before a jury the following occurred:

(a) After Peter told the court that "good little boys always tell the truth," Peter testified that David shot him in the eye with the rifle.

(b) Peter's father testified that the defendants had paid a substantial portion of Peter's medical bills and had offered to pay the rest.

(c) Bill, a neighbor, testified that: (i) David was "a vicious little bully with malicious tendencies"; and (ii) that when Bill, Bill's wife Clara, and David's mother were all standing together in Bill's yard after the incident, Clara stated to Bill that David's mother had said to her about one week before the accident that "she had tried to get David's father to put the air rifle in the attic where David couldn't get to it, before someone got hurt"; and that David's mother had said nothing in response to Clara's statement.

(d) Wilbur, an eyewitness, corroborated Peter's description of the shooting. On cross-examination Wilbur was asked:

"Aren't you addicted to the use of heroin?"

"Aren't you in fact now under the influence of a narcotic?"

"May I look at your arm?"

The court sustained plaintiff's objections to each of these three questions.

In each instance all appropriate objections were timely made and in (a), (b) and (c) the court permitted the testimony over objection and in (d) sustained the objections to each of the three questions.

Were the rulings of the court correct? Discuss.

Question 23

While traveling north through an intersection governed by a traffic light, Ann's car was struck on the driver's side by a dark blue sports car which sped from the scene of the collision.

Rick, the only pedestrian eyewitness, took photographs of the accident and of the sports car as it left the scene, but he did not observe the license plate on the car. Rick gave the undeveloped film to police who developed the photographs and were able to read the license plate number XJY-134 on the car. It was determined that Dave owned the car with license number XJY-134.

Ann commenced a negligence action against Dave seeking compensation for property damage and personal injuries to herself and her passenger, her four-year-old daughter Jane. Dave's answer alleged that this car was not involved in the accident, but if it was, it was used without his knowledge or permission. Dave also counterclaimed, alleging that Ann was negligent.

At the jury trial, the following occurred:

1. Ann's first witness, Bob, testified that he arrived at the scene within minutes of the accident, heard Jane crying, and heard Jane state that "the blue car went through a red light and hit us." A stipulation has been entered in the record that Jane is incompetent to testify at trial solely because of her age.

2. Ann testified that, prior to commencing suit against Dave, she spoke to him about settlement of her claim for $20,000. He stated, "I will settle with you if it isn't covered by insurance."

3. Rick, as a witness for Ann, testified as to the taking of the photographs developed by the police, and the photographs were admitted into evidence.

4. In the defense case, Dave introduced testimony by a properly qualified expert that three days after the accident and before the expert had an opportunity to examine the possibly faulty brake system on Ann's car, the car was repaired. Further, the expert testified that the repair included substantial brake work.

Assume timely and appropriate objections were made to the foregoing.

(1) Was the testimony in items 1, 2 and 4 properly admitted? Discuss.

(2) Were the photographs in item 3 property admitted? Discuss.

Question 24

In a rape prosecution against Roe, the following events occurred at the trial by jury:

1. Adam, a neighbor of the victim, Tess, testified that, within five minutes after the rape was alleged to have occurred, Tess ran to his house sobbing and said that she had just been raped by a man with a large brown blemish on his left arm.

2. Detective Cable testified that, on receiving Tess' report, he examined the file of known sex offenders, and that Roe was described as having a blemish on his left arm.

3. Roe's wife voluntarily testified for the prosecution that Roe returned home on the night in question with scratches on his arm.

4. Roe testified in his defense and denied the act, saying that he had never been near Tess' house. In rebuttal, the prosecution offered one of Roe's shoes, seized in an illegal search of Roe's house. The shoe was introduced together with expert testimony that a shoeprint identical to the shoeprint made by Roe's shoe had been located outside the window the rapist had used to enter Tess' house.

5. At the prosecution's request, the judge ordered Roe to bare his left arm for the jury's inspection. Roe refused. The judge allowed the prosecutor to argue in closing argument that Roe's refusal was an attempt to hide evidence, from which the jury might infer guilt.

Assume all proper motions and objections were timely made.

Did the court err in admitting the testimony in items 1 through 3, in admitting the shoe and testimony in item 4, or in permitting the prosecutor's argument in item 5? Discuss.

Essay Exam Answers

Answer to Question 1

(1) Testimony of Mr. Charles

Dan ("D") could contend that the testimony of Mr. Charles (C) is not relevant (*i.e.*, does not tend to prove or disprove a material fact of consequence). He may have run away simply because he desired to avoid an altercation with someone who was erroneously charging him with having committed a crime. The Prosecution ("P"), however, probably successfully argued in rebuttal that D's conduct does indicate a consciousness of guilt.

D could next assert that C's statement is hearsay. He is testifying as to what his wife stated, and what D did in response. Hearsay statements are those made out-of-court by someone other than the witness which are offered to prove the truth of the matter asserted. As to D's conduct, P could contend that in many states (and under the FRE), assertive conduct is not hearsay at all. Even if it is, the party-opponent admission exception to the hearsay rule would be applicable (anything said or done by the opposing party which is inconsistent with his litigation position is admissible).

Mrs. C's statement is arguably admissible as an adoptive admission (*i.e.*, an out-of-court statement made in the party-opponent's presence which a reasonable person would have objected to or denied). P would contend that a reasonable person, hearing a false criminal accusation, would have protested his innocence to the speaker. D could argue in rebuttal, however, that a reasonable person, confronted with a false accusation by a total stranger in a park would simply leave the area (as D did). However, P should prevail on this issue.

Mrs. C's statement would probably fall within the "excited utterance" exception to the hearsay rule. Such a statement must ordinarily be made about a startling event by someone who observed it, while the event is occurring (or while the declarant was still under the stress of the event.) The "startling event" in this instance was seeing D wearing her jacket. Since Mrs. C's statement was made watching this startling event, this testimony should be admissible. (*See* ELO Ch. 6-11(D)(3) & IV(D).)

Thus, C's testimony was probably properly admitted.

(2) The testimony of Yank ("Y")

D could have initially asserted that Y's testimony is not admissible because the latter testified as an expert without any foundation having been laid that he had any specialized expert knowledge. Y is, apparently, an ordinary dentist. P could argue that any dentist who constantly analyzes teeth, has sufficient specialized knowledge to give an expert opinion about dental impressions.

Assuming Y is qualified to testify as an expert, D could respond that no evidence was introduced to show that this type of comparison-testing is scientifically valid.

Since P apparently did not show that the comparison method used by Y is scientifically valid (which would be shown by factors such as error rate, peer review, general acceptance in the field, and whether the test can be reliably tested), the court erred in admitting Y's testimony. (*See* ELO Ch. 10-III(A)(2)(f).)

(3) Bob ("B")'s testimony

The P could contend that B's testimony was hearsay since it described what D said out-of-court.

D could respond that D's desire to use the cabin for two days is admissible under the "present state of mind" exception to the hearsay rule, since it describes what D indicated he would do in the future.

D's returning the key and commenting that the stove had exploded when the pipe was hit by lightning during the early morning hours of April 17 (when C's home was burglarized) is arguably not hearsay, since it is offered into evidence by D simply to show that he was aware that the cabin's stove had been damaged (rather than for the purpose of establishing that the item had, in fact, been damaged). (This is sometimes referred to as the "place and time" exception to the hearsay rule.) D's knowledge of the damaged stove would tend to corroborate his assertion that he was 200 miles away when the crime occurred. (*See* ELO Ch. 5-II(C)(6)(a) & Ch. 6-IV(C)(2).)

Thus, B's testimony was properly admitted.

The party-opponent exception to the hearsay rule would not be applicable to D's statements in this instance since B was D's witness.

(4) Able ("A")'s testimony

A's testimony appears to be offered for impeachment (the prosecution and D have each already presented the case-in-chief). Thus, a hearsay objection is not appropriate because A's statement was not offered to prove the truth of the matter (*i.e.*, that B, had not, in fact, seen D during the month of April); but rather, to impugn B's credibility by showing that he had made an earlier inconsistent statement. It is ordinarily proper to impeach a witness in this manner by extrinsic evidence (*i.e.*, A's testimony); provided the impeachment does not go to a collateral matter. The "I was far away" alibi asserted by D is certainly *not* collateral to the case (it is the essence of D's defense).

In some jurisdictions, however, a foundation must be laid before impeachment by extrinsic evidence as to a prior inconsistent statement is admissible (*i.e.*, the P should have asked B, while he was on the stand, "Isn't it a fact that you told A that you had not seen D during the month of April?"). If such was the rule in this jurisdiction, A's testimony should not have been admitted.

In a few jurisdictions, prior inconsistent statements are not deemed to be hearsay. In that event, A's testimony would (assuming no foundation was necessary) have been admissible as substantive evidence upon the P's case-in-chief. Such is ***not***, however, the case under the FRE unless the prior inconsistent statement was made under oath; FRE 801(d)(1)(A). (*See* ELO Ch. 4-X(B)(1) & Ch. 6-XIV(B)(6).)

Answer to Question 2

(1) Witt ("W")'s testimony

Don ("D") could have contended that W's testimony was hearsay (*i.e.*, he described what Payne and D had said out-of-court). Hearsay statements are those made by an out-of-court declarant which are offered into evidence to prove the truth of the matter asserted. However, Payne ("P") could have argued in rebuttal that (1) his statement is admissible as an operative fact (*i.e.*, it had a legal significance in itself, apart from whether the matter was true or not), in that it proves words of offer were made by P, and (2) D's response was admissible as either a party-opponent admission (a statement made by an opposing party which is inconsistent with his litigation position) or as an operative fact (simply to show that D was aware that a contractually binding offer had been made to him). Although D could have argued in rebuttal that his statement ("I'll let you know…") is not inconsistent with his position that P's offer was never accepted, it would probably still be admissible as an operative fact. (*See* ELO Ch.5-II(C)(3).)

W's testimony was properly admitted.

(2) Maida ("M")'s testimony

D could have contended that M's testimony was (1) irrelevant (*i.e.*, did not tend to prove or disprove a fact of consequence) since his expression of an intent to accept P's offer on May 2 would not preclude a change of mind prior to actually communicating an acceptance to P; (2) privileged (under both the marital communications and the attorney-client privileges); and (3) hearsay.

P could have responded in rebuttal that (1) the statement was relevant because it was made at a time close to the purported acceptance (the next day), which tends to increase the likelihood that D actually accepted P's offer; (2) at common law, at least the last phrase ("I'm going…") is admissible under both the party-opponent admission and the present state of mind (*i.e.*, statements by a declarant about his intention to undertake an act in the future) exceptions to the hearsay rule. Admission of the initial phrase, even if erroneous, would not appear to constitute reversible error.

As to D's claim of privilege, P could have contended that (1) at common law, eavesdroppers could testify about privileged communications (presently, however, many jurisdictions take a contrary position); (2) assuming D should have realized that their maid might be near the bedroom as he was speaking, the communication was not "confidential;" and (3) as to the attorney-client privilege, D's discussion with his wife was arguably not with the purpose of securing legal services within the context of a professional relationship. Assuming the common law view is followed, M's testimony was properly admitted. (*See* ELO Ch. 6-II(C) & IV(C); Ch. 8-II(C) & IV(C)(4)(a).)

(3) Admission of a portion of the Telephone Log

D could have argued that this evidence was inadmissible because (1) it was not properly authenticated (*i.e.*, Belle admitted that she did not recognize D's voice, and so there is no assurance that the caller was actually D); (2) it is double hearsay (the Log made by Belle is describing what D purportedly said).

P could have initially argued in rebuttal that authentication occurred by reason of the fact that D was probably the only person (other than his wife) who was aware of P's offer to paint the portrait.

As to the double hearsay objection, P could have argued that the initial level of hearsay (the Log itself) is admissible under the "business records" exception. Under this theory, a statement recorded in the regular course by a business whose usual practice was to record such statements, by one under a duty to make such entries who had personal knowledge of the matter, is *not* inadmissible under the hearsay rule. Since the job of an answering service is to take and record messages, and Belle ("B") personally received the information in question, this exception to the hearsay rule is applicable. The second level of hearsay (D's statement) is admissible as a party-opponent admission. (*See* ELO Ch. 5-II(F)(3) & Ch. 9-II(C)(7)(c)(ii).)

(4) The motion to exclude the Log after B's death

Where, as a consequence of death or physical disability, a witness cannot be cross-examined, it is within the court's discretion to strike her testimony. Since B merely testified that she accurately recorded the message received from someone purporting to be D and authenticated the Telephone Log, it is highly unlikely that any meaningful impeachment of B could have been undertaken by D. Thus, the court's refusal to exclude the Log was correct. (*See* ELO Ch. 7-II(D).)

Answer to Question 3

1. Dr. Jones ("J")'s testimony

D could have objected to J's testimony upon the grounds that (1) it violated the physician-patient privilege; (2) it was irrelevant (*i.e.*, did not tend to prove or disprove a fact of consequence), since D may have been motivated to take P to J's office from a humanitarian impulse, rather than as a result of feelings of culpability; (3) it was hearsay (J described what D said out-of-court); and (4) in nearly all states (as well as federal courts; FRE 409) offers to pay for medical assistance are not admissible to prove liability.

First, P could have argued that (1) the physician-patient privilege is not applicable because it pertains only to statements made for medical diagnosis and treatment, and D's instructions to J did not refer to these aspects; and (2) even if applicable, this privilege is held only by the person who received the diagnosis or treatment, P *not* D.

Second, P could have contended that D's conduct in taking him to a physician and promising to pay P's medical bills is relevant in that it evidences a recognition of responsibility for P's condition (*i.e.*, people don't ordinarily inconvenience themselves and incur liability for a stranger unless they feel responsible for the latter's situation).

Third, the hearsay objection would be overcome by the "party-opponent" admission exception to the hearsay rule.

Finally, in most states as well as the federal courts, an offer to pay medical expenses is not admissible to prove liability.

On analysis, the evidence probably should not have been admitted since (1) the act of taking P to J's office is probably not relevant (any kindhearted person would have done this); and (2) the majority view is to exclude offers to pay medical expenses (the rationale being that aid to accident victims should not be discouraged). (*See* ELO Ch. 2-II(A); Ch. 3-XIV(I); Ch. 6-II(C); Ch. 8-III(B)(1) & (3).)

2. P's testimony

D could have objected to this testimony on the grounds that (1) it is hearsay (P is describing what D said out-of-court); (2) settlement offers (D's offer to pay $5,000 in settlement of the action) are generally inadmissible; and (3) admissions of fact made during a settlement offer, while admissible under the common law, are inadmissible under the Federal Rules of Evidence (FRE 408).

The hearsay objection can be overcome by the party-opponent admission to the hearsay rule. The second objection can be overcome by the fact that, under the common law as well as the FRE, evidence that a party has offered to settle a claim may not be admitted on the issue of the claim's validity. Therefore, D's promise to pay $5,000 for a release is inadmissible. Whether D's statement about "going through a red light" would be admissible depends upon whether this jurisdiction adheres to the FRE view (excluding *all* statements made in the course of settlement negotiations) or not. Assuming the FRE is followed in this state, P's entire testimony should not have been admitted. (*See* ELO Ch. 3-XIV(A)-(E).)

3. Testimony of Mrs. D

D could have objected to this testimony as (1) violating the spousal privilege (in some states, one spouse can prevent the other from testifying against him), (2) violating the marital communications privilege, (3) hearsay, and (4) opinion pertaining to an ultimate issue of fact (*i.e.*, that D's conduct fell below the applicable standard of care).

P could have argued in rebuttal, however, that (1) many jurisdictions apply the spousal privilege only to criminal cases; (2) the marital communications privilege is not applicable since D's statement was not "confidential" (*i.e.*, it was made while the butler was present); (3) the party-opponent exception would overcome any hearsay objection; and (4) most jurisdictions permit lay witness opinion upon an ultimate issue of fact. FRE 704 specifically provides that testimony in the form of an opinion which is otherwise admissible is not objectionable because it embraces an ultimate issue of fact.

Assuming this jurisdiction permits lay witness opinion upon ultimate issues of fact and D was (or reasonably should have been) aware of the butler's presence, Mrs. D's testimony would be admissible. (*See* ELO Ch. 6-II(C); Ch. 8-V(B)(2) & (C)(4); Ch. 10-I(D)(2).)

4. Testimony of Bystander ("B")

D could have objected to B's testimony as (1) being hearsay (*i.e.*, B testified as to what X said out-of-court), (2) containing a reference to insurance, and (3) including lay witness opinion (*i.e.*, the portion of the testimony dealing with X's fault in the accident).

P could have contended in rebuttal that the statement is admissible under the dying declaration, statement against interest, or excited utterance exceptions to the hearsay rule.

As to the "dying declaration" exception, even assuming there is sufficient evidence for the jury to conclude that X sincerely thought he was going to die, D could have argued that this exception is not present because (1) some states limit this rule to cases involving homicide; and (2) the statement must pertain to the circumstances or cause of the declarant's death (*i.e.*, simply saying, "It was my fault," does not pertain to the cause or circumstances of X's death). As to the "statement against interest" exception, P could contend that since B believed that death was imminent, the statement was actually *not* against his pecuniary interest. Finally, even assuming that the "excited utterance" exception to the hearsay rule in this jurisdiction extends to statements made while still under the stress of the event (as opposed to requiring that the statement be made contemporaneously with the occurrence of the incident or condition): (1) there is insufficient indication that X was "excited," and (2) again, the statement must pertain to the startling event or condition.

Since (1) X's statement could be taken as referring to the accident, or (2) the statement could have diminished his estate and could be viewed as being against his interests, the hearsay objection should have been overcome.

The objection to that portion of B's testimony pertaining to X's statement about insurance should have been sustained (1) as irrelevant (it doesn't tend to prove or disprove whether D or X was responsible for P's injury); and (2) under public policy grounds (a jury's decision-making might be affected by the fact that X's insurance could more easily compensate P for his injuries).

Finally, the portion of B's testimony pertaining to fault should also have been inadmissible as opinion (if this jurisdiction does not permit lay witness opinion pertaining to an ultimate issue by a non-party).

In summary, although an exception to the hearsay rule exists, B's testimony should *not* have been admitted. (*See* ELO Ch. 3-XIII(A); Ch. 6-IV(D); Ch. 6-XI(B)(3)(b) & (B)(5); Ch. 6-XII(B)(2).)

Answer to Question 4

1. (a) The contract (minus the missing page)

There would be little substance to any objection made by Dan ("D") to the introduction of this document, assuming that Alex ("A"), besides negotiating the transaction, had viewed a final copy of the agreement. If this were so, A would possess the first-hand knowledge necessary to authenticate the contract. No hearsay objection could successfully be raised since the understandings embodied in the document would be admissible as operative facts (*i.e.*, statements which have a legal significance in themselves, without regard to the truth of the matters asserted). (*See* ELO Ch. 9-II(C)(1).)

(b) Testimony as to the contents of the missing page

Under the Best Evidence Rule, the original document is ordinarily required to prove the contents of a writing. P could have therefore contended that A's testimony was inadmissible. However, one is ordinarily permitted to introduce other evidence of a writing when there is no indication that the proponent has deliberately caused the original document to become unavailable. Since A has testified that the missing page was "inadvertently" destroyed, permitting A to testify was probably proper (if Corp had no other copies of the contract within its possession and D's copy was unavailable). (*See* ELO Ch. 9-IV(A)(4).)

Again, no hearsay contention would be feasible since the items described on the missing page would constitute operative facts.

2. D's cross-examination

Corp may have contended that details of other contracts entered into by it were not relevant (*i.e.*, have a tendency to prove or disprove a fact of consequence) to this case. Under the Uniform Commercial Code, which applies to contracts for the sale of merchandise, "usage of trade" may be relevant in determining the meaning of contract terms. Most jurisdictions have adopted the U.C.C. terms.

The question was probably appropriate for impeachment purposes *if* the other contracts referred to were reviewed by A at about the same time as or earlier than the agreement in question. A's ability to recollect would be discredited if he could not recall other contracts which he had made at approximately the same time with equal precision. Thus, the question should have been admitted. (*See* ELO Ch. 4-XII(A).)

3. The computer print-out

D could have objected to this evidence as (1) contravening the Best Evidence Rule (the "best evidence" being the original receipts, invoices and credits slips); (2) constituting hearsay (out-of-court statements offered into evidence to prove the truth of the matter asserted), since the printout is describing statements made in other documents — the receipts, invoices and credit slips; and (3) not being properly authenticated (*i.e.*, no foundation was laid to show that the key-punch cards actually reflected transactions with D, that the key-punching itself was done accurately, or that the process by which the information was entered into, and printed out of, the computer was reliable.

Corp could have argued in rebuttal that many jurisdictions (and the FRE) permit voluminous writings to be presented in a summarized format, provided the original back-up materials are made available to the other side (FRE 1006). However, it is unclear whether the delivery receipts, invoices and credit slips were so numerous as to come within this rule. FRE 1003 provides that a duplicate is admissible to the same extent as an original unless a genuine question is raised as to the authenticity of the original.

Corp could have asserted the "business records" exception to the hearsay rule. Under this doctrine, where a statement is recorded in the regular course of a business whose regular practice is to record such statements, by one who is under a duty to make such entries and has personal knowledge of the matters recorded (or which information was transmitted to such person by someone with personal knowledge of the matters recorded), it is admissible as an exception to the hearsay rule. The office manager would have to testify to the regularity of the procedure and to the accuracy of the method of transcription.

Computer records are admissible if the equipment is standard and the procedures used to input data are reliable. The court can determine that the sources of information are unreliable. Finally, D's authentication objections seem to be well taken since no proof has been offered to show that (1) the original receipts, invoices and credit slips were genuine (*i.e.*, properly identified); or (2) the process by which the information was assimilated and disclosed upon the computer print-out is reliable. (*See* ELO Ch. 6-VI(K)(2) & Ch. 9-IV(H)(2).)

Thus, the computer print-out should not have been admitted.

4. Prex ("P")'s testimony

D could have objected to this testimony upon the ground that (1) it was made during a settlement conference; (2) it was hearsay (P is testifying as to what someone from Corp said, and then as to what D stated his bookkeeper had told him.

The traditional common law view was that statements made during settlement conferences which did not constitute offers of settlement were admissible. However, a majority of jurisdictions today (as well as the federal courts - FRE 408) makes such statements inadmissible.

If P, himself, made the statement attributed to Corp, his statement would **not** be hearsay since he is on the witness stand and may be cross-examined. Even if someone else representing Corp made the $6,200 settlement offer, her statement would probably still *not* be considered hearsay since it was not offered to prove that Corp would actually settle its claim for $6,200; but rather, to show the context in which D's responsive comment was made.

D's statement at the conference would be admissible under the party-opponent exception to the hearsay rule. (Such statements are not considered hearsay at all in federal courts - FRE 801.) The statement of D's bookkeeper was probably admissible as an adoptive admission (*i.e.*, a statement about which the party-opponent has manifested her adoption or her belief that it is true. Since business persons ordinarily rely upon and accept statements made to them by their bookkeepers as accurate, this exception to the hearsay rule would probably apply.

Thus, D's hearsay objection would probably *not* be successful.

Thus, unless this jurisdiction excludes all statements made during the course of compromise negotiations, P's testimony was properly admitted. (*See* ELO Ch. 3-XIV(E); Ch. 5-II(C)(6); Ch. 6-II(C) & (D).)

Answer to Question 5

(1) Officer Jones ("J")'s testimony

Moses ("M") probably contended that J's testimony was hearsay (an out-of-court statement offered into evidence to prove the truth of the matter asserted therein), since J was testifying as to what Adams ("A") had told him. Peter ("P") probably argued in rebuttal that A's statement constituted an admission by the agent or servant of a party-opponent. However, M could have responded that (1) it had not been established that A was acting on behalf of M (*i.e.*, in fact, M had asserted that A was involved in the latter's own business); and (2) traditionally, an agent or servant has no right to speak for his principal, and therefore the former's statement could not be attributed to the latter. Nevertheless, the emerging view is that statements made by agents or servants in the course of their agency or employment are attributable to their principal; FRE 801(d)(2)(D). Thus, the court could have permitted the testimony with a limiting instruction (*i.e.*, that it was to be disregarded if the jury did not conclude that A was, in fact, acting on behalf of M when the accident occurred). However, A's statement that he was performing an errand for M probably constitutes sufficient evidence for the jury to infer that A was acting on behalf of M for a business purpose. (*See* ELO Ch. 6-II(E)(2)(b).)

(2) J's testimony (opinion)

M probably objected to this testimony upon the grounds that no foundation had been laid to the effect that (1) J had sufficient expertise to reconstruct an accident from skid marks, and (2) the process of interpreting a car's speed by skid marks is a scientifically valid basis for evaluating a vehicle's speed. The fact that J had been a police officer for 15 years would *not* necessarily establish that he had the special expertise presumably required to interpret skid marks. But, assuming that J was qualified to testify as an expert, the process by which skid marks are used to measure a vehicle's speed must be proven to be scientifically valid before it can be admitted into evidence. Scientific validity can be shown by factors such as error rate, peer review, general acceptance in the field, and whether the test can be reliably tested. Thus, unless additional evidence was presented by P's attorneys which addressed these objections, J probably should *not* have been permitted to offer an opinion as to the speed of M's vehicle. (*See* ELO Ch. 10-III(A)(2)(f).)

(3) Dr. Medic's testimony

M probably contended that Medic's testimony was hearsay (Medic is testifying as to what P told him). The initial portion of Medic's testimony (*i.e.*, that P complained to him of a severe headache) is probably admissible under the "present sensation" exception to the hearsay rule. Although M might have contended that this statement was untrustworthy (*i.e.*, P obviously realized that Medic would be testifying as to P's condition the next day), this concern is probably more appropriate in assessing the weight of Medic's testimony (rather than its admissibility).

FRE 803(4) makes statements for the purpose of medical diagnosis or treatment exceptions to the hearsay rule. The committee notes to FRE 803 say that statements made for the purpose of preparing the doctor to testify also qualify. This exception includes both past and present symptoms, such as P's complaints of headache. The testimony is admissible. (*See* ELO Ch. 6-IV(B)(5).)

(4) Cross-examination of Medic

Since bias in favor of a party is a proper basis for impeachment, the fact that Medic had received a substantial sum to testify on P's behalf was an appropriate subject of inquiry. Thus, the court correctly overruled P's objection. (*See* ELO Ch. 4-XI(B)(3).)

(5) Testimony of Walter ("W")

M probably objected to the rehabilitation of Medic's testimony by evidence of the latter's reputation for truth and veracity because Medic had been impeached only with respect to possible bias. Since there must ordinarily be some relationship between the area of impeachment and that which is being rehabilitated, M's objection should have been sustained. (*See* ELO Ch. 4-XV(C).)

(6) The cross-examination of W

A witness who testifies as to another person's character for truthfulness or veracity in the community may ordinarily be questioned about specific acts of the latter which pertained to those qualities. Since the falsification of income tax returns and the concealment of assets would (if true) discredit W's testimony by suggesting that W was not well informed as to Medic's notoriety in the community, the question was proper. (*See* ELO Ch. 4-IX(C)(1)(c)(i).)

Answer to Question 6

(1) F's testimony

F's initial testimony (that P had told him he was meeting a friend for lunch on June 15 at Front and Elm) would be relevant (*i.e.*, it tends to prove or disprove a material fact), since it would corroborate that P was at the scene of the accident.

D could have objected to this testimony, however, on the grounds that it was hearsay (an out-of-court statement offered into evidence to prove the truth of the matter asserted therein). However, P could probably successfully argue in rebuttal that F's statement was admissible under the "present intention" exception to the hearsay rule. (*See* ELO Ch. 6-IV(C)(2).)

D probably objected to F's second statement (that P had advised F that the bus had driven onto the sidewalk) as hearsay also. Since P's statement was made one week after the accident, it would **not** qualify as an excited utterance. Since there does not appear to be any exception to the hearsay rule which would justify the admission of F's second statement, the description of how the accident occurred should **not** have been admitted.

(2) L's testimony

The substance of L's testimony is unclear. If L had corroborated P's version of the accident, it would be relevant. Otherwise, however, L's assertion that he was in C City for a vacation and was staying at M Motel would not appear to be pertinent to the *prima facia* issues of the case. In the latter instance, a relevancy objection to the testimony should have been sustained.

D's offer of evidence pertaining to L's prosecution, permanent residency and failure to stay at the M Motel, was apparently offered for impeachment.

D's counsel could have contended that proof of the prosecution of L for letting air out of bus tires was proper impeachment, since it tended to show bias by L against (1) D (if D's buses were the subject of L's actions, or (2) bus companies in general (even if D's buses were not the subject of L's actions). While the alleged bias is more tenuous in the latter instance, D's question would probably still be permissible. In some jurisdictions, however, a foundation must be laid prior to the admission of **extrinsic** (*i.e.*, the facts indicate that counsel for D "offered evidence") evidence of bias (*i.e.*, L should have been asked, while he was on the stand, if he had been prosecuted for letting the air out of bus tires). In those states, the "evidence" would **not** be admissible.

P could have responded that the proffered evidence was impeachment through prior bad acts. It is not clear from the facts whether the prosecution of L had resulted in a conviction. If it had not, L's "prior bad acts" would not be a proper basis of impeachment since (1) the acts complained of in this instance arguably do not pertain to truthfulness or veracity; and (2) impeachment with respect to prior bad acts not resulting in a conviction ordinarily cannot be accomplished by extrinsic evidence.

D could have contended that the evidence showing that L had resided in C City all of his life and had never stayed at the M Motel, impeached L. However, P's attorney probably could have asserted in rebuttal that one can never impeach by extrinsic evidence with respect to a collateral matter. (*See* ELO Ch. 4-VIII(B)(1), XI(B)(2) & XIII(D).)

Thus, the court probably should *not* have permitted D to impeach L in this manner.

(3) X's testimony

P probably objected to X's testimony on the grounds that (1) it constitutes layperson opinion pertaining to the causal relationship between P's injuries and his actions, and (2) it is violative of the accountant-client privilege (assuming this privilege is recognized in this state). D could have argued in rebuttal that (1) layperson opinion is often admissible if it is based upon firsthand knowledge and helpful to a determination of the issues by the factfinder, and (2) the accountant-client privilege ordinarily extends only to communications (statements made by the client to the accountant), rather than the accountant's observations of the client's physical condition. However, X's testimony probably should not have been admitted since he does not have the expertise to offer an opinion as to the causal relationship between P's medical condition and his actions. (*See* ELO Ch. 10-I(C)(6).)

(4) Dr. Q's testimony

P could have contended that Dr. Q's testimony was violative of the physician-patient privilege. However, virtually all jurisdictions view this privilege as not being applicable to situations where the patient has placed his physical condition into issue. Since Dr. Q is a "brain specialist," there appears to be little doubt that he was qualified to testify as to the causes of P's memory lapse and insane behavior. Thus, Dr. Q's testimony was properly admitted.

D could have objected that P's cross-examination of Dr. Q was improper because (1) the work relied upon by P was not established as a learned treatise, (2) Dr. Q did not rely upon the work in giving his testimony, and (3) the statements in the book were hearsay. However, P could have successfully argued in rebuttal that (1) Dr. Q's own statement that the work was a reference book on brain injuries would establish the work as a learned treatise; (2) the modern rule is that an expert may be impeached by statements contained in a learned treatise regardless of whether he has relied upon them; and (3) since the statements contained in the work are being offered to contradict Dr. Q (rather than for the truth of the matter contained therein), the hearsay rule is inapplicable. It therefore appears that the cross-examination of Dr. Q was appropriate. The FRE recognizes an exception to the hearsay rule for statements contained in a learned treatise; FRE 803(18). (*See* ELO Ch. 10-II(B) & (E)(1)(c).)

Answer to Question 7

(1) Abel ("A")'s testimony

Peter ("P") might properly have objected that A's testimony was opinion, and therefore not admissible. However, a witness may ordinarily offer his opinion with respect to another's signature for the purpose of authenticating a document, as long as the witness possessed firsthand familiarity with the handwriting. Since A had seen Dan ("D")'s signature "hundreds of times" and his testimony is pertinent in proving that D had *not* signed the contract, the court correctly admitted this evidence. (*See* ELO Ch. 9-II(C)(5)(c).)

(2) The cross-examination of A

Assuming P's counsel had a good faith basis for his question, the inquiry would appear to be proper since bias is a proper ground for impeachment. While D could have objected on relevance grounds that P's lawsuit against A's employer would not necessarily cause bias by A towards P, actions which impair a business often affect its employees. If P's against the bank were successful, it might affect the bank substantially. Thus, D's objection should *not* have been sustained. (*See* ELO Ch. 4-XI(B)(2).)

Although P's counsel has asked a leading question, this mode of interrogation is ordinarily proper with adverse witnesses.

(3) The cross-examination of D

D's counsel could have objected to this cross-examination upon the grounds that (1) it was a leading question; (2) it was a compound question (D is being asked to answer two questions by a single inquiry — what P stated and how he responded); and (3) it calls for a hearsay response (*i.e.*, for D to testify as to what P said out-of-court). P could have responded in rebuttal, however, that (1) leading questions are permissible upon cross-examination; (2) the two inquiries were easily distinguishable (*i.e.*, did P make a particular statement, and did D respond in a specific manner?); and (3) P's statement was not offered to prove the truth of the matter therein (*i.e.*, that P had stated, "You know…"), but merely to describe the statement to which D acquiesced by not disputing P's statement (such acquiescence being inconsistent with D's testimony). (*See* ELO Ch. 5-II(C)(5).)

Thus, the objection to D's cross-examination was properly overruled.

(4) Row ("R")'s testimony

D could have objected to R's testimony on the grounds that (1) an attorney in a particular case should not be competent to testify, since a jury would have a tendency to give too much weight to his statement; and (2) it is hearsay (R is testifying with respect to P's statement and D's lack of response). However, P could respond that (1) most jurisdictions permit anyone (other than the presiding judge) to testify in a legal proceeding, and (2) R's statement is an adoptive admission by D, because a reasonable person would have denied R's allegation.

In any event, R's testimony would be admissible for impeachment purposes to contradict D (*i.e.*, to show that D had previously behaved in a manner which contradicts his testimony).

There would be no difficulty in impeaching D through extrinsic evidence, since this testimony was *not* collateral to the issues of the case (*i.e.*, whether D signed the contract is a central issue in the litigation). (*See* ELO Ch. 4-XIII(D) & Ch. 6-II(D)(3).)

(5) *The judge's instruction*

Where a presumption affects only the burden of producing evidence (as opposed to the burden of proof), the modern rule is that once the party against whom the presumption operates offers evidence sufficient for a jury to infer a finding contrary to the presumption, the presumption is overcome. Consequently, the burden of proving the applicable fact is upon the party attempting to establish it. Since A and D testified that the latter did not sign the contract, there was sufficient evidence for the factfinder to conclude that D had *not* executed the agreement. Thus, the court's instruction was erroneous. The judge should have instructed the jury that it should not conclude that D signed the contract, unless it was persuaded of such fact from a preponderance of the evidence (rather than indicating that D had the burden of persuading the jury by a preponderance of the evidence that he had *not* signed the agreement). (*See* ELO Ch. 11-II(B)(3)(b).)

Answer to Question 8

1. *(a) The carbon copy of the script, after Pete ("P")'s testimony*

Doe ("D") could have objected to this evidence on the grounds that (1) it is irrelevant (it does not tend to prove or disprove a material fact), since the fact that an item was mailed to a particular entity does not assure that it was actually received by it; (2) it violates the Best Evidence Rule, since it is merely a carbon copy (rather than the original manuscript); and (3) it is hearsay. (No authentication objection appears to be viable since P has stated that the script was his story.) P could have contended in rebuttal, however, that (1) the testimony is relevant because a jury could infer the script was actually received by D from the fact that it was mailed (items which are sent through the mails ordinarily reach the addressee); (2) P no longer has the original since it was sent to D, and, in many jurisdictions, a carbon copy of an item qualifies as an original for purposes of the Best Evidence Rule; and (3) the script is not offered for the "truth" of its contents, but as evidence that the script existed; therefore, it is not hearsay. (*See* ELO Ch. 9-IV(A)(4)(c).)

Thus, the carbon copy of P's script was properly admitted.

(b) P's testimony

D probably objected to this testimony upon the grounds that it is simply P's opinion as to the value of his script, and only an expert with respect to literary items could evaluate the story's worth. P could have argued in rebuttal, however, that some jurisdictions permit a layperson to offer his opinion about the value of his property where no better evidence is readily available. Since the value of P's story would, in any event, be a matter of some conjecture (even if estimated by an expert), P's testimony was probably properly admitted. (*See* ELO Ch. 10-I(C)(6).)

(c) The motion picture and statement of production

D could have objected to this evidence upon the grounds that it was (1) hearsay, and (2) not properly authenticated (*i.e.*, it was not shown that D, in fact, produced the motion picture). The hearsay exception is overcome by the operative facts doctrine (*i.e.*, the picture is not offered into evidence to prove the truth of the matters described therein, but rather to show a similarity with P's manuscript). P could have argued that the picture was properly authenticated because some jurisdictions view trade inscriptions as being self-authenticating (*i.e.*, items which are utilized in commerce and which bear the name of a manufacturer or producer are presumed to have been manufactured or produced by that party; unless evidence to the contrary is produced by the party against whom the item is offered). However, unless such an exception existed in this jurisdiction, the motion picture was not properly authenticated and should not have been admitted. (*See* ELO Ch. 9-II(D)(2)(c).)

(2) P's testimony

D probably objected to P's testimony about what Alex ("A") purportedly said upon the grounds that it was not given an opportunity to contest P's assertion that A was D's literary agent. Without the establishment of this fact, P's testimony would be irrelevant (*i.e.*, A would presumably have no firsthand knowledge as to D's procedures), and also hearsay (P is testifying about what A stated out-of-court). If A was D's agent and this jurisdiction viewed statements by a party in the course of her agency as a vicarious admission, the hearsay objection would be overcome.

FRE 602 provides that a witness may not testify unless sufficient evidence is introduced to show she has personal knowledge of the matter. While a court could probably conclude that there was sufficient evidence for a jury to determine that A was D's agent by reason of the former's representation to that effect, D should nevertheless have been given (1) the opportunity to contest P's assertion that A was its literary agent, and (2) a jury instruction to the effect that if the jurors did ***not*** believe that A was D's agent, P's testimony in this regard should be disregarded in its entirety by the jury in arriving at a verdict. Thus, the refusal to permit D's president to testify was error.

(3) Ed's testimony

P probably contended that Ed's assertion that he had never seen P's script was irrelevant because it would have been entirely possible for the script to have been received at D's premises and opened by another mailroom employee. Nevertheless, this testimony was probably properly admitted, subject to D's establishing that Ed was employed during the time when P's script would have been received. The fact that Ed, himself, never saw D's manuscript would tend to prove that D never received it. Even if other persons worked in the mailroom, this fact would affect only the weight to be given Ed's testimony.

D probably also argued that the refusal to allow Ed to testify that D always returned unsolicited mailed manuscripts was improper because evidence of a business custom is ordinarily admissible to prove the non-occurrence of a particular event. While a few jurisdictions do not admit business practices to prove the completion of an act (*i.e.*, mailing the script back to P) without independent corroboration of some type, the majority view is probably to the contrary (FRE 406). Since (1) Ed would appear to be sufficiently familiar with this practice by D, and (2) the practice was sufficiently specific, this testimony should have been allowed. (*See* ELO Ch. 3-X(E)(1).)

Answer to Question 9

(1) Testimony of the police officer

D probably objected to the officer's testimony upon the grounds that it was hearsay (an out-of-court statement offered into evidence to prove the truth of the matter asserted.) P might have contended that Carpenter ("C")'s statement constituted an excited utterance (a statement made by a witness about a startling event, while the event was occurring). Many jurisdictions have extended this exception to the hearsay rule to statements made after the event, provided that the declarant is still under the stress of the exciting event. Assuming this jurisdiction follows the latter rule, P could contend that since C was in a "dazed" condition, he was still under the influence of the accident.

P could also have contended that C's statement constituted a dying declaration (a statement made by an unavailable declarant who believed that his death was imminent and which concerned the cause of his impending death). While some jurisdictions limit this doctrine to homicide cases, it is assumed that this qualification is not applicable in this instance. While it is unclear whether C actually believed that his death was imminent, his inquiry ("You don't…") does suggest an awareness of that possibility. (*See* ELO Ch. 6-IV(D)(4) & XI(B)(1)-(5).)

(2) The death certificate

D could have objected to this evidence upon the grounds that it was hearsay and violated the Best Evidence Rule. (No authentication objection appears to be appropriate, since the document was certified.) The Best Evidence objection was probably overcome by the facts that (1) the original item was not removable from the public office in which it was deposited (*i.e.*, the coroner's office); and (2) in most jurisdictions, a duplicate is permissible to the same extent as an original, unless the circumstances indicate some question as to its genuineness; FRE 1003.

As to the hearsay objection, the initial statement ("If caused by injury…") is admissible since it was offered, not to show the truth of the matter asserted therein, but only to describe the directive to which the writer responded.

P might have contended that the public records exception to the hearsay rule is applicable to allow admissibility of the latter portion of the document ("Rung.…"). Under this doctrine, reports made by a public agency about matters which such agency was under a duty to report are admissible, unless the circumstances indicate a lack of trustworthiness; FRE 803 (8). However, since the person who prepared the certificates presumably did not observe the accident (and therefore did not have firsthand knowledge how C died), he must have obtained his information from another source. Since there was no way of ascertaining the identity or reliability of that source, the information should probably have been deemed untrustworthy. Thus, the court was correct is sustaining the objection to this evidence. (*See* ELO Ch. 6-VII(F)(4) & Ch. 9-IV(A)(4)(c).)

(3) Dr. Able ("A")'s testimony

Since A is an expert in the field of accident reconstruction, he appears to be qualified to render an opinion that one of the breaks in the ladder existed before it was smashed by the ambulance.

D probably objected to this evidence upon the grounds that A's opinion was based upon unauthenticated hearsay (the police report, the wood fibre analysis report and the ladder company's records). Many jurisdictions permit an expert to base his testimony upon information which is reasonably relied upon by experts in that particular field in formulating opinions, even if those facts or data are otherwise inadmissible in evidence. Since the items described above would seem to be the type of data upon which an accident reconstructionist would rely in formulating his opinion, the testimony was properly admitted. (*See* ELO Ch. 10-II(C)(4)(b)(i).)

(4) Baker ("B")'s testimony

P probably objected to B's testimony upon the grounds that it was hearsay (B is testifying as to what Hood had told him out-of-court). However, the "statement against interest" exception to the hearsay rule was probably applicable. Under this doctrine, where an unavailable declarant made a statement which was contrary to his proprietary or penal interests, it may be reiterated by another party; FRE 804(b)(3). At common law, the exception applies solely to statements against the declarant's financial interest; some states, and the FRE, have expanded the exception to cover statements against penal interest. It is assumed that this jurisdiction allows statements against penal interest to be admitted into evidence as an exception to the hearsay rule. Although P could have contended that Hood is not "unavailable" since he is in the courtroom, the latter's assertion of the Fifth Amendment privilege would probably satisfy the element of "unavailability"; FRE 804(a)(1). Thus, the court properly admitted B's testimony. (*See* ELO Ch. 6-XII(B)(3).)

(5) Cross-examination of B

Since the inability to recall is a proper basis of impeachment, P had the right to question B about the latter's recollection of events which occurred at approximately the same time as Hood's statement. However, the question to which D objected appears to be argumentative. Nevertheless, D's objection probably should ***not*** have been sustained since the cross-examiner was entitled to an explanation why B could recall only a solitary event upon the date about which he was testifying. (*See* ELO Ch. 4-XII(A)(2).)

Answer to Question 10

(1) Clerk's testimony

D could have objected to this testimony on the grounds that: (1) it was not relevant (tending to prove or disprove a material fact), since people often file guilty pleas to minor traffic violations simply to avoid the expense and inconvenience of a trial; (2) the statement is hearsay (an out-of-court statement offered into evidence to prove the truth of the matter asserted), since the plea suggests that D had, in fact, driven through the red light; (3) the plea document was not submitted; and (4) testimony about a withdrawn plea violates the presumption of innocence.

P could have replied that (1) the evidence is relevant, since it tends to show a recognition of culpability; (2) the plea is admissible under the party-opponent admission exception to the hearsay rule; (3) the requirement that convictions be proved by certified copies does not apply to pleas; and (4) the plea's withdrawal does not negate the previous admission.

The court should have excluded that evidence because once an accused is allowed to withdraw a plea, she is entitled to the presumption of innocence. It might be noted that in federal courts this type of evidence is explicitly made inadmissible (FRE 410). (*See* ELO Ch. 3-XIV(H)(2).)

(2) Oliver ("O")'s testimony

D probably objected to O's testimony upon the grounds that it was opinion pertaining to an ultimate issue of fact. By stating that it was "impossible" for P to avoid the accident, O was, in effect, stating that P was not contributorily negligent. P could argue in rebuttal that layperson opinion is often permitted where the subject matter is otherwise difficult to describe (*i.e.*, he was "drunk," "speeding," etc.). However, O's impressions can be described without resorting to opinions (*i.e.*, O could have testified that, "D crossed P's line of sight at the intersection prior to the crash at a distance of only 10 feet"). Thus, this evidence should not have been admitted. (*See* ELO Ch. 10-I(D)(3)(c).)

(3) White ("W")'s testimony

(a) The initial statement (D confided to him that he had gone through the red light) might have been objected to as hearsay; but P would have successfully argued in rebuttal that it is admissible under the "party-opponent admission" exception to the hearsay rule.

(b) As long as D had a good-faith basis for asking the question ("Aren't you related to P?"), the cross-examination of W appears to be proper since bias in favor of a party is a well established mode of impeachment. (*See* ELO Ch. 4-XI(B)(1) & Ch. 6-II(C).)

(4) Brown ("B")'s testimony

B's testimony (that W said "he was going to get D for...") constitutes impeachment through bias by extrinsic evidence (*i.e.*, calling B as a witness). However, P probably objected to B's testimony upon the ground that no foundation had been laid while W testified earlier (*i.e.*, W was never asked, "Didn't you tell B that..."). Assuming this jurisdiction required a foundation to impeach by extrinsic evidence with respect to bias, B's testimony should not have been admitted. There are, however, a number of states which do not require a foundation to impeach in this manner. In these jurisdictions, B's testimony would have been proper. (*See* ELO Ch. 4-XI(C)(1)-(3).)

It should be noted that no hearsay objection could be sustained, since B's testimony was not offered to prove the truth of the matter asserted therein (but rather, to demonstrate only that W had made statements that showed bias).

(5) Cross-examination of B

D might have objected to P's cross-examination of B upon the grounds that (1) it exceeded the direct (B was asked only about W's statement pertaining to "getting even" with D); and (2) the description of the accident in the newspaper would constitute hearsay (and possibly, opinion, depending on how the story itself was phrased). While the majority view is that cross-examination is limited to the subject matter of direct, there is a minority position which permits cross-examination pertaining to any relevant matter. Thus, in most states, B's testimony would ***not*** have been admissible. As to the second (*i.e.*, hearsay) objection, most courts permit a witness's recollection to be refreshed by any type of material. Since the item is not actually offered into evidence, it is not subject to an objection on grounds of hearsay or opinion. (*See* ELO Ch. 4-II(C) & IV(A)(2).)

Answer to Question 11

A. Wilson ("W")'s testimony

Traditionally, a witness was incompetent to testify if insane or otherwise incapable of accurately relating what he had seen or heard on a particular occasion. Today, however, a witness is competent if he understands the obligation to testify truthfully, has firsthand knowledge of the incident and has the ability to communicate.

While O probably objected to W's testimony upon the grounds that a psychiatrist had testified that W was sometimes unable to distinguish between his independent recollection and what others had described to him, the court's decision to permit W to testify was probably appropriate. W's shortcomings as a witness could be brought to the attention of the jury by O's counsel. The jury could then evaluate from W's demeanor whether he had a clear recollection of the incident in question or seemed to be parroting the statements of others. Thus, W's mental handicap affects merely the weight of his testimony, rather than his competency to testify. (And, W's mental impairment could be used to impeach his credibility, if there was evidence that the defect impaired the accuracy of his observation, recall or narration.) (*See* ELO Ch. 1-IV(C)(2)(b).)

B. (1) Jones ("J")'s statement

It should initially be noted that Olson ("O") would have no standing to assert any Fifth Amendment rights which Jones might be able to assert. (*i.e.*, that he had not received his "Miranda" rights).

O could have objected to this evidence upon the grounds that, assuming J (himself) did not take the stand (1) it was hearsay (an out-of-court statement offered into evidence to prove the truth of the matter asserted therein), and (2) it violated his Sixth Amendment right of confrontation.

As to the hearsay objection, the prosecution ("P") could have initially argued that the "statement against interest" exception to the hearsay rule is applicable. Under this doctrine, where an unavailable declarant has made a statement which is against his proprietary or penal interest, it is admissible. Since (a) assuming J has indicated he will assert his Fifth Amendment right against self-incrimination, J is, in effect, unavailable; and (b) assuming this jurisdiction has extended this hearsay exception to statements which would subject the declarant to criminal culpability (traditionally, the exception was limited to statements against proprietary interests, such as comments pertaining to the ownership of property or the existence of a debt), P properly prevailed on this issue.

The P could have also asserted the "excited utterance" exception (statements made about a startling event while under the stress of excitement caused by the event) to the hearsay rule. Since J's statement was made under the stress of excitement caused by the chase and subsequent arrest, this statement should be admitted.

The P could also have asserted the "present sense impression" exception (statements describing or explaining an event while the declarant is perceiving the event) to the hearsay rule. J's statement described the conditions under which his arrest was made while the arrest was actually taking place.

Finally, assuming O and J were charged with conspiracy, in some jurisdictions a statement made by a co-conspirator is attributed to everyone involved in the conspiracy. In such event, J's statement would be admissible under the "party-opponent admission" exception to the hearsay rule. However, many courts limit this exception to statements made "during the course and in furtherance of the conspiracy"; FRE 801(d)(2)(E). Since J's statement would not appear to be "in furtherance" of the conspiracy, this exception to the hearsay rule would probably *not* be applicable. (*See* ELO Ch. 6-II(F), IV(D) & (E), & XII(B)(3)(c).)

The P would argue that statements of a co-conspirator who has taken the Fifth Amendment have been admitted where such declarations have sufficient "indicia of reliability" to be placed before the jury; *Dutton v. Evans*, 400 U.S. 74 (1970). Since (1) J's statement appears to be a spontaneous "blurt out," and (2) J would be in a unique position to identify the other persons involved in the crime, the P correctly prevailed on this issue.

(2) O's statement and other evidence

O's statement is relevant (tends to prove or disprove a material fact), since his whereabouts on the date of the crime are crucial.

It is unclear from the facts that "other evidence" was offered to prove that "Hellcats" was not playing on the date he asserted. If O had identified a particular theater, the P could have had the manager of that establishment testify that "Hellcats" was not playing on that date.

If the P simply introduced, after proper authentication, the "movie" page of the local newspaper on that date, a hearsay objection, could have been raised by O. However, the "commercial publications" exception to the hearsay rule followed in some states and in federal courts (FRE 803(17)) appears to be applicable, since movie information contained in a newspaper is generally relied upon by the public. If this exception was not applicable, the P would have been obliged to bring in the managers and operators of every movie theater in the downtown area to testify that "Hellcats" was not playing on the evening in question.

Finally, while O might have contended that his statement ("Hellcats") was hearsay, it was, in any case, an admission, which is "non-hearsay" under the FRE, and an exception to the hearsay rule in state courts. Unlike "statements against interest", admissions need not be inconsistent with a party's interests. (*See* ELO Ch. 6-II(C) & VIII(B)(3).)

(3) The reporter's testimony

O could have objected to the reporter's testimony upon the grounds that it (1) was hearsay, (2) was irrelevant (*i.e.*, it does not tend to show that O was a participant in the burglary) and (3) violated the marital communications privilege. However, the P could have contended in rebuttal that (1) the party-opponent admission exception to the hearsay rule is applicable in this instance; (2) the evidence does tend to show that O was a participant in the crime (why else would he express disgust with J's statement); and (3) the statement was apparently not "confidential" because the reporter could overhear it. While O did not actually sees the reporter, there is no indication that she attempted to hide her presence from him. Thus, even if this was a jurisdiction which precludes the testimony of an eavesdropper, the evidence was admissible because O's personal carelessness permitted the statement to be overheard. (*See* ELO Ch. 8-V(C)(4)(a).)

(4) Police officer's testimony and map

Since the facts are silent, it will be assumed that the warrant was properly issued and authorized seizure of any items pertaining to the burglary. Thus, O could not object to testimony about the map upon the grounds that it was illegally obtained.

O could have contended that testimony about the map of Wilson ("W")'s premises was inadmissible because (1) it was not authenticated (the facts do not show how the police officer knew that the map depicted W's premises); (2) it is hearsay; and (3) it violates the Best Evidence Rule (the map itself). However, the P could have argued in rebuttal that (1) if the testifying police officer had viewed W's premises, he would have had sufficient firsthand knowledge to verify that the map described the burglarized premises; (2) the map did not constitute a "statement" for purposes of the hearsay rule (rather, it was merely a picture of another's premises); and (3) the map was a collateral document, since it was offered to show only motivation and opportunity on the part of O. However, since (1) the map is a significant piece of evidence in establishing O's culpability, and (2) there is no indication that the map itself is unavailable, the court probably erred in permitting testimony about the map and not insisting on production of the map itself. (*See* ELO Ch. 9-IV(A)(4) & (C)(3).)

Answer to Question 12

(1) Proof that Acme ("A") had not received any prior complaints

Mary ("M") could have objected to this evidence on the grounds that it was irrelevant (did not tend to prove or disprove a material fact) because (a) the fact that other persons had not complained of injuries due to Hairoff would not tend to prove that the particular tube purchased by M was not defective in some manner; and (b) it is entirely possible that other persons were adversely affected by Hairoff, but simply elected not to make a formal complaint. However, A could have replied that, given the large quantity of Hairoff tubes sold, the absence of complaints (other than M's) would tend to prove that its product was not the source of M's injuries. M might have some special type of allergy or condition which resulted in her injury. The relevance of the evidence depends on the similarity between the other Hairoff applications and M's application. Authorities are split on whether to accept such evidence, but here the prior lack of complaints was probably persuasive.

In many jurisdictions, where an inference is to be drawn from silence (*i.e.*, the lack of complaints), such silence is considered hearsay. The evidence is viewed as if those who had purchased Hairoff in the past had, in effect, by their silence stated that the product was safe. In some jurisdictions, including the Federal Courts and California, conduct not intended as an assertion is not hearsay. (*See* ELO Ch. 2-II(A) & Ch. 5-II(D)(3)(a).)

Even if the lack of complaints were hearsay, A could attempt to introduce this evidence for impeachment (*i.e.*, it contradicts M's assertion that she was injured by Hairoff). Since impeachment evidence is not offered to prove the truth of the matter asserted (but rather, for credibility) it is not hearsay.

(2) Dr. White ("W")'s testimony

M could have contended that W's testimony was inadmissible because it was (1) hearsay, and (2) violative of the physician-patient privilege. With respect to the first objection, A probably argued in rebuttal that M's statement to W was admissible under either the "party-opponent admission" or the "medical diagnosis and treatment" exceptions to the hearsay rule. Under the latter doctrine, a statement made by the declarant for the purpose of obtaining medical treatment is admissible despite the hearsay rule. With respect to the doctor-patient privilege, A could have argued that where a party has placed her physical condition into issue, testimony by the physician constitutes an exception to the rule precluding patient-doctor communications. Assuming this view was adhered to in this state, W's testimony would be admissible. (*See* ELO Ch. 8-III(B)(4)(a).)

Finally, A could contend that this evidence would be admissible to impeach M. However, since M never testified that she told W that her infection was caused by a rusty pitchfork, a foundation for impeachment through prior inconsistent statements (if required in this jurisdiction) was not laid.

(3) Dr. Spencer ("S")'s testimony

M probably objected to this testimony upon the grounds that (1) impeachment by drug addiction is impermissible (*i.e.*, the fact that M has had possession of an illegal substance on previous occasions does *not* suggest that she would lie under oath); (2) there is no recognized basis of impeachment by associating a witness with a particularly untrustworthy group; and (3) the fact that S was a specialist (and therefore presumably competent to render an opinion) would result in the jury's giving too much weight to his testimony. Since A does not appear to have a viable response to these arguments, the testimony should *not* have been admitted. (*See* ELO Ch. 4-XII(A)(3)(b).)

(4) M's prior lawsuits

M might have objected to the testimony about her prior litigation against cosmetic companies upon the grounds that (1) it is irrelevant, since her claims against other entities does not tend to prove that her present action is not legitimate; (2) it is hearsay (the witness is testifying about statements (the complaints) made out-of-court; (3) the complaints were not authenticated; and (4) the testimony violates the Best Evidence Rule (the witness testified as to the contents of documents). A could argue that (1) some jurisdictions permit this type of evidence (even absent proof of fraud) where coincidence appears unlikely, and arguably proof of seven different lawsuits over a ten-year period against cosmetic manufacturers satisfies this standard; (2) the hearsay rule is overcome by the "party-opponent admission" exception; (3) the witness might have testified that she saw these documents in the courthouses where the actions were filed, and so the complaints were authenticated; and (4) the complaints are collateral elements, and therefore the testimony is admissible despite the Best Evidence Rule. Since there has been no showing that the other claims asserted by M are similar to those in the present action (*i.e.*, that M suffered an infection as a consequence of using the product), the court should *not* have admitted this evidence. (*See* ELO Ch. 2-II(A).)

(5) Louise ("L")'s testimony

A could have objected to this evidence upon the grounds that (1) it is a prior consistent statement, which is usually not considered a proper subject for rehabilitation (except to rebut an assertion of *recent* fabrication or influence); and (2) it is hearsay. A few jurisdictions permit rehabilitation by prior consistent statements. Assuming, however, that this state adheres to the majority view, L's testimony would be inadmissible since there is no testimony that M had recently decided to testify in an untruthful manner.

Even if this jurisdiction permits prior consistent statements, the hearsay rule appears to be applicable. A few jurisdictions, however, view prior consistent statements of a witness as not being hearsay. Assuming, however, that this minority view is **not** followed in this state, M could still have contended that L's testimony is admissible for the purpose of rehabilitation, rather than as substantive evidence (*i.e.*, simply to show that M had made a statement consistent with her original testimony, rather than to prove that the statement is actually true or not). Assuming prior consistent statements are admissible for rehabilitation, L's testimony could be admitted for this purpose. A would, however, be entitled to a limiting instruction (*i.e.*, that the jury be advised to consider the prior consistent statement only for the purpose of evaluating M's credibility, rather than as substantive evidence pertaining to her *prima facie* case). (*See* ELO Ch. 3-XV(C)(3)(d) & Ch. 6-XIV(A)(4)(c).)

Answer to Question 13

(1) Abner ("A")'s testimony

Peter ("P") could initially have objected to A's testimony upon the grounds that (1) it was violative of the Best Evidence Rule, since A testified about the contents of a writing (the notice of cancellation); (2) it was irrelevant (did not tend to prove or disprove a material fact), since (a) the fact that it was Defender ("D")'s practice to mail cancellation notices on the date they were written does not prove that this particular notice was actually sent, and (b) even if the notice was sent, this fact would not prove that it had actually been received by P (the insured had to actually receive the notice that his policy had been canceled); and (3) A's statement that "it (the notice) must have been mailed" constitutes only his opinion as to what occurred, since he does not have firsthand knowledge.

With respect to the initial objection, D might have responded that it could not produce the original document since it had been mailed to P (who is now, apparently, denying receipt of the notice). However, most jurisdictions require the best secondary evidence in such a situation, and therefore D would have to submit a copy or to assert that it had not retained a copy of the cancellation notice (a highly unlikely proposition) to avoid application of the Best Evidence Rule.

As to the second objection, D could have argued in rebuttal that (1) evidence of a routine business practice is ordinarily admissible to prove conduct in conformity therewith on a particular occasion, and (2) a factfinder could infer from the fact of mailing that the notice had actually reached its destination. However, P could have successfully responded that an insufficient foundation for establishing the existence of a business custom existed in this instance since (1) A, an insurance agent, never testified that he was familiar with the day-to-day practices of D (*i.e.*, that it is the practice of the particular office *at which he works* to send out such notices); and (2) the business practice itself has not been described with sufficient specificity (presumably, the letters must be placed in a particular receptacle, from which they are later removed and mailed by an identifiable person). Additionally, some jurisdictions require corroborating evidence where a general business custom is introduced to prove performance of particular conduct (*e.g.*, requiring that a witness testify that the outgoing letters were, in fact, placed into the U.S. mail on the day in question). (*See* ELO Ch. 3-X(E) & Ch. 9-IV(A)(4)(c).)

Finally, D does not appear to have a successful response to P's "opinion" objection.

Thus, the court was probably incorrect in admitting A's testimony.

(2) Baker ("B")'s testimony

P might have objected to B's testimony upon the grounds that it was irrelevant, in that the failure to answer B does not tend to prove or disprove that P had received D's cancellation notice.

D could have responded that (1) D's silence does tend to prove that the letter was actually received, since most persons would assist a governmental employee in carrying out his functions (although a reasonable person could arguably choose to avoid gratuitous involvement in a criminal investigation of another individual); and (2) P's non-response to B's statement is an adoptive or tacit admission (*i.e.*, P, in effect, answered B's inquiry in a positive manner by not denying B's insinuation when a reasonable person in P's position would have done so). (*See* ELO Ch. 6-II(D)(3)(a).)

The court was probably correct in admitting B's testimony.

(3) Charlie ("C")'s testimony

P could have objected to C's testimony upon the grounds that it was irrelevant, since P's permitting insurance policies to lapse with another company for non-payment of premiums would *not* indicate that the policy in question had been canceled for the same reason. Additionally, evidence of prior conduct to prove conformity therewith on a particular occasion is ordinarily inadmissible. While D might have argued in rebuttal to the second objection that P's conduct in permitting other insurance policies to lapse rises to the level of a habit (a person's regular response to a particular type of situation), and is therefore admissible; it is unlikely that permitting insurance to lapse on three separate occasions over an individual's lifetime would constitute sufficient regularity to be characterized as a habit. Thus, the court was correct in refusing to permit C to testify. (*See* ELO Ch. 3-X(B)(1)(a)-(c).)

(4) Debbie's testimony

In most jurisdictions, there is no minimal age which a witness must have attained to be competent to testify. The judge must, however, believe that a potential witness (1) has sufficient maturity to be capable of receiving correct impressions through his senses, and (2) understands the necessity of telling the truth in the context of a legal proceeding. The facts are unclear as to Debbie's age at the time she purportedly transferred the mail from the mailperson to P. (The facts state only that she is *now* five years old.) However, assuming this matter came to trial in a relatively prompt period of time (*i.e.*, within one year), the judge could have concluded that Debbie was capable of testifying as to a manual act which she had undertaken one year before. Additionally, her statement that untruthful persons "get spanked," tends to show a recognition of the importance of being honest (since she presumably would not desire to have this form of physical punishment applied to her). Thus, the court's decision that Debbie was competent was probably correct. (*See* ELO Ch. 1-IV(C)(2)(b).)

(5) Ethel ("E")'s testimony

D probably objected to this testimony upon the grounds that it was (1) irrelevant, because E has not adequately described how Harvey ("H") determined what was "junk" mail (D's letter should not have been viewed as being in that category); and (2) hearsay, since E has testified as to the out-of-court statement of another.

P probably argued in rebuttal to the first objection that regardless of the selection process utilized by H to discard letters, D's item **might** have been amongst the portion viewed as "junk" mail. As to the hearsay objection, the portion of H's statement pertaining to his back is probably admissible under the "present sensation" exception to the hearsay rule. His statement pertaining to destroying items of "junk" mail is arguably admissible under the "statement against interest" exception to the hearsay rule, since he could presumably be terminated from his job and imprisoned for such conduct. However, the latter doctrine is applicable only where the declarant is unavailable. The facts are silent as to whether H could have been compelled to appear at the trial. If not, this element would be satisfied. Also, while many jurisdictions extend this theory to statements against penal interest (*i.e.*, H was presumably subject to criminal sanctions for his conduct in discarding mail), some jurisdictions restrict this doctrine to statements against pecuniary or proprietary interests. Assuming, however, that this jurisdiction extends the "statements against interest" doctrine to comments which would expose the speaker to criminal sanctions, the court was correct in permitting E's testimony. (*See* ELO Ch. 6-XII(B)(3).)

Finally, the portion of E's testimony pertaining to H's being in prison is arguably pertinent to the factual determination whether the declarant was "unavailable" or not.

Answer to Question 14

(1) Patterson ("P")'s testimony

(a) Label on Bottle

Don ("D") could have contended that testimony as to the writing on the bottle was not admissible because (1) it was hearsay (an out-of-court statement offered into evidence to prove the truth of the matter asserted); (2) the bottle was not authenticated (*i.e.*, no evidence was introduced, other than testimony as to the bottle label itself, to prove that D produced the item).

P could have argued in rebuttal, however, that (1) the label is an admission, "non-hearsay" under the FRE, and an exception to the hearsay rule in other jurisdictions; (2) many jurisdictions view "trade inscriptions" (*i.e.*, statements on items sold in commerce) to be self-authenticating. Assuming trade inscriptions are self-authenticating, P's testimony with respect to the bottle label was properly admitted. (*See* ELO Ch. 9-II(D)(2)(c).)

(b) Jack ("J")'s statement

D probably objected to P's testimony about J's statement on the grounds that (1) it was hearsay, and (2) the portion asserting that D should be "run out of business" was opinion. P could contend that J's statement was admissible under the "adoptive admission" exception to the hearsay rule. Under this doctrine, a statement made in the presence of the party-opponent is admissible if it contains assertions that a reasonable person would deny. If J simply accosted D and made the statement without D's having prior knowledge of the incident involving P, D's non-response would be perfectly understandable. (*See* ELO Ch. 6-II(D)(3)(a).)

(2) Cross-examination of P

Impeachment of P by inquiring about his smoking habits was probably proper since, given the well-known correlation between smoking and respiratory difficulties, the evidence would tend to contradict P's assertion that muriatic acid was the cause of his physical disability. (*See* ELO Ch. 4-VI(A).)

(3) Dr. Walton ("W")'s testimony

(a) P has chronic bronchitis

This testimony appears to be pertinent since it pertains to the extent and nature of P's injury. While it is W's opinion, because he is a specialist in internal medicine, this form of testimony would be admissible. (*See* ELO Ch. 10-II(A)(1).)

(b) The laboratory experiment and opinion based upon it

D probably objected to this evidence upon the grounds that there was no proof that (1) there was a substantial similarity of conditions (*i.e.*, that the amounts of water, sodium hypochlorite and muriatic acid utilized in W's experiment were proportionately equivalent to the amount of these substances in P's swimming pool at the time he was purportedly injured); and (2) the methodology, itself, was "scientifically valid" (*i.e.*, that the test can be reliably tested; that it was subject to peer review; that it has a low error rate; and that this method is generally accepted in the field). Since P does not appear to have an adequate rebuttal to these objections, W's experiment and his opinion that P's condition resulted from exposure to muriatic acid probably should *not* have been admitted by the court. (*See* ELO Ch. 10-III(A)(2)(d)-(f).)

(4) Cross-examination of W

It is assumed that this jurisdiction follows the modern view which permits cross-examination of an expert by a scholarly writing, whether or not she relied upon it in rendering an opinion.

P probably objected to the cross-examination upon the ground that articles appearing in the Wall Street Journal and Reader's Digest cannot be characterized as scholarly works, and therefore could not be utilized to impeach W through contradiction. Since the accuracy of articles appearing in daily or monthly periodicals is probably not independently verified by persons with expertise in a particular field, the court's refusal to permit cross-examination of W in this manner was probably correct. (*See* ELO Ch. 6-VIII(B)(2)(c).)

(5) Viewing of the pool

It is in the discretion of the Court whether the time-consuming and disruptive nature of a viewing is justified by the likelihood of obtaining highly probative evidence which could not feasibly be reproduced in the courtroom. Since little evidentiary light upon whether D had mislabeled a bottle of muriatic acid as sodium hypochlorite could be shed by visiting the pool, the court's denial of P's motion to inspect the filterhouse was probably appropriate. (*See* ELO Ch. 2-II(A).)

Answer to Question 15

(a) Testimony of Dr. Alienist ("A")

The prosecution ("P") could have objected to A's testimony upon the grounds that (1) assuming this jurisdiction follows the McNaughton definition of insanity, A's opinion goes directly to an ultimate issue of fact; (2) A's opinion is partially based upon hearsay (*i.e.*, Dave's out-of-court statements to him); and (3) three interviews did not constitute adequate opportunity upon which to form a credible opinion as to Dave's sanity.

However, Dave ("D") could have responded that (1) experts (A is a qualified psychiatrist) are permitted to offer opinions upon an ultimate issue of fact; and (2) in many states an expert may base his opinion upon information which would not otherwise be admissible into evidence, if the data is of the type which is "reasonably relied upon" by experts in a particular field in forming inferences or opinions. Thus, while it is entirely possible that D made self-serving statements to A, A's testimony was probably properly admitted. The P could prove the untrustworthiness of D's statement to A upon cross-examination. Finally, the paucity of interviews goes primarily to the weight of A's testimony (rather than to its admissibility). (*See* ELO Ch. 10-II(C)(4)(b).)

(b) The hospital record

The hospital record appears to have been properly authenticated by the librarian.

The P probably objected to this evidence upon the grounds that it was double hearsay (an out-of-court statement offered into evidence to prove the truth of the matter asserted), since the writing embodies the nurse's recitation about what D told her.

The "business records" doctrine states that a record is admissible as an exception to the hearsay rule if it is made at or near the time of an event by someone with firsthand knowledge and is kept in the course of a regularly conducted business activity whose normal practice is to make such a writing, unless the source of information indicates a lack of trustworthiness). Since a hospital is a business and it is the practice of hospital nurses to promptly make entries of this type in the course of their duties, the "business records" doctrine would arguably be satisfied.

The P could have argued, however, that the statements made to the nurse were "untrustworthy." This contention should be successful if D's statement was made *after* the date upon which the crime was committed (*i.e.*, in that event, D's statements could have been made for the purpose of laying a factual basis for his subsequent insanity plea).

As to D's statement, his counsel could have probably successfully contended that it was not being offered to prove the truth of the matter asserted therein (*i.e.*, that D would not "void until Noah finished the ark"). Rather, it was offered into evidence only for the purpose of proving that the statement was actually made (*i.e.*, the comment would not be made by a sane person).

Finally, the patient-physician privilege would not apply since the statement in question was apparently not made by D for the purpose of obtaining diagnosis or treatment.

In summary, if D's hernia surgery was performed *prior* to his arrest, the hospital record was probably correctly admitted. (*See* ELO Ch. 6-VI(E)(2)(b) & (K)(1).)

(c) Dr. Bromide ("B")'s testimony

D probably objected to B's testimony on the grounds that (1) it violates the physician-patient privilege; (2) examining D on approximately two occasions per year was insufficient opportunity for B to have formulated a credible opinion as to D's sanity; and (3) character evidence must ordinarily be in the form of reputation in the community (rather than opinion).

The P could have answered that (1) even assuming P's mental state constituted a communication for purposes of the physician-patient relationship (a point with respect to which there is a division of authority), this privilege is ordinarily *not* extended to criminal cases or situations where the patient has placed his mental condition into issue; (2) the fact that the opinion was predicated upon relatively few examinations goes to its weight (rather than admissibility); and (3) opinion evidence ordinarily is admissible when rendered by an expert when a party's physical or mental condition is in dispute.

The court could properly admit B's testimony. (*See* ELO Ch. 8-III(B)(4)(a).)

(d) Dr. Cyko ("C")'s testimony

D probably objected to C's testimony on the grounds that (1) impeachment as to character for truthfulness and veracity must ordinarily be done by reputation in the community (rather than by opinion); and (2) observing D's mother testify for presumably a relatively short period of time (*i.e.*, one to two hours) is an insufficient basis to form an opinion that she has a psychopathic personality.

The P probably argued in rebuttal, however, that (1) some jurisdictions permit opinion evidence with respect to character; (2) an expert witness (a status for which C would qualify, since he is a psychiatrist) is often permitted to give testimony based upon observations made at the trial; and (3) the relatively brief observation upon which C premised his testimony goes to its weight (rather than its admissibility).

C's testimony was incorrectly excluded. (*See* ELO Ch. 10-II(C)(2).)

Answer to Question 16

(1) Neighbor ("N")'s statement

Dan ("D") probably objected to N's testimony upon the grounds that it was (1) irrelevant (did not tend to prove or disprove a material fact of consequence), because Harvey could have been speaking emotionally, instead of from personal knowledge; and (2) hearsay (an out-of-court statement offered into evidence to prove the truth of the matter asserted), since N is testifying as to what H said.

The prosecution ("P") could have contended that N's statement and D's failure to reply were relevant because an innocent person would have objected to even an ambiguous accusation of murder. As to the hearsay objection, D's non-response constituted an adoptive admission (a statement made in the presence of a party-opponent, which, if untrue, the latter would be expected to deny). By failing to refute the statement made to him, D, in effect, adopted it. (*See* ELO Ch. 6-II(D)(3)(a).)

(2) Jack ("J")'s testimony

D could have objected to this testimony upon the grounds that (1) it was irrelevant, since D may have attempted to take his life as a consequence of the depression and despair which follow an arrest for murder; (2) it was hearsay (*i.e.*, D's conduct is being offered into evidence as a statement that he killed F); and (3) its probative value was outweighed by the highly prejudicial impact this evidence might make upon a jury.

The P probably contended in rebuttal, however, that (1) it is relevant, since one may infer a consciousness of guilt from the fact of attempted suicide; (2) the "party-opponent admission" exception to the hearsay rule would overcome D's second objection; and (3) since there were apparently no eyewitnesses to the crime, the probative value of this evidence outweighs its possible prejudicial impact.

J's testimony should be admissible. (*See* ELO Ch. 6-II(C)(3)(a).)

(3) Rita ("R")'s testimony

The P probably objected to this testimony upon the grounds (1) that it violated the Best Evidence Rule, since R is testifying about the contents of a writing, (2) the writing was not authenticated (*i.e.*, no showing was apparently made that R was familiar with F's handwriting), and (3) the testimony was hearsay (*i.e.*, F's alleged statement is being offered into evidence for the purpose of proving that she committed suicide).

D does not appear to have any viable response to the Best Evidence Rule objection, unless the crumpled-up letter was discarded. The authentication objection could be overcome by having R testify that she was familiar with F's handwriting. Finally, the hearsay objection could probably be overcome as follows: (1) the initial phrase of the statement ("I have nothing to live for…") is probably admissible under the present state-of-mind exception to the hearsay rule; and (2) the balance of the writing is *not* being offered into evidence to prove the truth of the matter therein, but rather to explain the motivation behind the initial phrase of the letter.

Assuming the letter is no longer in existence, the testimony should be admitted by the court. (*See* ELO Ch. 5-II(C)(6)(c).)

(4) Dr. Slade ("S")'s testimony

D could have objected to S's testimony upon the grounds that (1) it violated the psychotherapist-patient privilege; (2) it was hearsay, since S's testimony was based upon what F had told him; and (3) where character evidence is admissible, it must ordinarily be in the form of reputation in the community (rather than opinion).

The P could initially argue in rebuttal, that, even assuming this jurisdiction extends the patient-client privilege to psychologists in criminal cases, the privilege must be asserted by the patient.

The hearsay objection would probably also be unavailing because in most jurisdictions an expert may base an opinion upon data which would otherwise not be admissible, if the information is of the type which is "reasonably relied upon" by experts in that particular field.

While some jurisdictions restrict character evidence to the subject's reputation in the community, many states permit an expert to offer an opinion about the person in question where mental condition is in issue. (*See* ELO Ch. 3-I(A)(4)(b)(iii); Ch. 8-III(C)(3); Ch. 10-II(C)(4)(b).)

Thus, S's testimony should be admissible.

(5) Cross-examination of S

A witness' credibility can sometimes be attacked through acts of misconduct not resulting in conviction. The acts must show untruthfulness, and their probativeness must outweigh potential unfair prejudice. FRE 609(a)(2) defines crimes of dishonesty and false statement. Generally, shoplifting has not been included in these crimes.

Defense counsel's second question was probably improper because impeachment as to prior bad acts which have not resulted in a conviction may not be accomplished by extrinsic evidence. The reference to the investigative report was therefore inappropriate. Additionally, the second question was argumentative (phrased in a manner which would compel a response which takes issue with the inquiry). (*See* ELO Ch. 4-VIII(B)(3)(b) & (B)(5)(b).)

Answer to Question 17

1. *The statements by Helico ("H")'s officer*

H's officer made two separate statements (the offer to settle and the admission).

(a) *The offer to settle*

H probably contended that the offer to settle was inadmissible because (1) it is irrelevant (does not tend to prove or disprove a material fact), in that H may have just proposed the settlement offer to avoid the expense and inconvenience of litigation (rather than out of a belief of legal responsibility for the incident); (2) many states have evidentiary rules which preclude such evidence; and (3) it is hearsay (an out-of-court statement offered into evidence to prove the truth of the matter asserted therein). Paul ("P") probably argued in rebuttal that (1) settlement offers (which in this instance were probably substantial) are not usually made unless the offeror believes that he was legally culpable; and (2) the party-opponent exception to the hearsay rule is applicable (statements made by a party to the litigation, other than the party introducing the evidence, are ordinarily admissible as an exception to the hearsay rule).

Nevertheless, both the common law and the FRE hold that the fact that a party has offered to settle a claim may not be admitted on the issue of the claim's validity. Admission of such settlement offers would give the parties a strong disincentive to pursue settlement negotiations.

The evidence was improperly admitted. (*See* ELO Ch. 3-XIV(A) & (B).)

(b) *The admission of defective design*

In some jurisdictions, **any** statement made within the course of settlement negotiations is admissible, while under the FRE, evidence of statements made in settlement offers is not admissible. Therefore, the admissibility of this evidence depends upon whether the common law approach or the FRE are followed. However, we'll assume that no rule against admissibility exists in this state.

H's initial argument was probably that the statements made by the corporate officer were hearsay and did not constitute a party-opponent admission since he was not authorized to comment upon H's liability. Additionally, H probably contended that the officer's statement was an opinion as to an ultimate fact by a layperson (ordinarily, only the opinions of experts are admissible). P probably argued in rebuttal that, in some states, statements by corporate employees are admissible so long as they are "within the course and scope of their employment." In addition, most courts have abandoned the rule barring opinion testimony on ultimate issues. Therefore, the second part of the officer's statement should have been admitted. (*See* ELO Ch. 10-I(D)(2).)

2. Are the statements of Jason ("J") admissible?

We'll assume that (1) the photographs were properly authenticated (*i.e.*, that the proponent of the evidence testified that the pictures were, in fact, what they purported to be); and (2) J was actually qualified as an expert witness by the court (*i.e.*, the judge determined and advised the jury that J was to be considered an expert).

H probably contended that J should *not* have been qualified as an expert because (1) whether the tail rotor was conspicuous or not is not a matter upon which special expertise is needed; and (2) while J may have been knowledgeable about aircraft engineering, navigation and operation, the matter about which he testified involved aircraft design and construction. P could have argued in rebuttal, however, that (1) whether the rotor was "conspicuous" within the FAA rules is a matter of expert opinion, and (2) aircraft engineering, navigation and operation are sufficiently related to aircraft design and construction so that opinion evidence by J was proper. Experts can give their opinions upon ultimate facts. The testimony of J was proper.

Assuming the pictures were authenticated, H could have argued that there was not a sufficient basis for J's opinion that the tail rotor was not conspicuous under the FAA regulations ("regs") because (1) the photographs of other helicopters were irrelevant for purposes of determining if H's helicopter failed to meet FAA regs; and (2) there was no showing that J was familiar with the FAA regs. P probably argued in rebuttal, however, that (1) J's opinion that the helicopter rotor was not conspicuous within the FAA rules wasn't necessarily predicated upon the pictures of other helicopters, and (2) an expert can usually give an opinion without describing his basis for it (the foundation can be dealt with on cross-examination).

In summary, J's testimony was properly admitted. (*See* ELO Ch. 10-II(B).)

3. Sam ("S")'s testimony

H could have initially contended that S's testimony is inadmissible as double hearsay (S is testifying as to what Al said that P stated). However, P's statement would be an admission. (It might also be a spontaneous statement, since it occurred "immediately" after P was struck - although in most states the declarant must be describing the incident as it is actually occurring). With respect to Al's statement, the "past recollection recorded" or "business records" exceptions do *not* seem to be available, since there is no indication that S wrote down P's statement. Public records and reports are exceptions to the hearsay rule, however. S, an FAA investigator, had a duty to report accurately, and Al, a pilot had a similar duty. [*See* FRE 803(8).] Therefore, S's testimony should not be excluded by H's hearsay objection. The report itself should be admitted under the Best Evidence Rule.

P could have also contended that S's first and third sentences are layperson conclusions of law and therefore inadmissible. Additionally, the statement that he "goofed" arguably shows only contributory negligence ("CN'), which would *not* be relevant in a products liability action. However, many states permit a lay witness to give an opinion where he has personal knowledge of the occurrence and the opinion would be helpful to the factfinder. Also, evidence of CN is arguably admissible since P had also asserted a cause of action for negligence. Thus, evidence of CN probably should have been admitted with a limiting instruction (*i.e.*, that the jury only consider it with respect to the negligence action).

It therefore appears that S's testimony was properly admitted. (*See* ELO Ch. 6-II(C) & (D); Ch. 10-I(C)(6).)

Answer to Question 18

1. Lab report

Tim ("T") probably contended that the lab report was inadmissible because (1) it was not properly authenticated (there was no chain of continuous custody which satisfactorily established that the substance tested was the same item which was taken from T; nor was there adequate proof that the report itself was genuine); (2) it was hearsay (an out-of-court statement offered to prove the truth of the matter stated therein or inferable thereby); (3) no proof was introduced that the process by which the substance was tested was "scientifically valid" ; and (4) the admission of the report violated T's Sixth Amendment right of confrontation (since Smith was not present).

The Prosecution ("P") probably argued in rebuttal that (1) implicit in the report is that Jencks ("J") gave the substance directly to Smith, since the latter stated that he had tested the substance taken by J, and the seal (plus signature) upon a document by the officer who was the custodian thereof ordinarily establishes a writing's genuineness; (2) the hearsay objection is overcome by the (i) "public records" (*i.e.*, a document which sets forth matters observed pursuant to a duty imposed by law), *or* (ii) "business records" (a matter observed in the course of a regularly conducted activity whose regular practice is to make such a report) exceptions to the hearsay rule; (3) the process of determining if a substance is heroin may be so well established that evidence of its scientific validity was unnecessary; and (4) assuming Smith was available to be called as a witness and cross-examined by P, P's opportunity for confrontation was preserved.

However, since the chain of custody with respect to the substance tested by Smith was *not* established, the report should *not* have been admitted. (*See* ELO Ch. 9-II(B)(1)(b)(i).)

2. The cross-examination of T

It is assumed that P had a good faith belief that T was in possession of heroin on the date mentioned (if this were not the case, a mistrial could have been ordered).

At common-law, courts generally allow impeachment by bad acts that did not lead to conviction. However, many states (and the Federal Rules, see FRE 608(b)) limit bad-act evidence to bad acts that pertain to *truthfulness*. Since the incident about which T was cross-examined did not pertain directly to truthfulness (*i.e.*, the fact that one possessed heroin on a particular occasion would not necessarily suggest that she would lie under oath), most jurisdictions would probably disallow the question on that grounds. Also, there is a great potential for prejudice here, especially in view of the similarity between the bad act and the act charged on the present occasion. (That is, the jury might desire to punish T for his previous act, rather than for the act with which he is now charged; also, the jurors may reason that because T possessed heroin in the past, he's likely to be guilty of the same thing now.) Therefore, the P's question should *not* have been permitted. (*See* ELO Ch. 4-VIII(B)(1)(b).)

3. Sue ("S")'s initial testimony

The P could have objected to S's initial testimony on the grounds that (1) it was irrelevant (did not tend to prove or disprove a fact of material consequence), because the fact that T had utilized powdered milk during the eight times she and T had dined out would not tend to disprove that T had heroin in his possession on the occasion in question (especially since S did not testify that she and T intended to dine out after meeting with J); (2) prior conduct is inadmissible to prove conduct in conformity therewith on a particular occasion; and (3) the testimony was hearsay, since S was testifying about T's out-of-court conduct to permit the inference that T did not have heroin on the date in question.

T might have contended, in rebuttal, that (1) having powdered milk with him on prior occasions does tend to indicate that the substance taken by J was not heroin (the relatively small number of times S had seen T utilize powdered milk goes to the weight of her testimony, rather than its admissibility); (2) carrying powdered milk was a habit (a routine response to a particular set of conditions), and therefore is evidence admissible in most jurisdictions; and (3) non-assertive conduct is not considered hearsay in many jurisdictions. It is unlikely that possession of powdered milk eight times over a one-year period is sufficient to establish a habit. Thus, S's initial testimony should *not* have been admitted as direct evidence.

Alternatively, T might have argued that S's testimony was given for the purpose of impeaching J by contradiction (in which event, no relevancy or hearsay objection could be successfully made). However, the P could have argued in rebuttal that (1) T had already contradicted J, and so this additional impeachment was superfluous; and (2) S's testimony would not necessarily contradict J (the fact that T brought his own powdered milk when he dined out with S on prior occasions would not directly contradict J's testimony that T had possession of heroin on September 13). Again, the P should have prevailed.

Finally, T might have asserted that S's initial testimony was rehabilitation (since the P had tried to impeach T's prior testimony). The fact that T sometimes carried powdered milk would tend to corroborate his earlier testimony that the substance which was taken from him on the date in question was *not* heroin. However, since S had *not* testified that they were going out to dinner after meeting with J, and she cited only eight occasions over a one-year period, her testimony probably would *not* sufficiently corroborate T's assertion that he had powdered milk with him on the occasion in question. (*See* ELO Ch. 3-X(D)(2); Ch. 4-XIII(A)(1)(d) & XV(C)(3)(c).)

Thus, S's initial testimony should *not* have been admitted.

4. S's testimony about J

If this statement was offered as direct evidence, the P probably objected on the grounds that it was not relevant and also hearsay. However, it probably is relevant in that it bears upon the issue of whether the substance which J took from T was actually heroin. Although T might contend that J's statements were within the "party-opponent admission" exception to the hearsay rule, the majority view is that an employee's statements must be authorized by an employer to constitute a statement by the latter. Even the minority view requires that the statements pertain to matters within the scope of the employee's employment (which the comments of J do not). Thus, this testimony was *not* admissible as direct evidence.

Assuming, however, that T offered the statements as impeachment, the P probably contended that (i) the first statement (J's offer to release S in return for a bribe) is not admissible since impeachment through prior bad acts cannot be accomplished by extrinsic evidence (*i.e.*, S's testimony); and (ii) while bias is a proper ground for impeachment, many states require that a foundation must first be laid before extrinsic evidence to impeach on this basis is permitted. Such a foundation (*i.e.*, asking J "didn't you once attempt to bribe S and then threaten to get her friends when she refused?"), does not appear to have occurred. Thus, unless no foundation was required, S's testimony should *not* have been admitted as impeachment. (*See* ELO Ch. 4-XI(C)(1) & (2); Ch. 6-II(E)(2)(b).)

5. Dr. Walt ("W")'s testimony

Since the P had already put on its case-in-chief, the testimony in question is apparently an attempt to impeach T by contradiction. Thus, no hearsay objection can successfully be made since W's testimony is offered only for the purpose of contradicting T's earlier statement that he possessed only powdered milk when arrested.

T probably objected to this testimony upon the grounds that (1) it was not legally relevant, since it possessed too great a potential to prejudice the jury, and (2) it violated the physician/patient privilege. The P probably responded that (1) the potentially prejudicial impact is outweighed by the fact that this statement was made only with respect to impeachment of T's earlier testimony; and (2) in many states, the physician-patient privilege is not extended to criminal proceedings in which the patient is the accused. Additionally, the privilege pertains only to statements relating to diagnosis or treatment. Although the initial statement (that T was a drug addict) might arguably be pertinent to treatment of his insomnia and anxiety, T's second statement ("would W like to buy drugs?") is not. Assuming that impeachment by contradiction does *not* require a foundation in this jurisdiction, W's testimony was probably properly admitted. (*See* ELO Ch. 8-III(A) & (B)(1).)

Answer to Question 19

(1) Carl ("C")'s report

Owner ("O") could have objected to this evidence on the grounds that it is multiple hearsay, since Bob ("B")'s statement ("stmt") to C, and C's stmt, were both made out-of-court.

Paula ("P") could have contended that C's declaration (*i.e.*, the report) is admissible under either the "past recollection recorded" or "business records" exception to the hearsay rule. However, O could have argued in rebuttal that (1) the "past recollection recorded" exception is inapplicable because the declarant must have firsthand knowledge of the event he reported, and C wrote only what B had told him (*i.e.*, C had not seen the accident himself); and (2) the "business records" exception is not appropriate because the source of the information must be "trustworthy," and B was hardly an unbiased party.

Assuming, however, P prevailed on either of the above theories, B's stmt to C must also come within an exception to the hearsay rule. There is nothing to indicate that the "excited utterance" doctrine is applicable (*i.e.*, that B was under the emotional stress of the accident at the time he made his statement to C), especially since B's description of the incident was made in response to C's question. The "dying declaration" exception also appears to be inapplicable because the facts do not indicate that B believed death was imminent. No other exception seems applicable to B's stmt.

Thus, C should *not* have been permitted to read the report into evidence. (*See* ELO Ch. 5-II(F)(3)(b).)

(2) Flo ("F")'s testimony

O probably objected to the initial portion of B's stmt about stomach and head pains as being irrelevant (not tending to prove or disprove a fact of consequence), since any mental anguish suffered by B prior to his death would not be recoverable by P. Thus, this portion of F's testimony should *not* have been admitted. Although the same objection was probably made by O with respect to B's second stmt ("getting even"), this comment probably tends to show that B did not consider the accident to be his fault.

O probably also made a hearsay objection to F's testimony (F testified as to what B told her). B's stmt about head and stomach pains, if relevant, would probably be admissible under the "present sensation" or "medical diagnosis or treatment" exceptions to the hearsay rule. The portion of B's comments pertaining to "getting even" with the driver are probably admissible under the "present intention" exception. The part pertaining to being "hit by a speeding car" is probably also admissible under the "medical diagnosis and treatment exception" (especially since it was made in response to F's question as to "what happened?"). While B's use of the word "speeding" is layperson opinion, many jurisdictions permit such descriptions if they are based upon firsthand knowledge and helpful to the factfinder's understanding of factual circumstances. However, B's contention that the car was driven by a "drunken lunatic" should not have been admitted since it (1) was hearsay, and did not pertain to B's medical diagnosis or treatment, and (2) was opinion which was not based upon B's visual perception of Chauf.

Thus, only B's promise of revenge and his comment that he was hit by a speeding car should have been admitted. (*See* ELO Ch. 6-IV(B),(E) & Ch. 10-I(C)(6).)

(3) Chauf's writing

This evidence was probably objected to by O upon the grounds that (1) it was not properly authenticated (how did Earl know that the signature upon the document was Chauf's?); (2) it was hearsay (Chauf is speaking through the writing); and (3) it contained opinion ("intoxication" is an opinion, since Chauf did not know if he was legally intoxicated or not).

P probably contended in rebuttal, however, that (1) Earl may have seen Chauf's handwriting on other writings, and thus may have gained sufficient familiarity with it (we'll assume that Earl had not actually seen Chauf write the stmt in question); and (2) the writing comes within the "dying declaration" or "stmt against interest" exceptions to the hearsay rule. However, the "dying declaration" doctrine would probably *not* be applicable because Chauf's stmt was *not* about the cause of his death (*i.e.*, the knifing). Additionally, some states limit this exception to criminal cases. O would also contend that the stmt was not against Chauf's pecuniary interest because Chauf was about to die (and therefore he had no apprehension of legal liability). However, if C left an estate of any significance, P should have prevailed on the hearsay question on the basis of the "stmt against interest" exception.

Assuming the authentication problem can be overcome, Chauf's written stmt was properly admitted. (*See* ELO Ch. 6-XII(B)(3).)

(4) Frank's testimony

O probably objected to Frank's testimony upon the grounds that it was (1) character evidence (character evidence is ordinarily not admissible to prove conduct in conformity therewith on a particular occasion); and (2) hearsay (Frank was testifying about what B did out-of-court for the purpose of permitting the inference that B acted in a safe manner on the occasion in question). P probably contended in rebuttal, however, that (1) Frank's testimony described a habit (a consistently repeated response to a particular situation), and such evidence is ordinarily admissible. Since Frank's testimony probably pertained to a habit, it was properly admitted. (*See* ELO Ch. 3-X(B)(1) & X(D).)

(5) P's question and O's response

(It will be assumed that P had some reason to believe that Chauf had, in fact, received traffic citations for driving under the influence of alcohol. If P had no basis for his inquiry, it would have been improper and a mistrial could have been declared.)

O might have contended that P's question was not proper, since it pertained to prior specific acts of misconduct by Chauf, and prior misconduct is not admissible to prove that Chauf was driving in a similar manner on the occasion in question. P probably argued in rebuttal, however, that the prior traffic citations are admissible to show that O was negligent in not having learned about Chauf's prior misconduct (and therefore the evidence is *not* being offered to show that Chauf drove negligently on the occasion in question).

P probably complained to the court that O's answer was non-responsive (O was asked only for a "yes" or "no" answer, but volunteered that the basis of the question was false). This objection was probably proper, and so the judge should have (1) admonished O to answer the precise question which was asked; and (2) advised the jury that it should disregard the portion of O's response which followed his "No." (*See* ELO Ch. 3-XI(B)(1)(d).)

Answer to Question 20

1. Paul ("P")'s prior lawsuits

P probably contended that Dexter ("D")'s cross-examination was not proper because it did not tend to impair his credibility (the fact that one has filed previous actions against food or drug manufacturers does not tend to show that these actions were undertaken fraudulently, and therefore that the witness is untrustworthy). While D probably argued in rebuttal that it is unlikely that an "honest" person would bring that many lawsuits against food and drug manufacturers (and therefore an inference of untrustworthiness could be drawn), the objection to D's question was correctly sustained. (*See* ELO Ch. 3-XI(A)(2)(a).)

2. Deposition of Dr. Box

We'll assume the videotape was properly authenticated.

D probably contended initially that the statute permits only transcriptions, not a videotape. However, P could have argued in rebuttal that (1) the statute should not be viewed as being restrictive, and (2) a videotape should be preferred over a transcript, since it permits the jury to actually observe the declarant's demeanor. P properly prevailed.

D could have argued that Box was not "unavailable" within the meaning of the statute, since he would have appeared if P had paid the required fee. However, since Box deliberately avoided P's attempt at service, P properly prevailed on this issue too. (FRE 804).

Finally, D probably contended that the videotape was hearsay (the videotape is reproducing what Box said). Hearsay is an out-of-court statement offered into evidence for the purpose of proving the truth of the matter asserted therein. P would initially argue that the statute says that testimony within its parameters is usable "for any purpose," and so Box's statements were admissible even though the hearsay rule would otherwise be applicable. Secondly, if the hearsay rule is applicable to Box's statements, P could contend that the evidence is admissible under the "prior testimony" exception to the hearsay rule (*i.e.*, a statement made under oath by an unavailable declarant, provided the party against whom it is offered had a motive and opportunity to cross-examine the declarant). While this exception is ordinarily applied to statements which have been memorialized in a writing (usually, a transcript), it would be logical to apply it to videotaped testimony since the jury has the benefit of observing the declarant's demeanor.

In summary, the videotape was properly admitted. (*See* ELO Ch. 6-X(A)(2)(a).)

3. Modification of the pill

D probably argued that this testimony was (1) irrelevant (*i.e.*, did *not* tend to prove or disprove a material fact), since the fact that D recently removed a particular chemical that often accumulated in the liver does not necessarily mean that the initial pill was defective; and (2) inadmissible on public policy grounds (many states prohibit evidence of subsequent remedial measures, since defendants would be discouraged from making their products safer if their efforts could be introduced into evidence against them).

P probably argued in rebuttal, however, that (1) the testimony is relevant, since business entities rarely improve non-defective products; and (2) a few jurisdictions do permit evidence of subsequent remedial measures in products liability cases (since fault is not at issue). Unless this state adheres to the latter view, this evidence should *not* have been admitted. (*See* ELO Ch. 3-XII(A)(3) & (4).)

4. Abel ("A")'s testimony

D probably contended that the cross-examination was improper because (1) it exceeded the scope of direct (A testified about D's pills, not sleeping pills in general); and (2) while cross-examination of an expert by a *learned treatise* is permissible, newspaper articles are not learned treatises (since they *are* not extensively checked for accuracy and are usually written with a view towards being interesting (rather than authoritative). While P probably contended that A's knowledge (or lack of it) of sleeping pills does pertain to his ability to testify that D's pills were *not* defective, there doesn't appear to be an adequate response to D's second objection. Thus, D's objection should have been sustained. (*See* ELO Ch. 10-II(E)(1)(c).)

5. Carl ("C")'s testimony

P probably contended that C's testimony is hearsay (C was repeating P's out-of-court statement) and was privileged (*i.e.*, a confidential statement made for the purpose of obtaining legal services). D could have argued in rebuttal, however, that (1) the party-opponent admission to the hearsay rule is applicable, since the alleged statement was made by P; (2) since P never retained C, the privilege never accrued; and (3) the privilege is not applicable, in any event, if legal counsel was sought for the purpose of perpetuating a fraud. D will prevail on issue (1). With respect to (2), P probably responded that so long as legal services were being solicited, the privilege applies (even if the attorney involved was not retained). With respect to (3), P probably argued that no foundation was laid that P's suit was fraudulent, since P's remark to C could have been intended to imply only that, although P had previously suffered liver damage, he had suffered a new, but similar type of disability as a consequence of D's pills. The court's ruling was correct. (*See* ELO Ch. 8-II(C)(1) & (H)(1).)

Answer to Question 21

(a) The transcript of Oats' testimony

The transcript is relevant because it would tend to prove Dick ("D") took 2 bottles from Phil's store.

D can be expected to contend that the transcript was hearsay (an out-of-court statement offered to prove the truth of the matter asserted.) The prosecution will argue in rebuttal that Oats' testimony satisfies the "prior testimony" exception to the hearsay rule (*i.e.*, an unavailable declarant gave testimony, under oath, against the party against whom the testimony is being offered, and the latter party had an opportunity and similar motive to question the declarant): Oats is dead, his testimony was under oath, and D had the same motivation to question Oats because throwing objects out of a window supports the contention that D was driving recklessly (*i.e.*, it evidences a desire to hide the reason or cause of the allegedly reckless driving). D could contend that in his reckless driving case there was no reason to question Oats' testimony, since throwing objects out of a car could have been viewed as irrelevant (*i.e.*, not tending to prove or disprove that he was driving recklessly).

In summary, the transcript was properly admitted. (*See* Ch. 6-X(A)(1).)

(b) Phil ("P")'s testimony

D could have objected to P's testimony upon the grounds that (1) it is violative of the Best Evidence Rule; (2) there was no authentication of the DLD label (proof that the bottle actually did contain DLD); and (3) the DLD label was hearsay. In rebuttal, P would have contended that (1) the Best Evidence rule is satisfied because D had thrown away the bottles in question; (2) a few states view trade inscriptions as self-authenticating, absent any evidence of forgery; and (3) the "business records" exception to hearsay is applicable (the DLD label was printed in the ordinary course of the manufacturer's business).

P's testimony was properly admitted. (*See* ELO Ch. 6-VI(B)(3); Ch. 9-II(D)(2)(c) & IV(E)(3).)

(c) Judicial notice

A court may take judicial notice of facts which are easily verifiable from indisputable sources. The "standard" pharmacological dictionary, if well researched and written by persons prominent in the pharmaceutical field, would satisfy this standard. Generally, the judge is not required to give advance notice to the parties that he plans to take judicial notice of a fact. However, D could argue that the court should not take judicial notice of facts essential to conviction in a criminal case. D should prevail since whether DLD is an opium derivative is central to D's criminal conviction. (*See* ELO Ch. 12-II(F)(1).)

(d) Win ("W")'s testimony

D would have argued that W's testimony comes within the "marital communications" privilege. The prosecution could have responded, however, that conduct is not a "communication" and, even if it were, it was not "confidential" in this instance (D attempted to *conceal* his drug use from W, rather than confide in her about it). The prosecution properly prevailed on this issue.

A witness may ordinarily testify only as to facts observed. However, where lay witness opinion is based upon personal observation and is helpful to a clear understanding of the relevant testimony, it is often admitted. D probably argued that W's testimony that D "concealed" his drug use constituted an opinion. However, the prosecution could have contended in rebuttal that W's testimony described her impressions in the most practical way. The prosecution properly prevailed. (*See* ELO Ch. 8-V(C)(3)(b).)

Answer to Question 22

a. Peter ("P")'s testimony

Presumably, the defendants ("Defs") objected to P's testimony on the grounds that a 4-year old boy is not competent to testify. However, a child is usually considered able to testify so long as he understands the nature of his obligation to tell the truth. Since P stated that "good little boys tell the truth" the judge's determination that P was competent would be proper. (*See* ELO Ch. 1-IV(C)(2)(b).)

b. P's father's testimony

The Defs probably objected to this testimony on the grounds that (1) the offer of future payments and the prior payment are irrelevant (do not tend to prove or disprove a material fact), since these gestures could have been made out of humanitarian reasons (rather than as an acknowledgment of culpability); (2) the offer of future payments was a compromise, and in most states and the FRE such offers are *not* admissible; and (3) Defs' conduct was hearsay. Plaintiff's ("Pls") could have contended in rebuttal that (1) paying another's medical bills does suggest legal responsibility; (2) no compromise was actually "offered" since Defs didn't condition payment upon receiving a release; and (3) the party-opponent admission to the hearsay rule is applicable. The evidence was improperly admitted. (*See* ELO Ch. 3-XIV(A), (B) & (I).)

c. Bill ("B")'s testimony

B's testimony is relevant since it tends to prove that D's mother was aware of the risk posed by the firearm, which in turn permits an inference that Defs failed to act reasonably in not taking affirmative measures to extinguish the risk. (*See* ELO Ch. 2-I(B)(3).)

(i) That D was a bully

While character evidence is ordinarily not admissible to prove conduct in conformity therewith on a particular occasion, it may be admitted for any other relevant purpose. Pls probably argued that proof of D's character is appropriate to show that Defs knew, or should have known, of his dangerous tendencies (and therefore they acted negligently in permitting him to gain possession of an air gun).

Defs might, however, also have contended that B's statement reflects his personal opinion of D, rather than the community's view of him. While some states permit opinion testimony as to character, this is a minority view. Thus, B's testimony as to his opinion of D probably should have been admissible. (*See* ELO Ch. 3-II(C)(1).)

(ii) Clara ("C")'s statement

The defs probably attacked this statement as double hearsay (B was testifying as to what C told him D's mother had said). But D's mother arguably "adopted" C's statement by not objecting to it (where a reasonable person in the party-opponent's position would have denied an assertion made in her presence, she is deemed to have adopted the statement.

The "spontaneous declaration" exception to the hearsay rule does not appear to be applicable to C's statement, since (1) the facts fail to indicate that, as a consequence of the shooting, she was under an emotional strain; and (2) her statement was not "about" the shooting incident. (*See* ELO Ch. 6-II(D)(3)(a).)

d. Impeachment of Wilbur ("W")

The Pls could have contended that the initial question was ***not*** proper impeachment because W's prior bad act (possession of an illegal drug) has no bearing upon whether he would be likely to be truthful or not under oath. While Defs probably argued that one who would engage in criminal conduct is likely to lie, the court was probably correct in sustaining the objection.

Pls probably made the same objection to the second question. However, one who is under the influence of a drug while testifying might ***not*** be able to (1) recall an incident which occurred some time before, and (2) coherently relate what had occurred. Assuming Defs had a good faith basis for their question, this objection probably should ***not*** have been sustained.

Finally, the Pls probably objected to the last question upon the grounds that (1) it did not concern truthfulness (it was merely another way of asking if W was a heroin addict); and (2) it constituted impeachment by extrinsic evidence (impeachment by prior bad acts not reflected in a conviction can only be done intrinsically). Defs could have argued in rebuttal that heroin addiction does bear upon truthfulness and the arm was a means of showing that W was presently under the influence of the drug (if the needle marks were fresh). However, the objection to this question was probably correctly sustained. (*See* ELO Ch. 6-VIII(B)(1).)

Answer to Question 23

1. Bob's testimony

Dave ("D") probably contended that Bob's testimony is hearsay (an out-of-court statement, other than one made by the declarant while testifying, offered into evidence to prove the truth of the matter asserted), since Bob is testifying as to what Jane ("J") stated for the purpose of creating the inference that D was negligent.

However, under the "excited utterance" exception to the hearsay rule, a statement made about a startling event while the declarant was under the stress of that event is admissible. (We'll assume that this jurisdiction requires only that the out-of-court statement have been made while the declarant was under the stress of the event, as opposed to requiring that the statement have been made *while* the event was occurring.) Since J was crying, Ann ("A") would argue that J was under the effect of the accident when she made her statement to Bob. D, however, probably responded that the "excited utterance" exception was not applicable because several minutes had passed before Bob appeared, and so A might have had adequate time to advise J to make the statement in question to anyone who inquired about the accident. Furthermore, since Jane is incompetent to testify at trial because of her age, any other statements made by her should be inadmissible. The statement should *not* have been admitted. (*See* ELO Ch. 6-IV(D).)

2. D's statement to A

D probably objected to A's testimony upon the grounds that it (1) was hearsay; (2) was not relevant, since D may simply have desired to avoid time-consuming and expensive litigation; (3) was an offer of settlement (and such offers are ordinarily inadmissible). In rebuttal, however, A could contend that (1) the hearsay objection is overcome by the party-opponent exception to the hearsay rule; (2) A's statement did tend to prove a fact of material consequence (*i.e.*, that D was responsible for the accident); (3) D's statement was made *in response* to a settlement proposal, and so does not fall within the rule which excludes compromise offers (although in some states and under the FRE, any statement made in the course of settlement negotiations is inadmissible); and (4) evidence of liability insurance (while not admissible to prove culpable conduct) is ordinarily admissible for other purposes. Since D has denied that his car was involved in the accident, the fact that he had insurance which pertained to the vehicle should be admissible to show that D owned the car or had responsibility for it. In summary, then, D's statement was properly admitted. (*See* ELO Ch. 3-XIII(A)(3).)

3. The photographs

D probably objected to the admission of the photographs as not being properly authenticated, since A (via Rick) has not established a clear chain of continuous custody. While Rick testified as to taking the photographs at the scene and giving the photographs to the police, there has been no testimony that the film developed by the police and delivered back to Rick was the same film which Rick had given to them. If, however, Rick testified that the picture appeared to be an accurate representation of the situation which he photographed, the photographs would be authenticated and therefore properly admitted. (*See* ELO Ch. 9-V(A)(1)(a).)

4. The expert's testimony

Since D alleged that A was negligent, evidence as to A's faulty brakes (if they were so) is relevant. It would tend to prove that, if the light was against A, she might have failed to stop at the intersection because her brakes failed.

A probably contended that repairs made following an accident are ordinarily inadmissible to prove negligence. However, D could have argued in rebuttal that an exception to this rule exists where the evidence is offered to show simply that a condition existed prior to the accident (not that, in fact, the condition caused the accident). Since the facts indicate that A's repairs were made within three days of the accident, the court was probably correct in admitting the testimony of D's expert witness. (*See* ELO Ch. 3-XII(B)(1) & (2)(c).)

Answer to Question 24

1. Adam ("A")'s testimony

Roe ("R") probably contended that A's testimony about Tess ("T")'s statements is not admissible because it is hearsay (an out-of-court statement introduced into evidence to prove the truth of the matter asserted). The State ("St.") could argue that the statement is admissible under the "excited utterance" exception to the hearsay rule. In some jurisdictions, the statement must have been made while the event was occurring; but in others (including federal courts), the statement must only have been made while "under the stress" of the startling event. Assuming the latter rule is followed in this state, five minutes is probably *not* too long a period of time to end the stress of such a dramatic event. The court did not err in admitting A's statement. (*See* ELO Ch. 6-IV(D)(4)(a).)

2. Cable ("C")'s testimony

R probably contended that C's testimony was not admissible because (1) it violated the Best Evidence Rule (to prove the contents of a writing — the police file — the original is required); (2) the testimony is hearsay; (3) the file was not authenticated (no foundation was laid that the writing was what it purported to be); and (4) the portion of the file showing that R had previously been convicted of rape is inadmissible because evidence of prior criminal convictions to show action in conformity therewith on a subsequent occasion is usually not admissible.

The St. might have argued in rebuttal that (1) the file was authenticated by C's testimony that he obtained it from the location where the file of known sex offenders was supposed to be located (*i.e.*, testimony of a witness with knowledge); (2) the "business records" (writings kept in the ordinary course of the profession) and "public records" (writings compiled by public officers about matters observed pursuant to a duty imposed by law) exceptions to the hearsay rule are applicable; (3) the prior convictions tend to identify R as T's assailant, and thus fall within the rule that other-crimes evidence may be used for identification purposes; and (4) the evidence is not too prejudicial in light of its crucial probative value. However, there appears to be no satisfactory response to the Best Evidence objection and the evidence of prior rape convictions was probably too tenuous a connection to prove R's identity. Therefore, C's testimony should *not* have been admitted. (*See* ELO Ch. 9-IV(A)(4).)

3. Testimony of R's wife

R probably contended that the adverse testimony privilege permits him to prevent his wife from testifying. The majority rule is that, in a criminal case, the defendant can prevent his spouse from testifying. However, in a minority of jurisdictions, this privilege belongs to the testifying spouse. If this state adheres to the latter view, R's wife should have been permitted to testify.

Confidential communications made during a marriage can be precluded by a spouse. The St. probably contended that actions (R's agitated appearance and the scratches on his arm) are not communications; and even if they are deemed to be communications, a party's physical appearance is ordinarily not deemed to be "confidential" in nature (since persons other than his spouse could presumably observe him and his condition).

Assuming the adverse testimony privilege is not available to R in this state, R's wife's testimony was properly admitted. (*See* ELO Ch. 8-V(B)(1) & (C)(3).)

4. R's testimony

The court was correct in admitting the shoe which was obtained in an illegal search of R's house. Illegally seized evidence is admissible to impeach a criminal defendant who has elected to testify.

Where a procedure or test is utilized, there must usually be some foundation that the process is scientifically valid. The facts fail to indicate that the expert gave any testimony about the scientific validity of the shoeprint comparison procedure. Thus, this portion of the evidence probably should not have been admitted. (*See* ELO Ch. 10-III(A)(2)(d).)

5. Prosecutor's request and closing argument

A witness may be impeached by extrinsic evidence showing a contradiction in his testimony provided such impeachment does not pertain to a collateral matter. While R's arm is extrinsic evidence, the blemish upon it would tend to contradict R's statement that he did not rape T. This is not a collateral matter since it pertains to the essence of the St.'s case against R.

The facts are silent as to whether this jurisdiction requires that a foundation be laid before impeachment by this type of extrinsic evidence may occur. R apparently was not asked, "Do you have a large brown blemish on your left arm?" Thus, if a foundation was required, this evidence arguably should *not* have been admitted.

While no comment may be made upon a criminal defendant's refusal to testify on his own behalf, once an accused takes the stand any legitimate comment about his testimony may be made. Thus, the prosecutor's comment was proper. (*See* ELO Ch. 4-XIII(D)(1), (2) & Ch. 8-IV(F).)

Multiple-Choice Questions

1. There had recently been complaints about the price of gasoline. Exton Corporation was accused of price-gouging by the State of Utopia's Department of Commerce. Exton retained Gibelco & Bunn to defend it. Gibelco's attorney requested that Exton send her all pertinent records, so that the documents could be carefully reviewed. The Utopia Department of Commerce commenced an action against Exton to recover the millions of dollars which it claimed had been overcharged to citizens of that state.

   During the discovery stage of the case, the Department of Justice made a request for certain relevant documents. Gibelco's attorney responded that the documents requested were in its possession, and therefore privileged. The Utopia Department of Justice disagreed with this assertion.

   Based upon the foregoing, it is most likely that:

   (A) The records are discoverable, since they are not within the attorney-client privilege.
   (B) The records are discoverable, since any purported attorney-client privilege must be asserted by Exton at trial.
   (C) The records are not discoverable, since they are now in Gibelco's possession.
   (D) The records are not discoverable, since, if reviewed by Gibelco, the records now constitute Gibelco's work product.

2. Bill Sacamore and Joe Schmoe were two ex-convicts. Joe asked Bill to help him in "knocking over" a grocery store. When Bill vacillated, Joe promised that he would give Bill at least $1,000 for his participation. Bill then agreed. They agreed that Bill would drive the getaway car, and Joe would actually steal the money from the grocer. On the prearranged date, Bill and Joe drove to the grocery store. Joe went inside, while Bill waited in the car. Joe pulled a gun on the Owner, and removed $5,000 from the safe. However, as he was about to exit, a security guard at the store shot Joe in the leg. Joe was captured and arrested.

   When the paramedics arrived, Joe said to one of them, "Give Bill Sacamore this $1,000. If he doesn't get his money, his friends will get me in the slammer." Joe subsequently confessed, and Bill was arrested and charged with conspiracy to commit armed robbery. At Bill's trial, the paramedic is called to testify about Joe's statement to him. However, Bill's attorney objected to this testimony. (Assume the testimony is not hearsay.)

   Based upon the foregoing, it is most likely that the statement is:

   (A) Inadmissible, since it is not relevant.
   (B) Inadmissible, since it is within the physician-patient privilege.

(C) Inadmissible, since a paramedic is not a physician.

(D) Admissible, since Bill's participation in the robbery could arguably be inferred by Joe's statement.

3. Post sued Dean for personal injuries allegedly caused by Dean's negligence. A major issue at trial was whether Post's disability was caused solely by trauma or by a preexisting condition of osteoarthritis. Post called Dr. Cox, who testified that the disability was caused by trauma. On cross-examination, Dr. Cox testified that a medical textbook entitled *Diseases of the Joints* was authoritative and that she agreed with the substance of passages from the textbook that she was directed to look at, but that the passages were inapplicable to Post's condition because they dealt with rheumatoid arthritis rather than with the osteoarthritis that had inflicted Post. Dean then called his expert, Dr. Freed, who testified that, with reference to the issue being litigated, there is no difference between the two kinds of arthritis. Dean's counsel then asks permission to read to the jury the textbook passages earlier shown to Dr. Cox. The judge should rule the textbook passages

    (A) Admissible only for the purpose of impeaching Cox.
    (B) Admissible as substantive evidence if the judge determines that the passages are relevant.
    (C) Inadmissible, because they are hearsay, not within any exception.
    (D) Inadmissible, if Cox contended that they are not relevant to Post's condition.

4. Bill and Harry are accused of conspiring to commit a bank robbery. Bill was apprehended immediately after leaving the bank, and confessed to the crime. Under questioning, he advised police that Harry had supplied the gun and was to meet him afterward to receive one-third of the cash proceeds. Bill subsequently gave the police a note written by Harry, which stated: "Don't forget my share. If you get lost, I'll find you, and it won't be pretty." When the prosecution attempted to introduce this note at Harry's trial, Harry's attorney objected. (Assume the note is not hearsay.)

    Based upon the foregoing, it is most likely that the note is:

    (A) Admissible, but only if a handwriting expert corroborates the validity of Harry's signature.
    (B) Admissible, if the court determines there is adequate evidence of the letter's authenticity.
    (C) Inadmissible, since the letter is not relevant to whether Harry was a co-conspirator or not.
    (D) Inadmissible, since the letter was confidential in nature.

5. Darryl and Paul were motorists. One day, as Paul was driving to work, his car was struck by a vehicle driven by Darryl. Paul immediately got out of his car and, after getting Darryl's driver's license and other data, began asking people in the area if they had seen what had occurred. Although somewhat reluctant to "get involved," Martha told Paul that she had seen the accident, and that Darryl's vehicle was over the white line when the crash occurred. Three days later, an adjuster employed by Paul's insurer also asked Martha what had occurred, and was given the same response. Paul sued Darryl (who claimed that Paul's vehicle was over the white line). At trial, when Paul's attorney attempted to have the insurance adjuster testify as to what Martha had said to him, Darryl's attorney objected.

   Based upon the foregoing, it is most likely that the testimony will be:

   (A) Admissible, since it is an admission.
   (B) Admissible, since Martha's statement was an excited utterance.
   (C) Inadmissible, since there is no indication that Martha is unavailable.
   (D) Inadmissible, since Martha's statement is hearsay.

6. Jack was shot and killed by someone with a pistol. Michael is accused of the murder. The prosecution's case is premised upon the argument that Michael was greatly angered by Jack's constant banter, and reacted in a murderous manner. At the criminal trial, the prosecution sought to introduce testimony by Pete to the effect that he had heard Jack call Michael a "sissy" and "scaredy cat" on numerous occasions, and that Michael had objected to these characterizations. However, Michael's attorney objected to this testimony.

   Based upon the foregoing, it is most likely that Pete's testimony is:

   (A) Admissible, if it is offered to show Michael's alleged motivation.
   (B) Admissible, if Michael asserts his Fifth Amendment right against self-incrimination and there is no other means of admitting this evidence.
   (C) Inadmissible, since it is hearsay.
   (D) Inadmissible, since it is a statement pertaining to Michael's character.

7. Dick and Paul were motorists in the State of Utopia. One day, as Paul was backing out of his driveway onto the street, his car was struck by a vehicle driven by Dick. Paul was immediately taken by paramedics to a local hospital. Paul subsequently sued Dick. Dick denied liability, contending that Paul had illegally backed into the street. Dick also contested the extent of Paul's asserted injuries.

   In presenting Paul's case, his attorney called one of the paramedics, Mike, who attended to Paul in the ambulance which brought him to the hospital. Mike was asked to testify about the seriousness of Paul's injuries. However, before

Mike testified, he reviewed the report of the patient's condition which he is required by law to complete in such instances. This report was given to him by Paul's attorney. However, the report had not been admitted into evidence, and Dick's attorney objected to Mike's testimony.

Based upon the foregoing, it is most likely that Mike's testimony is:

(A) Admissible, under the doctrine of present recollection refreshed.

(B) Admissible, since it constitutes past recollection recorded.

(C) Inadmissible, since it is based upon a document which is hearsay.

(D) Inadmissible, if the report has not been authenticated.

8.   Pam owned a large house on Marlborough Street in the City of Alacon. She entered into a written agreement with Deborah whereby the latter agreed to add a second story onto Pam's home. The specific work which Deborah was to perform was described in detail in the written agreement. After the work was completed, Pam refused to pay the last installment, claiming that there were numerous deficiencies in Deborah's work. In fact, Pam sued Deborah for the sum of money which she paid to another entity to perform the work in question "correctly." At the trial, when Deborah sought to personally testify about various aspects (which requirements were set forth in the written agreement) of her performance, Pam's attorney objected.

Based upon the foregoing, Deborah's testimony about matters described in the written contract is:

(A) Admissible, since the "business records" exception to the hearsay rule is applicable.

(B) Admissible, since Deborah's testimony is based on firsthand knowledge.

(C) Inadmissible, since the Best Evidence Rule is applicable to this situation.

(D) Inadmissible, since the Parol Evidence Rule is applicable in this situation.

9.   Dora, an elderly woman, was walking down a city street toward a corner. Paul was jogging toward the corner from the intersecting sidewalk. Paul and Dora arrived at the street corner at the same time, and Paul inadvertently brushed against Dora. Dora, due to her elderliness, fell to the ground (breaking her left arm). Paul did not believe he was at fault, but advised Dora that he would "take care of her doctor bills, and that he was sorry the incident had occurred." George, a passerby, heard Paul's statements. When Paul failed to pay Dora's higher-than-expected medical bills, she sued him. At the trial, Dora's attorney attempted to have George testify about Paul's statements to Dora. Paul's attorney vigorously objected to this testimony.

Based upon the foregoing , it is most likely that George's testimony about Paul's statements is:

(A) Admissible, as a party-opponent admission.

(B) Admissible, since it is relevant upon the question of Paul's failure to act reasonably.

(C) Inadmissible, since Paul promised to pay Dora's medical bills.

(D) Inadmissible, since Paul did not intend for his statement to constitute an acknowledgment of culpability.

10. Paul was injured when the brakes on his 6-month-old Fordico Company ("Fordico") automobile abruptly failed to work. Paul commenced a products liability action against Fordico, contending that the latter had manufactured a defective vehicle. However, Paul was injured while driving on a rain-soaked street. In its defense, Fordico attempted to introduce evidence that, despite the poor weather, Paul was negligently exceeding the speed limit by at least 15 m.p.h. when he was injured. Fordico would like to call a witness, Rob, who witnessed the accident to testify as to the foregoing.

Based upon the foregoing, if Paul's attorney objects to the introduction of this evidence, it is most likely that:

(A) The objection will be sustained, since the evidence is not relevant.

(B) The objection will be sustained, since the evidence is hearsay.

(C) The objection will not be sustained, since the evidence is relevant.

(D) The objection will not be sustained, if there is rebuttal evidence that, even if Paul was exceeding the speed limit, his injuries would have occurred anyway.

11. On the way home from school one day, Dan's stepdaughter, Amy, failed to stop at a red light and crashed into Patricia's car. Under the applicable law, a vehicle "owner" is vicariously liable for its negligent operation by members of his or her household. Case law has defined a vehicle "owner" as the legal owner or person "in control" of the automobile. Patricia sued Dan and the legal owner (i.e., the person in whose name the vehicle was registered) of the car, Dan's second wife, Carol. In rebuttal, Dan claimed that the vehicle belonged to Carol, and therefore he has no personal liability to Patricia. At trial, Patricia attempts to introduce evidence that Dan had purchased liability insurance for the car which Amy was driving when the collision occurred.

Based upon the foregoing, if Dan objects to the introduction of this evidence, it is most likely that:

(A) The objection will be overruled, since Dan's purchase of insurance tends to show that it was more likely than not that Amy was at fault.

(B) The objection will be overruled, since Dan's purchase of liability insurance tends to show that he is the "owner" of the vehicle.

(C) The objection will be sustained, since the existence of insurance is irrelevant to who was at fault.

(D) The objection will be sustained, since the availability of insurance tends to bias a factfinder against the insured party.

12. Margaret was shopping at Frank's Market, when she slipped and fell on some liquid on the floor in one of the aisles. Mr. Jamison, the manager of Frank's Market, heard Margaret's fall and ensuing commotion. He did not, however, see the incident. Sensing what had occurred, Mr. Jamison walked over to Margaret and immediately said to her, "Frank's Market will pay you $5,000 to forget any claim." Margaret angrily refused this offer, and told Mr. Jamison that she was going to "Sue, sue, sue!" Soon afterward, Margaret did commence litigation against Frank's Market, which denied liability in its answer.

At trial, Margaret tries to introduce evidence that, immediately after her slip-and-fall, Mr. Jamison offered, on behalf of Frank's Market, to pay her $5,000 in settlement of her claim.

Based upon the foregoing, if counsel for Frank's Market objects to the introduction of this evidence, it is most likely that:

(A) The objection will be sustained, since Mr. Jamison's statement was a compromise offer.

(B) The objection will be sustained, since Mr. Jamison's statement is hearsay and not relevant (i.e., he hadn't even observed the incident).

(C) The objection will not be sustained, since Mr. Jamison's statement is pertinent to a determination of the culpability of Frank's Market.

(D) The objection will not be sustained, since Mr. Jamison's statement was not made in the course of formal settlement negotiations.

13. After Karen purchased her new, vanilla white Lexus car, she immediately drove it to a local shopping mall. Since the car was brand new, Karen parked it at the very end of the parking lot, far from any other vehicles. In this manner, she hoped to avoid having it being "nicked" by an uncareful driver. After she had finished her shopping, Karen returned to her car. She observed that a black van was parked next to it. As Karen walked to the driver's side of her car, she noticed a large black stripe on the rear portion of her car and some white paint on the right front fender of the van. Karen, understandably upset, took down the van's license plate number and sued the owner for damage to her vehicle.

At trial, Karen attempts to introduce testimony from the owner of the van that he had his vehicle painted only two days after the alleged incident.

Based upon the foregoing, if counsel for the defendant objects to this testimony, it is most likely that:

(A) The objection will be overruled, since the testimony shows that the van owner had attempted to conceal evidence.

(B) The objection will be overruled, since in negligence cases evidence of remedial measures is ordinarily admissible.

(C) The objection will be sustained, since evidence of remedial measures is not admissible.

(D) The objection will be sustained, since the evidence fails to show that the defendant was the driver of the vehicle at the time in question.

14. Alice and her friend Pam were walking downtown, on the way to a restaurant. They passed by a building which was under construction. As Alice and Pam were staring at the new masonry, they heard an ugly "scraping" sound. Immediately thereafter, a piece of masonry fell from the building, directly onto Alice's shoulder. Alice sued Mr. Moneybags, the owner of the building, and Cosgrove. In his answer, Moneybags claimed that the construction company, Cosgrove, Inc. ("Cosgrove") was an independent contractor, and that the building was completely under his control when the incident occurred. Thus, he had no liability. Moneybags further contended that he exercised no control over the construction at the time of the accident.

At trial, Alice attempts to introduce evidence that one day after the incident, Moneybags ordered Cosgrove to erect a screen on the portion of the roof over-looking the street; and that Cosgrove complied.

Based upon the foregoing, if counsel for Moneybags objects to the introduction of this evidence, it is most likely that:

(A) The objection will be sustained, since evidence of remedial measures is inadmissible.

(B) The objection will be sustained, since the evidence has no bearing upon Moneybags' alleged negligence.

(C) The objection will be overruled, since the evidence shows Cosgrove's pen-ultimate control of the construction.

(D) The objection will be overruled, since (with a limiting instruction) the evidence could be used to show that Moneybags retained control over the building's construction.

15. Marla wanted to buy some new diamond earrings. Accordingly, she drove down to "Ripoff's," a store recommended to her by a friend. Clyde Ripoff ("Ripoff"), the owner, showed her several pairs of beautiful earrings. He eventually sold Marla a pair of (what appeared to be) diamond studs. Ripoff told Marla that the earrings were "very" valuable, and that he was "giving her an excellent bargain." Later, when Marla attempted to insure the items, she was emphatically informed by her insurance agent that the earrings were

merely cubic zirconia. They were therefore of only minimal worth. Marla then commenced an action against Ripoff for "grossly" misrepresenting the value of the earrings.

At the trial, Marla's counsel seeks to introduce evidence that Ripoff had a well deserved reputation for being "unsavory and unethical" in his business dealings.

Based upon the foregoing, if counsel for Ripoff objects to the introduction of this evidence, it is most likely that:

(A) The objection will be sustained, since Ripoff's character is not directly in issue.

(B) The objection will be sustained, since the evidence is being offered to show that Ripoff acted in conformity with his usual character on the occasion in question.

(C) The objection will be overruled, since the evidence tends to show that Ripoff deceived Marla.

(D) The objection will be overruled, if Ripoff offers evidence of his character for honesty.

16. One Sunday afternoon, James was driving on a public street. Unfortunately, he was injured when a car driven by Paul went through a stop sign and crashed into the passenger side of James' car. James sued Paul's parents under a negligent entrustment theory, contending that they carelessly permitted Paul to borrow their car. Paul had been in several car accidents during the prior two years. In these incidents, Paul had been adjudged as either "negligent" or "reckless."

At trial, counsel for James attempts to introduce evidence of Paul's "negligent" and "reckless" character. Based upon the foregoing, if counsel for Paul's parents objects to the introduction of this evidence, it is most likely that:

(A) The objection will be overruled, if the evidence is offered to show that Paul's parents knew (or should have known) about his reckless or negligent tendencies.

(B) The objection will be overruled, if the evidence is offered to show that Paul had failed to act unreasonably.

(C) The objection will be sustained, since character evidence is ordinarily inadmissible to prove conduct in conformity therewith on a particular occasion.

(D) The objection will be sustained, since Paul's prior "negligent" or "reckless" conduct does not tend to prove that he was negligent in this case.

17. Theresa was charged with the attempted robbery of a beauty supply store. Theresa was a "make-up junkie," who had two prior convictions for robbing beauty supply and cosmetics stores, at gunpoint. Theresa had previously worked as an Avon representative, until the company discovered that Theresa was often keeping, rather than selling, their products. Theresa was arrested at the scene. She admits committing the crime, but claims that she was coerced into participating in it by her boyfriend, who threatened to "give her a thrashing" if she didn't "come through with some money."

At trial, the prosecution attempts to introduce evidence that Theresa had two prior convictions for the robbery of other beauty supply stores.

Based upon the foregoing, if Theresa's attorney objects to the introduction of this evidence, it is most likely that:

(A) The objection should be sustained, since prior convictions are ordinarily not admissible.
(B) The objection should be sustained, since Theresa's prior convictions are not relevant.
(C) The objection will be overruled, since Theresa's prior convictions are admissible character evidence in this situation.
(D) The objection will be overruled, since it is relevant to prove that Theresa (as opposed to anyone else) committed the crime in question.

18. Magda was shopping at Nordstrom's Department Store. She sees a lovely silk scarf, and ties it around her neck to see how it looks. After doing this, Magda sees some leather gloves and walks over to them. Then other items catch her attention while she continues to shop. Suddenly, Magda remembered that she was supposed to meet a friend for lunch at noon. She hurried out of the store, still wearing the scarf. However, as soon as she left Nordstrom's, Magda was arrested by security personnel for shoplifting. At trial, Magda contended that she had simply forgotten about the scarf she had tied around her neck.

At trial, the prosecution sought to introduce evidence that, on a prior occasion, Magda was stopped outside of a different store for neglecting to purchase an item which she was wearing (jeans she had purportedly "tried on" at a Gap store). However, no charges against Magda had been filed in this instance.

Based upon the foregoing, if Magda's attorney objects to the introduction of this evidence, it is most likely that:

(A) The objection will be overruled, since the evidence rebuts Magda's assertion that she had made an innocent mistake.
(B) The objection will be overruled, since prior similar conduct is admissible to prove conduct in conformity therewith on the occasion in question.

(C) The objection will be sustained, since it is irrelevant to Magda's conduct on this particular occasion.

(D) The objection will be sustained, since prior conduct is not admissible.

19. On July 1, John Adams executed a deed conveying a life estate in Blackacre to Charles Baker. Thereafter, Baker brought an action against Adams for reformation of the deed, contending that it was the intention of the parties that Blackacre be conveyed to Baker in fee.

Evans, a witness for Baker, testified that she worked in the office of Ladd, an attorney who handled a lot of Adams' business. She was shown a document which bore the printed letterhead, "John Adams, Bigtown." The document was dated June 12, and it read: "Dear Mr. Ladd: I have decided to sell Blackacre outright to Baker. In a few days, I'll call you about preparing the deed." At the bottom in longhand was written, "John Adams."

Miss Evans, upon examining the document, stated that it was a photographic copy of a letter which Ladd had received through the mail about the middle of June, that she had seen the letter at that time, and that the letterhead on it was the same as that which appeared in Ladd's office file of correspondence with Adams, who lived in Bigtown. Baker then offered the document into evidence.

The BEST objection that Adams should make against the introduction of this evidence is that it is

(A) Irrelevant.

(B) Violative of the Best Evidence Rule.

(C) Hearsay.

(D) Violative of the attorney-client privilege.

Questions 20-21 are based upon the following fact situation:

Bill Bungler was arrested for attempting to extort money from Harvey Hardin. The latter owned a large hardware store in Centerville.

20. After properly introducing into evidence Bungler's telephone registry which showed a call to 250-0000 on the day a demand for $50,000 was telephonically made upon Harvey, the prosecution sought to introduce into evidence a properly authenticated copy of the Centerville telephone book. This book contained a listing for Harvey's store at that number. The evidence is

(A) Inadmissible, because it is hearsay.

(B) Inadmissible, because it is entirely possible that Bungler called Harvey's store for a business purpose.

(C) Inadmissible, because of the Best Evidence Rule.

(D) Admissible, because it is relevant to show that Bungler might have been the extortionist.

21. To show that Harvey reasonably felt threatened with imminent harm, the prosecution sought to introduce into evidence an unsigned, hand-printed note received by Harvey reading "Deliver $50,000 to the phone booth on Main and Grand at 8:00 p.m. tomorrow, or you'll be out of business within a week." This evidence is

    (A) Inadmissible, because there has been no proof that it was Bungler's hand-writing.
    (B) Inadmissible, because it is hearsay.
    (C) Admissible, because it is not hearsay.
    (D) Admissible, because it is a party-opponent admission.

22. Bob Barker was arrested for burglary. At the trial, Barker testified in his defense that he was playing cards with Jack on the night of the burglary. Defense counsel also called Joseph Blow as a witness on the defendant's behalf. Blow testified that he lived in the same community as Barker, and that the latter had an excellent reputation for honesty and integrity. On cross-examination, the prosecution asked Blow if he was aware that Barker had been fired from his job as a supermarket cashier two years before for taking money from the cash register. The question is

    (A) Proper, because Blow testified as to Barker's character.
    (B) Proper, because a witness may always be cross-examined with respect to prior acts of misconduct committed by him.
    (C) Improper, because the prior misconduct was different from burglary.
    (D) Improper, because Barker was never asked about the supermarket incident.

23. Bob Brown had been employed as a miner for the ABC Mining Corp. for 12 years. He was recently killed when there was an explosion in the underground area in which he was working. His executor brought a wrongful death action against ABC, claiming the latter negligently permitted unsafe working conditions to exist, as a consequence of which Brown was killed. The executor called Jock as a witness. He testified that earlier on the day of the explosion, Brown had commented to him, "I could swear that I smell gas down here." Jock's testimony is

    (A) Admissible, as a party-opponent admission.
    (B) Admissible, as a dying declaration.
    (C) Admissible, as a present sense impression.
    (D) Admissible, as an excited utterance.

24. Arlene parked her relatively new car facing downward on a steep hill, turned her tires toward the curb, and set the parking brake. She then exited the vehicle. When Arlene returned approximately one hour later, the vehicle had moved forward and impacted upon the vehicle in front of her. While Arlene was surveying the damage, Clyde, the owner of the other vehicle, arrived. He subsequently sued Arlene, claiming that her negligence caused the damage to his vehicle. Arlene filed an indemnity action against the manufacturer of her car, alleging that the parking brake was defective.

At trial, Arlene attempts to testify that, when she parks her car, she invariably sets the parking brake.

Based upon the foregoing, if Clyde's attorney objects to the introduction of this evidence, it is most likely that:

(A) The objection will be sustained, since prior conduct to prove action in conformity therewith is inadmissible.

(B) The objection will be sustained, since it is inconsistent with Arlene's claim against the manufacturer.

(C) The objection will be overruled, since evidence of habit is admissible.

(D) The objection will be overruled, since prior conduct is admissible to prove action in conformity therewith on the occasion in question.

25. Mary is a 72-year-old retired junior high school teacher. She commenced an action against Matthew, a licensed stockbroker, claiming that he had deceived her into investing her life savings by fraudulently claiming that he would greatly enrich her via a series of stock transactions. Matthew has no history of disciplinary action or lawsuits against him with respect to stock transactions initiated by him. Matthew is generally known as an "honest" person by his friends, colleagues, and clients.

At trial, Matthew's counsel attempts to introduce evidence, via the testimony of another stockbroker who works closely with Matthew, that Matthew "has an excellent reputation for honesty in the business community."

Based upon the foregoing, if Mary's attorney objects to the introduction of this evidence, it is most likely that:

(A) The objection will be overruled, since character evidence is admissible in civil cases.

(B) The objection will be overruled, since Matthew's character is directly in issue in this case.

(C) The objection will be sustained, since the testimony is hearsay.

(D) The objection will be sustained, since evidence of Matthew's character is not admissible.

26. Carlyle always had a very fond relationship with his children. Prior to his death, Carlyle (a wealthy, 72-year-old man, who resided in a nursing home) changed his will to leave everything to his neighbor and friend, Jojo. After the will was read, Carlyle's two children, Maggie and April, were furious. They claimed that the modification was invalid because Carlyle was not mentally competent when the will was changed.

At trial, Maggie and April attempt to introduce evidence of specific acts of Carlyle which occurred about the time that his will was modified (i.e., neighbors will testify that Carlyle sometimes dressed as a cowboy and pretended to shoot Indians with a toy pistol, etc.).

Based upon the foregoing, if counsel for the executor of Carlyle's estate vigorously objects to the introduction of this evidence, it is most likely that:

(A) The objection will be overruled, since Carlyle's character is in issue.
(B) The objection will be overruled, since character evidence is ordinarily admissible.
(C) The objection will be sustained, since the evidence pertains to prior specific acts (rather than general character traits).
(D) The objection will be sustained, since character evidence is generally inadmissible.

27. Charley and Bill are two oil rig workers. Over time, they have developed an intense hatred of each other. They recently got into a barroom brawl. In the midst of the fight, Bill pulled a switchblade from his hip pocket, and slashed Charley across the throat. This cut ultimately caused Charley to bleed to death. Bill has been charged with Charley's murder. Bill claims that Charley had initiated the altercation, and that he had merely acted in self-defense.

At trial, Bill's attorney sought to introduce evidence to the effect that Bill had an excellent reputation for "honesty and dealing fairly with people."

Based upon the foregoing, if the prosecution objects to this evidence, it is most likely that:

(A) The objection will be sustained, since Bill cannot initially introduce evidence of his own good character.
(B) The objection will be sustained, since this evidence does not tend to rebut the commission of the crime for which Bill has been charged.
(C) The objection will be overruled, since a defendant may initially introduce evidence of his own positive character traits in a homicide case.
(D) The objection will be overruled, since character evidence pertaining to a defendant is admissible in criminal cases.

28. Jamie and Sharon have been college roommates for two years. One afternoon, Sharon stole one of Jamie's personal checks, and went to a local record store. She used the check to purchase several compact discs. At the time of purchase, Sharon forged Jamie's name on the check. As her roommate, Sharon was very familiar with Jamie's signature. Jamie eventually found out about the forged check, and pressed forgery charges against Sharon. Pursuant to the advice of her attorney, Sharon has claimed that she neither took the check, nor forged Jamie's name.

At trial, Sharon's attorney attempts to introduce evidence that Sharon had an excellent reputation for honesty and truthfulness.

Based upon the foregoing, if the prosecution objects to this evidence, it is most likely that:

(A) The objection will be overruled, since evidence of Sharon's character for honesty is pertinent to the crime for which she is charged.
(B) The objection will be overruled, since positive character traits pertaining to a defendant are admissible in criminal trials.
(C) The objection will be sustained, since only evidence of prior specific acts by Sharon is admissible.
(D) The objection will be sustained, since evidence of an accused's character must be initiated by the prosecution.

29. Kellie and Shawna are both exotic dancers at a striptease bar. Shawna has a history of fighting with the other dancers. While performing on stage, doing a mock "fight" routine, Shawna grabbed at Kellie's costume (what little there was) and pushed her to the ground. Kellie was extremely embarrassed by this incident. She sued Shawna for assault, battery and intentional infliction of severe emotional distress. Pursuant to her attorney's advice, Shawna claimed that Kellie had aggressively accosted her first; and therefore she had merely acted in self-defense.

At trial, Kellie's attorney attempts to introduce testimony that Shawna had a reputation for being "an aggressive bully."

Based upon the foregoing, if Shawna's counsel objects to this evidence, it is most likely that:

(A) The objection will be sustained, since this is a civil case.
(B) The objection will be sustained, since it is not relevant to whether Shawna committed the torts asserted.
(C) The objection will be overruled, since Shawna's conduct was arguably criminal in nature.

(D) The objection will be overruled, since it bears directly upon a major issue in the litigation.

30. Jimmy is a macho-type guy, who lived in a "rough" neighborhood. One day, while standing at the window of his apartment, Jimmy saw Slash slicing the tires of his car with a knife. Jimmy ran out of his house with a baseball bat. He swung the bat and hit Slash several times, breaking Slash's arms and legs. Although Jimmy's neighbors were impressed with his pronounced "law and order" style, Slash pressed criminal charges. Jimmy was taken into custody and charged with aggravated battery. In his defense, Jimmy claims Slash threatened him with the knife, resulting in his actually striking the latter with the bat.

At the criminal trial, Jimmy's counsel attempts to introduce evidence to show that he is "peaceable in nature."

Based upon the foregoing, if the prosecution objects to this evidence, it is most likely that:

(A) The objection will be sustained, since character evidence is not admissible.
(B) The objection will be sustained, since this is mere opinion evidence.
(C) The objection will be overruled, since this type of character evidence is admissible in this situation.
(D) The objection will be overruled, since only specific instances of Jimmy's peaceable character are admissible.

31. Tanya recently became a member of "The Roses," a female gang at her high school. Although Tanya is in high school, she was held back one year. She is 18 years old. As a manifestation of allegiance to her new gang, Tanya is told that she must "slash" a member of a rival gang. Tanya is mistakenly informed that Rita, another girl at the high school, is a member of "The Balabusters." In fact, Rita has no gang ties whatsoever. One day after school, Tanya pulled out a razor blade and slashed at Rita's arm. Rita attempted to avoid being cut by ducking. As a consequence, Tanya accidentally slashed Rita's neck, wounding her fatally. Tanya is arrested and charged with murder.

At the criminal trial, pursuant to her attorney's advice, Tanya testified that (1) she acted in self-defense (i.e., Rita had initially attacked her with a switch-blade), and alternatively (2) Rita provoked the situation by insulting Tanya. In response, the prosecution attempts to introduce character evidence of Rita's peaceable, non-violent nature.

Based upon the foregoing, if Tanya's attorney objects to the introduction of this evidence, it is most likely that:

(A) The objection will be overruled, since evidence of Rita's character is admissible to disprove Tanya's assertions.

(B) The objection will be overruled, since pertinent character evidence of the victim is admissible in criminal cases.

(C) The objection will be sustained, if the prosecution failed to introduce evidence pertaining to Tanya's character during its case-in-chief.

(D) The objection will be sustained, since the prosecution may only introduce evidence pertaining to Tanya's character.

32. Mark and Rick were both chefs at the Benita-Hanna Restaurant in Seattle. One night, while preparing dinner for customers of the restaurant, Rick and Mark started to argue about how much soy sauce to put in a particular type of dish. Mark lost his temper, picked up a Ginsu knife, and stabbed Rick in the hand, wounding (but not killing) the latter. Rick pressed charges against Mark, and Mark was arrested.

At the criminal trial, upon the advice of his attorney, Mark asserts that he acted in self-defense. The prosecution, as part of its case-in-chief, attempts to introduce evidence of Rick's peaceful character to rebut Mark's assertion.

Based upon the foregoing, if Mark's attorney objects to this evidence, it is most likely that:

(A) The objection will be sustained, since Mark did not commit homicide.

(B) The objection will be sustained, since, while any type of character evidence is admissible, it must initially be offered by Mark.

(C) The objection will be overruled, since Rick's character is pertinent to the question of Mark's guilt.

(D) The objection will be overruled, since only evidence of specific instances of peaceful character is admissible in this situation.

33. Betty was an 18-year-old entering student at Podunk College. She was invited to a Pi Rho fraternity party. There, she met Alan. After a couple of hours of dancing, Alan asked Betty if she'd like to "come upstairs" with him. Betty, naive to the sexual connotation inherent in Alan's invitation and having never been at a fraternity house, agreed to go "upstairs." Once inside Alan's room, Alan forced himself upon Betty and raped her. Although Betty seemed to protest, Alan assumed that she wasn't really serious. Betty pressed charges against Alan. Alan admitted having sexual relations with Betty, but claimed that she had impliedly consented to the act.

At the criminal trial, Alan's attorney attempts to introduce evidence that Betty had a well-known reputation at the campus for sexual promiscuity with college-age men.

Based upon the foregoing, if the prosecution objects to this evidence, it is most likely that:

(A) The objection will be sustained, since Betty's past sexual behavior is not admissible through reputation or opinion evidence.

(B) The objection will be sustained, since Betty's past sexual behavior is admissible, but only through specific acts with other men.

(C) The objection will be overruled, since Betty's past sexual behavior is relevant to the issue of her alleged consent.

(D) The objection will be overruled, since Betty had voluntarily gone into Alan's room.

34. Steve and Cindy have been "dating" for over three years. They have had sexual relations together on numerous occasions. Although Cindy had always assured Steve that she "couldn't get pregnant" and was having sexual relations with him alone, Steve had suspicions to the contrary. One day, Cindy informed Steve that she was pregnant with his child. Revealing an uncharacteristic chivalry not previously discernible, Steve unhesitatingly responded, "Adios amigo!"

In the paternity civil suit subsequently filed by Cindy against Steve, the latter's attorney attempts to introduce the testimony of several witnesses to the effect that Cindy bragged to them about past, specific sexual behavior with other men.

Based upon the foregoing, if Cindy's counsel objects to the introduction of this evidence, it is most likely that:

(A) The objection will be overruled, since evidence of Cindy's prior sexual behavior with other men directly pertains to the issue of whether Steve is the child's father.

(B) The objection will be overruled, since evidence of Cindy's prior sexual behavior with other men is pertinent to the issue of Cindy's consent.

(C) The objection will be sustained, since Cindy's past sexual encounters are not admissible.

(D) The objection will be sustained, unless Steve's attorney is limited to Cindy's sexual behavior with men during the time period during which she could have become pregnant.

35. Brenda, owner of Brenda's Bridal Registry Shop, ordered fourteen dozen glasses from Bill's House of Baccarat. Before the glasses were shipped, Bud, an

employee of Bill's House of Baccarat ("Bill's"), examined the glasses. In his opinion, they appeared to be in perfect condition. However, when Brenda opened the boxes of glasses after they had arrived, she discovered that many of them had tiny cracks. Brenda informed Bill's of her dissatisfaction. When Bill's refused to refund her payment price, Brenda sued Bill's for breach of contract.

At trial, Bill's attorney called Terry, Bud's supervisor, to testify that Bud had told him immediately before the glasses were shipped that "the glasses are in perfect condition."

Based upon the foregoing, if Brenda's counsel objects to the introduction of this testimony, it is most likely that:

(A) The objection will be sustained, since it is irrelevant if Terry personally inspected the glasses or not.
(B) The objection will be sustained, since Bud's statement to Terry is hearsay.
(C) The objection will be overruled, since Bud's statement to Terry is an admission of a party-opponent.
(D) The objection will be overruled, since Bud's statement to Terry is not offered to prove the truth of the matter asserted.

36. Lou and Jack are both farmers. They had been next-door neighbors for years. One day, Jack, who was not married and had no children, walked over to Lou's house, handed a completed deed to Lou and said, "Here, old friend, the farm is yours." The next day, Jack suffered a heart attack and died shortly thereafter. Lou subsequently took the deed to be recorded. At the Recorder's Office, however, he learned that it had been improperly executed. While Jack had signed the deed, he had forgotten to notarize it (as required by state law to record a deed). Lou has never recorded the deed.

At the quiet title action commenced by Lou concerning his ownership of the farm, Lou's counsel attempted to introduce into evidence Jack's manual delivery of the deed and statement, "Here, old friend, the farm is yours." This would be relevant in proving that Jack had intended the transfer to be "immediately operative," and therefore a conveyance had occurred.

Based upon the foregoing, if the executor of Jack's estate objects to the introduction of this evidence, it is most likely that:

(A) The objection will be sustained, since it is hearsay.
(B) The objection will be sustained, since it is irrelevant (unless the executor has contended that Jack was not competent).
(C) The objection will be overruled, since the testimony is admissible to show that Jack intended the conveyance to Lou to be immediately operative.

(D) The objection will be overruled, since the evidence constituted a dying declaration.

37. Carol works as a teller at Hometown Bank in Boise, Idaho. One day, while she was sitting behind the counter, Miss Gribbins, a wealthy, but well known eccentric, stormed up to Carol's window and shouted, "Your boss is a big crook." Miss Gribbins then promptly turned and left the bank. Several customers standing at the windows of the other tellers overheard Miss Gribbins' statement and knowingly smiled. Mr. Revered, the owner of Hometown Bank and Carol's boss, subsequently learned of Miss Gribbins' statement. He commenced an action for slander against Miss Gribbins, seeking damages of $1,000,000.

    At trial, Mr. Revered's counsel called Carol to the stand to testify that Miss Gribbins had said to her, "Your boss is a big crook."

    Based upon the foregoing, if counsel for Miss Gribbins objects to the introduction of this testimony, it is most likely that:

    (A) The objection will be overruled, since Carol's testimony is not hearsay.
    (B) The objection will be overruled, since Carol's testimony is hearsay, but constitutes present state of mind.
    (C) The objection will be sustained, since Miss Gribbins' statement was mere opinion (rather than fact).
    (D) The objection will be sustained, unless Mr. Revered's counsel has already proved that Miss Gribbins was competent.

38. Claire was watching television when a friend (Penny) told her that Susan, Claire's neighbor, had smacked her (Claire's) daughter Amy across the face for no apparent reason. This incident had supposedly occurred while Amy was playing on the sidewalk outside of Susan's house the day before. Claire immediately went to Susan's house to confront her. The altercation escalated until they got into a fight/wrestling match. During the struggle, Claire kicked Susan in the knee, and Susan subsequently filed a tort action (alleging assault, battery and false imprisonment) against Claire. Claire counter-claimed.

    At trial, Claire's counsel called Jane to the witness stand, and attempted to have her testify that she (Jane) overheard Penny telling Claire that she (Penny) had seen Susan, for no apparent reason, slap Amy's face the day before the fight between Claire and Susan.

    Based upon the foregoing, if Susan's attorney objects to the introduction of this testimony, it is most likely that:

(A) The objection will be overruled, since this testimony shows that Claire had a motive for accosting Susan.

(B) The objection will be sustained, since this testimony is irrelevant (i.e., it doesn't pertain to who actually commenced the altercation).

(C) The objection will be sustained, since it probably has too great a possibility to prejudice the jury against Susan.

(D) The objection will be sustained, since Jane's testimony is hearsay.

39. Conrad, Donald and Peter golf together each Wednesday afternoon. Conrad and Peter are medical students, and Donald works for MegaBank. One Wednesday while on the links, Donald casually mentions to Peter and Conrad that "MegaBank always has megabucks in it on Fridays, since Friday afternoon it takes its cash to the Feds." That Friday, Peter robbed MegaBank at gunpoint. However, he was apprehended the next day. Upon the advice of his attorney, Peter contended that his arrest was a case of mistaken identity, and that he's not "into" bank robbery.

At trial, the prosecution called Conrad to testify that he overheard Donald tell Peter that Megabank always has "megabucks in it on Fridays." Donald recently moved to Tahiti.

Based upon the foregoing, if Peter's counsel objects to the introduction of this testimony, it is most likely that:

(A) The objection will be overruled, if Donald is "unavailable" under FRE 804(a)(5).

(B) The objection will be overruled, since the evidence shows Peter's belief that MegaBank had a large amount of cash money in it when the robbery occurred.

(C) The objection will be sustained, since Conrad's testimony is hearsay.

(D) The objection will be sustained, since the testimony is irrelevant in that it does not pertain to whether Peter robbed MegaBank or not.

40. Winona was reading a book one evening. Harry, her husband, suddenly entered their home in a hasty manner. He was sweaty and out of breath. He walked past Winona, into the bathroom. Winona then heard the water running. She later noticed that Harry had put small bandages on several places of his arms. Soon afterward, Winona and Harry became divorced. One month later, Harry was charged with raping Cindy on the night in question. At the trial, the prosecution called Winona to testify about what she had seen that evening. (Assume that Winona is willing to recount what she had seen.)

If Harry's attorney objects to the introduction of this evidence, it is most likely that:

(A) Her testimony is inadmissible under the spousal privilege.

(B) Her testimony is inadmissible under the marital communications privilege.

(C) Her testimony is admissible, since Winona is not relating anything said by Harry.

(D) Her testimony is admissible, since only Winona holds the privilege of testifying or not (and she is amenable to do so).

41. Jack and Tina were involved in a car accident. Bob, who was standing on the sidewalk when the cars driven by Jack and Tina collided, was the only eyewitness. Jack sued Tina for the numerous injuries which he sustained in the incident, and Tina counter-claimed.

At trial, Bob testified on behalf of Jack that Tina ran a "Stop" sign and crashed into Jack's car. During the cross-examination, Tina's attorney asked Bob if he was related to Jack. In fact, Bob and Jack were cousins. Bob testified that he was related to Jack. After Bob left the witness stand, Jack's attorney called Morgan, who happened to come upon the scene moments after the accident occurred. Jack's attorney then asked Morgan to testify that Bob told him (Morgan) that Tina had failed to halt at the "Stop" sign.

Based upon the foregoing, if Tina's attorney objected to the introduction of this testimony, it is most likely that:

(A) The objection will be sustained, since the testimony is hearsay.

(B) The objection will be sustained, since the testimony is an improper means of rehabilitation.

(C) The objection will be overruled, since Morgan's testimony is admissible as rehabilitation evidence.

(D) The objection will be overruled, since Morgan's testimony is proper rehabilitation and substantively relevant to Jack's contention that Tina was negligent.

Questions 42-44 are based on the following fact situation:

Paul, the Plaintiff in a personal injury action, called Wes as a witness to testify that Dan's car, in which Paul had been riding, ran a red light. Wes, however, testified that Dan's car did not run the light. Paul then called Vic to testify that Dan's car ran the light.

42. The trial judge should rule that Vic's testimony is

(A) Admissible as impeachment because Paul was surprised by Wes's testimony.

   (B) Admissible as evidence of Paul's case-in-chief because Vic's testimony was relevant to material issues.

   (C) Inadmissible because Paul cannot impeach his own witness.

   (D) Inadmissible because Paul is bound by the testimony of his own witness.

43. On cross-examination of Vic, Dan's attorney asked Vic if he was drunk at the time he witnessed the accident. Vic responded, "No, I have never in my life been drunk." Dan's attorney then sought to prove by Yank's testimony that Vic was drunk on New Year's Eve two years ago. The trial judge should rule that Yank's testimony is

   (A) Admissible to impeach Vic by showing that he had an imperfect recollection of recent events.

   (B) Admissible to show that Vic is not a truthful individual.

   (C) Inadmissible because a witness cannot be impeached by proof of specific acts of misconduct.

   (D) Inadmissible because the question of whether Vic has ever been drunk is a collateral matter.

44. Dan called Zemo as a witness and asked him if he knew Vic's reputation for veracity in the community where Vic resided. The trial judge should rule that this question is

   (A) Objectionable because collateral to the issues on trial.

   (B) Objectionable because character cannot be proven by reputation.

   (C) Unobjectionable because a foundation for impeachment of Vic.

   (D) Unobjectionable because Zemo could be expected to know Vic personally if he knew his reputation.

45. The bus in which Pat was riding was struck from the rear by a taxi. He sued Cab Company for a claimed neck injury. Cab Company claimed the impact was too slight to have caused the claimed injury and introduced testimony that all passengers had refused medical attention at the time of the accident. Pat called a doctor from City Hospital to testify that three persons (otherwise proved to have been on the bus) were admitted to the Hospital for treatment within a week after the accident after complaining about severe neck pains. The trial judge should rule the doctor's testimony

   (A) Admissible, because a doctor is properly qualified as an expert in medical matters.

   (B) Admissible, if other testimony establishes a causal connection between the other passengers' pain and the accident.

   (C) Inadmissible, because the testimony as to the neck pain complained about by the other three passengers is hearsay, not within any exception.

(D) Inadmissible, because the testimony is not the best evidence of the other passengers' pain and these persons have not been shown to be unavailable.

46. Tim and Samantha were involved in a serious traffic accident. After settlement efforts failed, Tim sued Samantha for the injuries which he sustained as a result of the incident. During discovery, Beth testified at a deposition called by Tim's attorney. At the deposition, Beth stated that she saw the accident, and that Samantha had failed to come to a complete halt at a red light.

At trial, when asked by Tim's attorney whether Samantha had completely halted at the red light, Beth answered "Yes." Tim's attorney, after recovering from the shock of Beth's response, then attempted to introduce the portion of Beth's deposition which was inconsistent with her trial testimony. (Assume the writing was properly authenticated.)

Based upon the foregoing, if Samantha's attorney objects to the introduction of the deposition testimony, it is most likely that:

(A) The objection will be overruled, and Beth's deposition testimony can be utilized by the factfinder as substantive evidence (as well as for impeachment).

(B) The objection will be overruled, since Beth's deposition testimony is admissible for impeachment (but not as substantive evidence).

(C) The objection will be sustained, assuming Samantha's attorney was present and also had the opportunity to question Beth at the deposition.

(D) The objection will be sustained, since Beth's prior deposition is hearsay.

47. Gina sued Exico Company, a Delaware corporation which operated a toxic disposal plant. Gina claimed that fumes emitted from the plant had caused her to become sterile. At the trial, Exico's attorney called Dr. Evans, a medical expert, who testified that, in his opinion, Gina's sterility was an inherited condition. On cross-examination, Dr. Evans was shown a voluminous book written by Dr. Frank. Dr. Evans candidly acknowledged that Dr. Frank was considered an expert with respect to sterility by many in the medical field. Gina's attorney then attempted to read into the record a portion of Dr. Frank's book which indicated that, based upon his extensive research, sterility occasionally resulted from emissions emanating from toxic waste disposal plants.

Based upon the foregoing, if Exico's attorney objected to the introduction of this evidence, it is most likely that:

(A) The objection will be overruled, if Dr. Frank's book is a learned treatise.

(B) The objection will be overruled, since authenticated writings can be read into evidence for impeachment purposes only.

(C) The objection will be sustained, since Dr. Frank's book constitutes hearsay.

(D) The objection will be sustained, if Dr. Frank is available to testify.

48. Justin sued William for negligently causing a collision which occurred on a highway, in which Justin was injured and his car damaged. William had received several prior drunk-driving citations.

At the trial, Justin's attorney attempted to introduce a guilty plea for drunken driving entered against William pertaining to the incident in question as proof of William's unreasonable behavior. In this jurisdiction, driving under the influence is punishable by a maximum term of 5 years in prison and a $50,000 fine.

Based upon the foregoing, if William's attorney objects to the introduction of this evidence, it is most likely that:

(A) The objection will be overruled, since there is an exception to the hearsay rule for prior, serious criminal convictions.

(B) The objection will be overruled, if William's guilty plea was made under oath.

(C) The objection will be sustained, if the guilty plea was properly authenticated.

(D) The objection will be sustained, since the guilty plea constitutes hearsay.

49. An armed robbery occurred at the Abco Bank. The crime was accomplished by three men. Later, Mel was arrested and successfully tried for conspiracy to commit, and committing, an armed robbery at the Abco Bank. Subsequently, Duane was apprehended and prosecuted for the same crimes. As part of its case-in-chief against Duane, the prosecution offered evidence of its successful prosecution of Mel for conspiring with Duane and Ralph to rob the Abco Bank. Duane chose to assert his Fifth Amendment right to refrain from testifying at his trial. (Armed robbery is punishable in this jurisdiction by imprisonment for up to 10 years.)

Based upon the foregoing, if Duane's attorney objects to the introduction of this evidence, it is most likely that:

(A) The objection will be sustained, since the judgment against Mel is irrelevant to Duane's culpability for the crime charged.

(B) The objection will be sustained, since the judgment against Mel is being offered for purposes other than impeachment.

(C) The objection will be overruled, since a prior criminal conviction constitutes an exception to the hearsay rule.

(D) The objection will be overruled, since prior criminal convictions are a proper basis for impeachment.

50. Alvin was stabbed by Mitch during a fight at a local bar. Perceiving that he had been mortally wounded, Alvin told Carl, another patron at the bar, "I owe Jim a thousand dollars." Alvin then expired. Jim had previously sued Alvin to recover the $1,000. However, in his answer to that complaint, Alvin had contended that the $1,000 was actually a gift. This action was subsequently dismissed without prejudice before trial.

Jim has now filed another action, this time against Alvin's estate, for recovery of the $1,000. At trial, Jim's attorney called Carl to testify about Alvin's statement.

Based upon the foregoing, if the attorney for Alvin's executor objects to the introduction of this testimony, it is most likely that:

(A) The objection will be sustained, since Carl's testimony constitutes hearsay.
(B) The objection will be overruled, since Alvin's remark constitutes a dying declaration.
(C) The objection will be overruled, since Alvin's remark constitutes a declaration against interest.
(D) The objection will be overruled, since Alvin's remark evidences his present state of mind.

51. Tim (who was insolvent) was driving his friend's (Todd) car when he struck Mary, a pedestrian who was lawfully using a crosswalk at an intersection when injured. Two days after the accident, Tim told his friend Jeff that he had imbibed eight "shots" of tequila prior to commencing to drive Todd's car. Tim recently relocated to India.

Mary sued Todd, but not Tim, pursuant to a statute which made the owner of a vehicle vicariously liable for the negligent driving of persons using it with his/her permission. Todd is an extremely wealthy individual. He owns a Lexus and a yacht. Assume that persons convicted of "driving under the influence" are subject to imprisonment for a maximum term of 6 months.

At the trial, Todd's attorney sought to have Jeff testify about Tim's statement to him.

Based upon the foregoing, if Todd's attorney objects to the introduction of this testimony, it is most likely that:

(A) The objection will be overruled, since Tim's statement is admissible under the "statement-against-interest" exception to the hearsay rule.
(B) The objection will be overruled, since Tim's statement is an admission.
(C) The objection will be sustained, since there is no direct proof that Tim was intoxicated at the time of the incident.

(D) The objection will be sustained, since Jeff's testimony constitutes hearsay.

52. Daniel and his wife Margaret had been having a difficult time with their marriage for some time. One evening, while Daniel was supposedly working late, Margaret was stabbed to death. After a lengthy, extensive investigation, the police arrested and charged Daniel with killing Margaret. At the trial, Daniel's counsel attempted to have Ben, Daniel's neighbor, testify that his wife, Kerry, had told him (Ben) that she was having an affair with Daniel, and that she had murdered Margaret out of jealousy and a "passionate desire" to be with Daniel. Although aware of the trial, Kerry had decided to remain at home.

Based upon the foregoing, if the prosecution objects to Ben's testimony, it is most likely that:

(A) The objection will be sustained, since Kerry's statement to her husband was privileged.

(B) The objection will be sustained, since Ben's testimony about Kerry's statement is hearsay.

(C) The objection will be overruled, since Kerry's confession to Ben constitutes a statement against interest.

(D) The objection will be overruled, since Ben's testimony suggests that Kerry was a co-conspirator.

53. Megan sued BigCo, which manufactures breast implants. She claims that she contracted an unusual disease from a breast implant produced by BigCo, which she received several years earlier. At the trial, BigCo attempted to introduce a transcript describing the testimony of Dr. Peters, a recognized expert, which was given in a previous lawsuit against BigCo by Jane. Jane is another BigCo breast implant recipient, who had contracted a disease similar to that of Megan. Dr. Peters, who has long since died, had testified at that trial (in which BigCo prevailed) that BigCo's breast implants did not cause the disease contracted by Jane.

Based upon the foregoing, if Megan's attorney objects to the introduction of Dr. Peters' authenticated transcript, it is most likely that:

(A) The objection will be sustained, since Dr. Peters' transcript is hearsay.

(B) The objection will be overruled, since Jane's counsel had opportunity and similar motive to cross-examine Dr. Peters.

(C) The objection will be overruled, since Dr. Peters' transcript was properly authenticated.

(D) The objection will be overruled, if Dr. Peters' was an expert with respect to matters about which he testified.

54. Jimmy was a passenger in a car being driven by Martin. The automobile was struck at an intersection by a vehicle driven by Trish. Jimmy sued Trish under a negligence theory. However, Trish answered that Martin had "run a red light." At the trial, Jimmy's attorney called Martin to the stand to testify that Trish went through a yellow light and "was clearly speeding" when the collision occurred.

Based upon the foregoing, if Trish's attorney objects to this testimony, it is most likely that:

(A) The objection will be overruled, since Martin's opinion testimony is admissible (assuming he saw Trish coming at their vehicle).

(B) The objection will be overruled, since testimony regarding Trish's conduct (though hearsay) constitutes an admission.

(C) The objection will be sustained, since layperson "opinion" testimony is inadmissible.

(D) The objection will be sustained, since there is no independent means (i.e., a radar gun) of verifying Martin's opinion.

55. Angie was injured in a car accident. While crossing a street, she was struck by a car driven by Bill. After the accident, Angie was examined by Dr. Martin. He ordered a lab technician to take X-rays. The lab technician who took the X-rays subsequently advised Dr. Martin that the X-rays "clearly demonstrated" that Angie's back injuries were permanent in nature. Angie sued Bill under a negligence theory to recover for her extensive, painful injuries. At the trial, Angie's attorney attempted to have Dr. Martin testify that, based upon the evaluation of the X-rays as related to him by the lab technician, Angie's back injuries were permanent in nature. However, the X-rays had not been introduced into evidence.

Based upon the foregoing, if Bill's attorney objects to Dr. Martin's testimony, it is most likely that:

(A) The objection will be overruled, since Dr. Martin may base his opinion upon data perceived by him prior to or at the hearing.

(B) The objection will be overruled, assuming Dr. Martin is also testifying from his personal knowledge (i.e., he had personally examined Angie).

(C) The objection will be sustained, since the X-rays had not been authenticated and admitted into evidence.

(D) The objection will be sustained, since Dr. Martin's testimony is based upon hearsay.

56. Margaret was driving down Paramount Boulevard when her car was struck by a vehicle driven by Dennis. She sued Dennis under a negligence theory for the personal injuries which she sustained in the incident. William was a passenger in Dennis' vehicle at the time of the incident, but suffered no physical injuries.

At trial, William was called as a witness by Margaret's attorney. Surprisingly, he testified that Margaret "ran a red light." Margaret's attorney then called Jason to testify that William had, prior to the trial, told him (Jason) that "Dennis failed to see the red light."

Based upon the foregoing, if Dennis' attorney objects to Jason's testimony, it is most likely that:

(A) The objection will be sustained, since Jason's testimony is hearsay.

(B) The objection will be sustained, since Margaret cannot impeach her own witness.

(C) The objection will be overruled, if William was given the opportunity of explaining his statement to Jason and was available for re-direct examination.

(D) The objection will be overruled, since Jason's testimony was a proper mode of impeachment (whether or not William was available for re-direct examination).

57. Karen was injured when a car being driven by Stacey struck her. Tom, an eyewitness to the accident, testified at trial that Stacey "ran a red light," and collided into Karen's car. After Tom concluded his testimony, Stacey's attorney called Bob to testify. Bob attempted to testify that he lived near Tom; and that Tom had a reputation for having an "aggressive, impetuous nature."

Based upon the foregoing, if Karen's attorney objects to Bob's testimony, it is most likely that:

(A) The objection will be sustained, since Bob's testimony is irrelevant.

(B) The objection will be sustained, since Bob's testimony doesn't pertain to truthfulness or veracity.

(C) The objection will be overruled, no foundation for Bob's testimony was laid (i.e., Bob did not state that he was personally familiar with Tom's character).

(D) The objection will be overruled, since Bob's testimony impairs Tom's credibility.

58. Potts sued Dobbs on a products liability claim. Louis testified for Potts. On cross-examination, which of the following questions is the trial judge most likely to rule improper?

(A) "Isn't it a fact that you are Potts' close friend?"

(B) "Isn't it true that you are known in the community as 'Louie the Lush' because of your addiction to alcohol?"

(C) "Didn't you deliberately fail to report some income on your tax return last year?"

(D) "Weren't you convicted seven years ago of obtaining money under false pretenses?"

59. In an action to recover for personal injuries arising out of an automobile accident, Plaintiff calls Bystander to testify. Claiming the privilege against self-incrimination, Bystander refuses to answer a question whether she was at the scene of the accident. Plaintiff moves that Bystander be ordered to answer the question. The judge should allow Bystander to remain silent only if

(A) The judge is convinced that she will incriminate herself.

(B) There is clear and convincing evidence that she will incriminate herself.

(C) There is a preponderance of evidence that she will incriminate herself.

(D) The judge believes that there is some reasonable possibility that she will incriminate herself.

Questions 60-61 are based on the following fact situation:

Phillips purchased a suit of thermal underwear manufactured by Makorp from synthetic materials. While he was attempting to stamp out a fire, Phillips' thermal underwear caught fire and burned in a melting fashion up to his waist. He suffered a heart attack a half hour later. In a suit against Makorp, Phillips asserted negligence and breach of warranty theories. Phillips testified to the foregoing.

60. Dr. Jones, a physician, specializing in cardiovascular difficulties, having listened to Phillips' testimony, is called by Phillips and asked whether, assuming the truth of such testimony, Phillips' subsequent heart attack could have resulted from the burns. His opinion is

(A) Admissible, because he is an expert.

(B) Admissible, because the physician's expertise enables him to judge the credibility of Phillips' testimony.

(C) Inadmissible, because a hypothetical question may not be based on prior testimony.

(D) Inadmissible, because an expert's opinion may not be based solely on information provided by lay persons.

61. Dr. Black, a physician specializing in internal medicine, is called by Phillips to testify that, on the basis of her examination of Phillips and blood analysis reports by an independent laboratory, reports which were *not* introduced in evidence, she believes that Phillips has a permanent disability. This testimony is

(A) Admissible, because such laboratory reports are business records.
(B) Admissible, if such reports are reasonably relied upon in medical practice.
(C) Inadmissible, unless Dr. Black has been shown to be qualified to conduct laboratory blood analyses.
(D) Inadmissible, because Dr. Black's testimony cannot be based on tests performed by persons not under her supervision.

62. Penny sued Dion for personal injuries which she sustained when a car being driven by Dion struck her vehicle. At trial, on behalf of Penny, Walter testified that Dion had "ran a red light." On cross-examination, Walter was asked, "Why were you standing on 2nd and Maple?" (the viewpoint from which Walter purportedly observed the incident). Walter responded that he had gone "to the corner store to buy a paper." Dion's attorney then called Shirley, Walter's ex-secretary, to testify that Walter was at the corner waiting to meet her for a "private" lunch engagement.

Based upon the foregoing, if Penny's attorney objects to Shirley's testimony, it is most likely that:

(A) The objection will be overruled, since Shirley's testimony impeaches Walter's veracity.
(B) The objection will be overruled, since Shirley's testimony undermines Walter's moral character.
(C) The objection will be sustained, since Shirley's testimony is irrelevant to the issue of fault.
(D) The objection will be sustained, since Shirley's testimony pertains to a collateral matter.

63. Daniel was an attorney who primarily practiced estate planning law. Peggy, another attorney, sued Daniel for breaching an oral agreement to sell his legal practice to her for $300,000. At trial, on behalf of Peggy, her secretary, Desmond, testified that he overheard Daniel personally offer to sell his practice to Peggy for $300,000. On cross-examination, Daniel's attorney asked Desmond, "Isn't it true that you work for Peggy, and that ever since you watched most of the O.J. Simpson trial on television you hate attorneys?"

Based upon the foregoing, if Peggy's attorney objects to this questioning, it is most likely that:

(A) The objection will be sustained, since Daniel's attorney asked Desmond a leading question.

(B) The objection will be sustained, since the question's potential for prejudicing the jury outweighs its probative value.

(C) The objection will be overruled, since personal partiality/bias constitutes a proper basis for impeachment.

(D) The objection will be overruled, since Desmond's state of mind constitutes a proper basis for impeachment.

64. Doris had sued Brad for breach of an oral contract. At the trial, Clara testified on behalf of Doris. She confirmed that a contract had, in fact, been made. On cross-examination by Brad's attorney, Clara was asked, "Weren't you caught cheating at a poker game last Saturday night?" Clara responded to this question with an unequivocal "No." Brad's attorney then called Dahlia, who was playing poker with Clara at that time. Dahlia was asked if Clara was caught cheating at poker that Saturday night? (You may assume that it's a misdemeanor to gamble in this jurisdiction.) Dahlia was prepared to testify that Clara had been caught dealing herself an ace from the bottom of the deck.

Based upon the foregoing, if Doris' attorney objects to this testimony, it is most likely that:

(A) The objection will be sustained, since the misdemeanor in question clearly pertains to veracity.

(B) The objection will be sustained, since impeachment via extrinsic evidence is not permissible in this instance.

(C) The objection will be overruled, since it pertains to Clara's veracity.

(D) The objection will be overruled, since it pertains to whether or not Clara is law-abiding.

65. Larry sued Olivia for the serious injuries which he sustained when Olivia collided with him while he was driving home from work. Winifred testified in Olivia's defense that Larry had "run a red light." For the purpose of impeaching Winifred, Larry's attorney called Jeanine to the stand. Jeanine testified that Winifred had "a very poor reputation for truthfulness in the community," and that, in her opinion, "Winifred was not trustworthy." Olivia's attorney then asked Jeanine whether she was "aware that Winifred had recently brought a lost wallet containing $27 in cash to the police?"

Based upon the foregoing, if Larry's attorney objects to this question, it is most likely that:

(A) The objection will be overruled, since Jeanine may be cross-examined about specific instances of Winifred's conduct pertaining to truthfulness or untruthfulness.

(B) The objection will be overruled, since Jeanine may be cross-examined about the extent of her knowledge about Winifred's reputation for honesty in the community.

(C) The objection will be sustained, since it pertains to a collateral matter.

(D) The objection will be sustained, since the jury can determine whether or not to believe Jeanine.

66. Peter sued Don for breach of contract. The court admitted testimony by Peter that Don and his wife quarreled frequently, a fact of no consequence to the lawsuit. Don seeks to testify in response that he and his wife never quarreled. The court

(A) Must permit Don to answer, if he had objected to Peter's testimony.

(B) May permit Don to answer, whether or not he had objected to Peter's testimony.

(C) May permit Don to answer, only if he had objected to Peter's testimony.

(D) Cannot permit Don to answer, whether or not he had objected to Peter's testimony.

67. In a will case, Paula seeks to prove her relationship to the testator Terrence by a statement in a deed from Terrence, "I transfer to my niece Paula ... " The deed was recorded pursuant to statute in the office of the county recorder and was retained there. Paula called Recorder as a witness, who authenticated an enlarged print photocopy of the deed. The photocopy was made from microfilm records kept in the Recorder's office pursuant to statute. The photocopy is

(A) Admissible as a record of a document affecting an interest in property.

(B) Admissible as recorded recollection.

(C) Inadmissible as hearsay, not within any recognized exception.

(D) Inadmissible under the Best Evidence Rule.

Questions 68-73 are based on the following fact situation:

Driver ran into and injured Walker, a pedestrian. With Driver in his car were two of his friends, Paul and Ralph. Passerby saw the accident and called the police department, which sent Sheriff to investigate.

All of these people are available as potential witnesses in the case of *Walker v. Driver.* Walker alleges that Driver, while drunk, struck him as he walked in a duly marked crosswalk; and that he (Walker), as a consequence, suffered physical harm to his leg and foot.

68. Counsel for Walker calls Paul to testify that just before the accident, Ralph exclaimed, "Watch out! We're going to hit that man in the crosswalk!" The trial judge should rule that this testimony is

(A) Admissible as a spontaneous utterance reflecting Ralph's impression at the time his statement was made.

(B) Admissible since it constitutes a declaration against interest as to the declarant, Ralph.

(C) Inadmissible because Ralph is available as a witness.

(D) Inadmissible because the statement preceded the accident.

69. Walker's counsel calls Sheriff to testify that in Driver's presence Paul said, "We hit him while he was in the crosswalk," and that Driver remained silent. The trial judge should rule this testimony

(A) Admissible because Driver, by his silence, has made Paul his agent and would thereby be bound by any admission Paul made.

(B) Admissible because Driver's silence constitutes an admission of a party-opponent.

(C) Inadmissible as "double hearsay" in that Driver's silence is being used to prove the truth of what Sheriff said Paul had stated.

(D) Inadmissible unless Driver is first called and asked to admit or deny the incident.

70. Walker's counsel seeks to introduce the testimony of Joe concerning Walker's statement three days after the accident that, "My ankle hurts so much, I'd bet almost anything that its broken." The trial judge should rule that this testimony is

(A) Admissible as a statement of the declarant's pain and suffering.

(B) Admissible to prove that Walker's ankle was permanently injured.

(C) Inadmissible as a hearsay declaration.

(D) Inadmissible because proof of Walker's medical condition is a subject for expert testimony only.

71. Driver's counsel wants to introduce testimony from Sheriff concerning a discussion between Sheriff and Passerby at the police station 1/2 hour after the accident, wherein Passerby, in response to a question by Sheriff, excitedly exclaimed in a loud voice, "Walker ran out in the street and was not in the crosswalk!" Sheriff duly recorded Passerby's statement in an official police report. The trial judge should rule that Sheriff's oral testimony is

(A) Admissible as a spontaneous utterance.

(B) Admissible as based on past recollection recorded.

(C) Inadmissible because of the Best Evidence Rule.

(D) Inadmissible as hearsay, not within any exception.

72. Walker's counsel wants to have Sheriff testify to the following statement made to him by Ralph, out of the presence of Driver: "We were returning from a party at which we had all downed at least four beers." The trial judge should rule this testimony

(A) Admissible as an admission of a party.

(B) Admissible as a declaration against interest.

(C) Inadmissible as hearsay, not within any exception.

(D) Inadmissible as opinion.

73. On the evening of the day of the accident, Ralph wrote a letter to his sister in which he described the accident. After Ralph testified that he could not remember some details of the accident, Walker's counsel seeks to show him the letter to assist Ralph in his testimony on direct examination. The trial judge should rule that this is

(A) Permissible under the doctrine of present recollection refreshed.

(B) Permissible under the doctrine of past recollection recorded.

(C) Objectionable, if Driver's counsel was not shown the letter prior to the time it was shown to Ralph.

(D) Objectionable, unless the letter is read into evidence.

Questions 74-75 are based on the following fact situation:

Owner, the sole owner of Oscar's Restaurants, hired Bellman to manage the restaurants. Bellman did so for the next five years, sending regular reports to Owner's headquarters and receiving irregular phone calls and written messages from Owner in reply. A week ago, Waiter arrived unannounced at Bellman's office, carrying an Assignment which stated that Owner's restaurants and agreement with Bellman had been transferred to him (Waiter). Waiter notified Bellman that, effective immediately, he was fired and that Waiter was taking over the management of the restaurants. Bellman claimed that Waiter could not fire him and that Owner's signature on the purported Assignment was a forgery. He then brought an action to prevent Waiter from taking control of the restaurants.

74. Bellman was called to testify that he and Owner had signed a contract when he was hired, wherein they had agreed that (1) Bellman would manage the restaurants for a ten-year period, and (2) he could be terminated only for unsatisfactory performance during that period. Which of the following objections by Waiter to Bellman's testimony is most likely to be sustained?

(A) That the testimony violates the Statute of Frauds.

(B) That the testimony violates the Best Evidence Rule.

(C) That the testimony violates the parol evidence rule.

(D) That the testimony is irrelevant.

75. Waiter offered the Assignment into evidence. The trial judge can admit this document into evidence

(A) Subject to adequate proof of the genuineness of the signature.

(B) Only if, in the trial judge's opinion, the contested signature bears a reasonable facsimile to that of Owner's.

(C) Only if the trial judge finds that the genuineness of Owner's signature is established as a matter of law.

(D) Only if Waiter persuades the court that it is more likely than not that the signature is genuine.

Questions 76-77 are based on the following fact situation:

Lyons was on trial for the murder of his wife. The prosecution claimed that Lyons committed the murder by poisoning his wife with bichloride of mercury. Lyons' defense was that his wife committed suicide.

76. Lawyer, an attorney, was called by the prosecution to testify that the accused attempted to retain him as his defense counsel and during their preliminary discussions admitted having killed his wife. Lawyer had eventually declined to represent Lyons. The trial judge should rule Lawyer's testimony

(A) Admissible, because Lawyer declined to represent Lyons.

(B) Admissible, because Lyons had advised lawyer of a crime.

(C) Inadmissible, because the communication was privileged.

(D) Inadmissible, because Lawyer's testimony contains hearsay.

77. Lyons was called to testify on his own behalf concerning matters surrounding the death of his wife. On cross-examination he was asked, "Isn't it true that you were convicted of perjury five years ago?" Lyons denied having ever been convicted of perjury. The prosecution then offered into evidence a properly authenticated copy of the official court record of conviction. The trial judge should rule the record

(A) Admissible, because counsel may prove Lyons' conviction by extrinsic evidence.

(B) Admissible, because the perjury conviction helps to prove Lyons's guilt.

(C) Inadmissible, because the Best Evidence Rule requires that the original court record of Lyons' conviction be produced.

(D) Inadmissible, because specific instances of misconduct of the accused may not be proved by the use of extrinsic evidence.

Questions 78-79 are based on the following fact situation:

ABC agreed to do the inspection and testing needed during construction by XYZ of a complex conveyer belt for an industrial plant. XYZ estimated completion in four months.

During negotiations, the parties had agreed that if overtime became necessary, it should be paid on a time-and-a-half basis. Their written contract, however, merely called for (1) ABC to expend 150 hours per month, and (2) XYZ to pay ABC $8,000 in four monthly installments of $2,000 each.

After three months, and after XYZ had paid ABC $6,000 in monthly installments, it became obvious that the conveyer would not be completed on time by XYZ. ABC requested, and XYZ orally agreed to pay ABC, $2,000 per month until the job was finished.

ABC submitted invoices on this basis for the fourth through the sixth months, when the job was finished. XYZ, having previously not paid the invoices contending it was short of cash, then paid ABC $2,000; but repudiated the oral agreement relying on the parol evidence rule. ABC sued XYZ for $4,000.

78. Will XYZ's parol evidence defense probably succeed?

   (A) Yes, because the oral agreement purports to vary the written contract on a subject included in it.
   (B) Yes, because the oral agreement purports to add to the written contract.
   (C) No, because the oral agreement in question was entered into after the written contract.
   (D) No, because the second agreement relates to a subject which was not dealt with in the original agreement.

79. If ABC offered to introduce evidence that during negotiations prior to the written contract XYZ had orally agreed that overtime should be paid on a time-and-a-half basis, which of the following rules would provide the *most* support for ABC?

   (A) Parol evidence of collateral agreements is admissible where the writing was only a partial integration.
   (B) Parol evidence of negotiations is admissible in aid of interpretation.
   (C) Parol evidence is admissible to show an oral condition precedent to the existence of a contract.
   (D) Parol evidence is admissible to show fraud.

80. Alfred was charged with mail fraud. At trial, the defense called Joanna, who testified that she had known Alfred for 16 years, and that he was an honorable, honest human being. On cross-examination, the prosecuting attorney asked Joanna if she had not been caught cheating while playing cards three weeks before. Joanna replied that she had not. The prosecuting attorney then offered to have Bill testify that he, Joanna and four other persons were playing cards three weeks ago, and that Joanna was caught dealing an ace to herself from the bottom of the deck. Bill's testimony is

(A) Admissible, because it tends to discredit Joanna.
(B) Admissible, because Joanna had testified as to Alfred's character for honesty.
(C) Inadmissible, because Joanna has not been the subject of a criminal conviction as a consequence of the card-cheating incident.
(D) Inadmissible, if gambling is a federal crime.

81. John was charged with aggravated battery. At trial, the prosecution called Melvin to the stand to testify that he was present at a line-up and saw Jones point to John and state, "That's the guy who hit me with a tire iron just because I told him that the Celtics stink." Jones passed away between his identification of John and the latter's trial. Melvin's testimony is

(A) Inadmissible, because Jones has died.
(B) Inadmissible, because Jones' identification of John constituted an opinion relating to an ultimate fact (the identity of the perpetrator).
(C) Admissible, because Jones is unavailable.
(D) Admissible, because it is probative of John's motive for striking Jones.

82. Under the Mann Act, it is illegal to transport persons across state lines for the purpose of engaging in prostitution. Jack was prosecuted under this statute for taking Sue from Boston to New York to solicit "tricks" in the latter city. As part of its case-in-chief, the prosecution called Sue. However, she unexpectedly testified that (1) Jack hadn't driven her to New York, and (2) she had visited that city to shop for dresses. The prosecutor then offered into evidence a properly authenticated written statement made by Sue and delivered to the prosecution, wherein she had stated that Jack had driven her to New York City for the purpose of engaging in acts of prostitution at a Small Business Administration convention in that city. The written statement is

(A) Admissible, for any purpose because it is hearsay.
(B) Admissible as substantive evidence, but not for impeachment.
(C) Admissible for impeachment, but not as substantive evidence.
(D) Admissible for impeachment and as substantive evidence.

83. Josephina was arrested for driving under the influence of alcohol. At her trial, the prosecution seeks to introduce the written report of Officer Bones, one of the arresting officers. Officer Bones' report, made at the scene immediately after Josephina was handcuffed and placed in the back of the patrol car, stated that the defendant's speech was slurred at the time of the arrest. Officer Bones was not present at the trial since he had recently been in an accident. However, Officer Smith (Bones' partner for 8 years) testified that the signature on the report was that of Bones. The report is

    (A) Inadmissible, because it contains Bones' opinion as to an ultimate issue.
    (B) Inadmissible, because it is hearsay.
    (C) Admissible, because it has been properly authenticated.
    (D) Admissible, because Officer Bones was unavailable.

Questions 84-85 are based on the following fact situation:

Pedestrian was hit at a street crossing by an automobile driven by Driver. The accident was witnessed by Warren, a bystander, and Pedestrian's wife. Pedestrian's injuries were serious, but during the first few weeks following the accident he appeared to be recovering. However, his condition later grew worse, and when it was apparent that he was about to die, Pedestrian cried out in anguish, "Why didn't Driver stop for the red light?" Pedestrian died immediately after making the statement. Mrs. Pedestrian later brought an action for $50,000 against Driver for the wrongful death of her husband, alleging excessive speed, failure to observe traffic signals and defective brakes.

84. Warren was called by Mrs. Pedestrian to testify that Driver pleaded with him to testify falsely that Pedestrian ran in front of his car. The trial judge should rule that Warren's testimony is

    (A) Admissible, because Driver's offer was a declaration against interest.
    (B) Admissible, because Warren was called to testify by Pedestrian's wife.
    (C) Inadmissible, because it was hearsay, not within any exception.
    (D) Inadmissible, because it was not relevant to the issue of whether Driver was, in fact, negligent.

85. Samuel was called to testify. After Samuel stated that he and Driver had lived in the same community for 12 years, he testified that Driver enjoyed a reputation for being a safe and prudent driver. The trial judge should rule that Samuel's testimony is

    (A) Admissible, because character evidence is admissible to prove the Driver acted in conformity therewith at the time in question.

(B) Admissible, if Samuel first testifies that he has personal knowledge of Driver's driving habits.

(C) Inadmissible, because evidence of Driver's reputation as a safe and prudent driver cannot be used to prove that he acted in conformity therewith on the occasion in question.

(D) Inadmissible, because character evidence is never admissible in a civil lawsuit.

86. On March 1, Computer Programs (CP) orally agreed with Holiday Department Store (HDS) to write a set of programs for HDS's computer and to coordinate the programs with HDS's billing methods. A subsequent memo, signed by both parties, provided in its entirety: "HDS will pay CP $20,000 in two equal installments within one month of completion if, by July 1, CP is successful in shortening by one-half the processing time for the financial transactions now handled on HDS's Zenon 747 computer." Tests by CP cut processing time by 51%, but were not coordinated with HDS's Zenon 747 computer. However, if HDS would spend $5,000 to change its invoice preparation methods, as recommended by CP, the programs would cut processing time by a total of 58%, saving HDS $8,000 a year.

If HDS denies liability on the ground that CP had orally agreed to coordinate with HDS's methods of accounting, and CP seeks in litigation to bar testimony about that agreement because of the parol evidence rule, HDS's most effective argument is that

(A) The parol evidence rule does not bar the introduction of evidence for the purpose of interpreting a written agreement.

(B) The memorandum was not a completely integrated agreement.

(C) HDS detrimentally relied on the oral promise of coordination in signing the memorandum.

(D) The memorandum was not a partially integrated agreement.

87. Peter sued Dever, who was 19, for negligence after the former was hit by a car driven by the latter while crossing a street. Peter asserted that Dever was exceeding the speed limit as he turned a corner. Dever answered that he was not speeding and, alternatively, that Peter was contributorily negligent. Peter called James to the stand to testify that Dever always came around that corner at an excessive rate of speed. James' testimony is probably

(A) Admissible, to show that Peter was probably speeding on the occasion in question.

(B) Admissible, even though hearsay, because it would constitute an admission of the party-opponent.

(C) Inadmissible, because it is hearsay and opinion.

(D) Inadmissible, because it is character evidence.

88. Jerry sued Delbert for negligence, claiming that the latter drove through a red light and hit the former's car in an intersection. Delbert counter-claimed, contending that Jerry entered the intersection while the light against him was yellow. After Jerry gave his version of the events of the accident, Malcolm, an eyewitness, was called to the stand and testified that Jerry's description of the accident was correct. Delbert's counsel then sought to introduce a properly authenticated report made by an investigator for Delbert's insurance company, who had died prior to the trial. In the report, the investigator claimed that Malcolm had advised him that the light was green for Delbert when he drove into the intersection. The report is

    (A) Admissible, for purposes of impeachment only.
    (B) Admissible, for purposes of impeachment and as substantive evidence.
    (C) Inadmissible, because it is hearsay.
    (D) Inadmissible, because Malcolm was never asked about the report prior to Delbert's attempt to introduce it into evidence.

89. Jack Jones was tried for the murder of Arthur Godfried. Walter testified on behalf of the defendant that he and Jones were playing cards during the evening on which the homicide occurred. On cross-examination of Walter, the prosecuting attorney asked if Jones had not threatened to kill him (Walter) about one week before the trial. Walter replied that Jones had not. The defense then sought to have Officer Oates testify that shortly after the crime he had interviewed Walter, and that the latter had stated that he was playing cards with Jones on the evening in question. Walter's statement had not been recorded, nor was it made under penalty of perjury. Officer Oates' testimony is

    (A) Admissible, as substantive evidence.
    (B) Admissible, under the business records exception to the hearsay rule.
    (C) Inadmissible, since it was hearsay, not within any exception.
    (D) Inadmissible, because proof of prior consistent statements by a witness is ordinarily not a permissible form of rehabilitation.

90. Jim Decker recently died. A will written by Decker was admitted to probate. However, a dispute has arisen between Decker's two sons, Oscar and Otto. A line was drawn through a provision of the will giving Decker's sports car to Otto. If this action was done by Decker with the intent of revoking the gift to Otto, the car would fall into the residuary clause (and thereby be inherited by Oscar). Otto claims that Oscar, who found the will, drew the line through the clause in question. Oscar seeks to introduce into evidence a statement by Ray, one of Decker's golfing partners, that Decker had told Ray about one year

before he died that "I recently changed my will to leave the sports car to Oscar." Decker's statement is

(A) Admissible, since it pertains to the partial revocation of the declarant's will.
(B) Admissible, because it pertains to the declarant's then existing state of mind.
(C) Inadmissible, because it is hearsay, not within any exception.
(D) Inadmissible, because it is violative of the typical "Dead Man" statute.

91. Albert and Susan were involved in a traffic accident. Susan was taken away from the scene of the collision by paramedics. While traveling to the hospital, Phil, one of the paramedics, asked Susan, "What happened?" Phil was not a medical doctor. Susan, who sincerely believed that she was going to die, responded that, "I'm very angry with myself; I was trying to put out my cigarette and lost control of the wheel for a second." Susan survived the accident and has now regained her health. When Albert sued Susan to recover for his personal injuries, Susan counter-claimed for her injuries and damages to her car. Susan's statement to Phil is

(A) Inadmissible, under the patient-client privilege.
(B) Inadmissible, because it is hearsay, not within any exception.
(C) Admissible, under the dying declaration exception to the hearsay rule.
(D) Admissible, because relevant to a determination as to who was at fault with respect to the accident.

92. Alex was involved in a motor vehicle accident with Milton. When a police officer arrived, he detected the smell of whiskey on Milton's breath. Milton was subsequently prosecuted for drunken driving. At the trial, Milton took the stand in his defense and asserted his innocence. When asked on cross-examination how many drinks he had ingested before the accident, he stated "three beers." Milton was subsequently acquitted of the drunk driving charge. In a civil lawsuit by Alex against Jones (the owner of the car which Milton was driving) for negligent entrustment, Alex sought to introduce into evidence a properly authenticated copy of the transcript of the criminal case which contained the foregoing question and answer. Milton had left the jurisdiction prior to the trial, and Alex has been unable to procure his attendance by process or otherwise. The evidence is

(A) Admissible, under the former testimony exception to the hearsay rule.
(B) Admissible, under the party-opponent exception to the hearsay rule.
(C) Inadmissible, because it is hearsay, not within any exception.
(D) Inadmissible, because Milton was acquitted in the criminal case.

93. Mitchell and Karl had been drinking and playing pool at a local restaurant-bar. Mitchell suddenly accused Karl of cheating by changing the position of one of the balls when Mitchell's back was turned. Karl stood his ground and asserted that Mitchell was an inferior player and a very poor sport. Mitchell abruptly reached toward his pocket. He wanted to withdraw a dollar to pay for the game, and then leave. However, before Mitchell could remove the money from his pocket, Karl swung his pool stick and struck Mitchell across the head (causing a severe injury to the latter). Karl was charged with the crime of aggravated battery. Karl's answer asserted the privilege of self-defense. In his defense, Karl seeks to testify that his girlfriend, Sally, had told him that Mitchell usually carried a switchblade knife. In fact, this was incorrect and it is illegal to carry such an item in this jurisdiction. Sally died in an automobile accident about one week before the trial. Karl's testimony is

   (A) Admissible, to show his belief that Mitchell was often armed with a knife.
   (B) Admissible, because a defendant in a criminal case is always entitled to introduce evidence of the victim's character by specific instances of misconduct.
   (C) Inadmissible, because it is hearsay, not within any exception.
   (D) Inadmissible, because character evidence pertaining to the victim is not admissible in a criminal case which does not involve homicide.

94. John owned Blackacre. One year ago, he handed a properly completed deed to the property to Milt, saying at the time, "When I die; this land is yours." (The deed made no mention of any requirement that Milt pre-decease John.) Six months later, however, John purported to transfer Blackacre via a valid deed to his niece, Nellie. John has recently been declared to be incompetent and both Milt and Nellie claim ownership to Blackacre. A conveyance of land does not occur in this jurisdiction unless the grantor has completed a valid deed with the intent that the transfer be immediately operative. Although Milt claims that John said nothing when the deed was tendered to him, Arthur was present at that time. Nellie seeks to have Arthur testify as to John's words to show that John did not intend that the conveyance be immediately operative when the deed was manually give to Milt. The evidence is

   (A) Admissible, because it is not hearsay.
   (B) Admissible, because it is admissible under the "statement against interest" exception to the hearsay rule.
   (C) Inadmissible, under the parol evidence rule.
   (D) Inadmissible, because it is hearsay, not within any exception.

95. Albert and Banes were involved in a traffic accident. Garland witnessed the accident and told Officer Krupke (who arrived shortly after the incident

occurred) what he had seen. Krupke wrote this information into an Accident Report which he was required to write by law. Garland testified at the trial for Albert. On cross-examination, counsel for Banes asked Garland if he had looked at the Accident Report prior to the trial for the purpose of refreshing his memory. Garland admitted that he had. As a consequence,

(A) The entire report may be introduced on re-direct for the purpose of reha-bilitating Garland.

(B) Counsel for Banes may introduce into evidence the portion of the Acci-dent Report dealing with Garland's testimony.

(C) Counsel for Banes may inspect the report and cross-examine Garland with respect to it, but cannot introduce any portion of it into evidence.

(D) Counsel for Banes is not permitted to introduce any portion of the Acci-dent Report, if Garland's testimony was consistent with it.

96. You may assume that there is no "Dead Man" statute in this jurisdiction. Dr. Fine is suing the estate of Mr. Boone (who recently died), based upon an alleged oral contract pursuant to which Dr. Fine performed an operation upon the deceased. Mrs. Boone, the wife and executrix of Mr. Boone's estate, seeks to testify that her husband had told her that Dr. Fine had offered to perform the operation gratuitously if Mr. Boone (a prominent person within the town) would permit use of his name in an advertising campaign which Dr. Fine planned to undertake, and that he (Mr. Boone) had accepted this offer. If Dr. Fine objects to Mrs. Boon's testimony, it should be

(A) Admissible, because it is not hearsay.

(B) Admissible, under the "statement against interest" exception to the hear-say rule.

(C) Inadmissible, under the physician-patient privilege.

(D) Inadmissible, under the confidential marital communications privilege.

97. Mr. and Mrs. Ballow were in litigation for the custody of their 5-year old child, Arturo. Seven years ago, Mr. Ballow was convicted of child beating with respect to his son, Damien (the product of an earlier marriage). Although an authenticated copy of this conviction could easily be obtained, Mrs. Ballow seeks to have Damien personally testify as to the beatings administered to him by Mr. Ballow. This evidence is

(A) Inadmissible, because character evidence is admissible only in criminal proceedings.

(B) Inadmissible, because character evidence (even though admissible) can be proved only by reputation in the community or opinion.

(C) Admissible, because evidence of prior acts bearing upon whether Mr. Bal-low should be given custody of Arturo is proper.

(D) Inadmissible, because under the Best Evidence Rule the earlier conviction is the proper means of proving Mr. Ballow had struck Damien.

98. Paul was hurt when he was bitten by a large, unleashed, unusual-looking dog. Delmer, a person who lived about one mile from Paul, had an Australian Blue Hound. Paul sued Delmer for his injuries, but the latter denied that his dog was involved in the attack. Wally was a neighbor of Paul's who had seen the incident from a distance of about 100 feet away. He was called as a witness by Paul, and testified that the latter had been attacked by an Australian Blue Hound. He was asked on cross-examination how he knew the exact type of dog which had attacked Paul. Wally replied that after the incident he had looked at a chart of various breeds of dogs in a library, and the one which looked most like the animal that attacked Paul was labeled "Australian Blue Hound." On a motion to strike Wally's testimony, the best objection would probably be

(A) Lack of personal knowledge by Wally.

(B) Lack of adequate perception.

(C) Improper opinion.

(D) Bias in favor of Paul.

99. Paul sued Derrick for personal injuries which he sustained in an accident. Paul contended that Derrick had negligently collided with his vehicle. At the trial, on behalf of Paul, William testified that Derrick had "clearly run through a yellow light." On cross-examination, William was asked, "Why were you standing on 5th and Olive?" (the vantage point from which William supposedly observed the incident). William responded that he had just exited a pharmacy which he had visited at that street corner.

Derrick's attorney then called Sharon to testify that William (who was married) was with her, having an "intimate lunch" at a restaurant twelve blocks from the site of the collision when William supposedly saw the incident.

Based upon the foregoing, if Paul's attorney objects to Sharon's testimony, it is most likely that:

(A) The objection will be sustained, since Sharon's testimony would only impugn William's moral character (not his trustworthiness).

(B) The objection will be sustained, since Sharon's testimony is irrelevant to the issue of fault.

(C) The objection will be overruled, since Sharon's testimony constitutes a proper mode of impeachment.

(D) The objection will be overruled, since Sharon's testimony pertains to a collateral matter.

100. Jeffers, a police officer, shot and killed Roland in the line of duty. Jeffers was so traumatized by the incident that he retired from the police force and underwent counseling with Karen, a licensed clinical social worker. In all, Jeffers attended approximately 50 counseling sessions.

The administrator of Roland's estate filed suit in federal district court alleging that Jeffers had violated Roland's constitutional rights by using excessive force during the encounter. During pretrial discovery, the administrator of the estate learned of the counseling sessions and sought access to Karen's notes concerning the sessions for use in cross-examining Jeffers. On objection by Jeffers, the court should rule that Karen's notes are

(A) Inadmissible, because the need for the disclosure is outweighed by the patient's privacy interests.

(B) Inadmissible, because the psychotherapist-patient privilege applies to confidential communications made to a licensed social worker.

(C) Admissible, because the communications were made solely to permit Karen to serve as an expert witness in the litigation.

(D) Admissible, as a present sense impression.

101. Darby is on trial for raping Wanda. The prosecution seeks to introduce testimony by Maria that 15 years ago, Darby raped her, an act for which he was never charged. Maria would testify that the rape took place when Darby, a stranger to her, attacked her in a parking lot. The rape of Wanda is alleged to have occurred following a date between the two. There are no meaningful similarities between the two crimes other than the fact that Darby was the alleged rapist. The prosecution's theory in seeking introduction of the Maria rape is that because Darby raped before, he's likely to have raped on the present occasion. Darby has not taken the stand as a witness. Maria's testimony is

(A) Inadmissible, because it seeks to put into evidence separate, unrelated offenses.

(B) Inadmissible, because evidence of other crimes is not admissible to show that Darby acted in conformity with his character on this occasion.

(C) Admissible, and may be considered for its bearing on any matter to which it is relevant.

(D) Admissible, because the probative value of the evidence outweighs the danger of prejudice to the defendant.

102. Duane is charged with molesting Victor, a 10 year old boy. The prosecution seeks to present evidence that, fifteen years ago, Duane molested Kara, a 6 year old girl, and was arrested for it but never charged. If counsel for Duane objects to the introduction of this evidence, it is most likely that the objection will be

(A) Sustained, because Duane was never convicted of a crime.
(B) Sustained, because this incident took place fifteen years ago.
(C) Overruled, because the probative value of the evidence outweighs the danger of undue prejudice to the defendant.
(D) Overruled, because in this case, evidence of prior child molestation is admissible.

103. Derek is on trial for burglary in a federal district court. While investigating the crime scene, detectives discovered a piece of cheese left at the scene with teeth marks in it. The prosecution claims that the teeth marks were made by Derek, and seeks to offer testimony by Dr. Jacobs, a dentist who is an expert on dental identification. The prosecution would have Dr. Jacobs testify that there have been tests of the accuracy of such identifications, that the technique has been written up in peer-reviewed forensic journals, that it has a very low false positive rate and that it is generally accepted by criminalists as a method of identification. Dr. Jacobs' testimony is

(A) Admissible, because there has been an adequate showing that bite mark identification is scientifically valid.
(B) Admissible, because there has been an adequate showing that bite mark identification is generally accepted in the field.
(C) Inadmissible, because the evidence is not relevant to an issue in the case.
(D) Inadmissible, because Dr. Jacobs is not qualified to be treated as an expert.

Multiple-Choice Answers

1. **A**   Ordinarily, the attorney-client privilege is assertable by a party's counsel on behalf of the client. The client may be a corporation. Since the records in question were already in existence when the Department of Commerce commenced its action against Exton, the work product privilege cannot be successfully asserted, since these documents were not prepared in anticipation of litigation or for trial. Also, since the communications are routine reports generated in the ordinary course of the corporation's business, they do not constitute confidential communications between an attorney and her client. Thus, the records are discoverable. (*See* ELO Ch.8-II(G)(4) and (I)(2).) Choice **B** is incorrect, since the attorney-client privilege can be asserted at the discovery stage. Also, the attorney (as well as his client) can ordinarily assert this privilege. Choice **C** is incorrect because documents do not become insulated from discovery simply because they are delivered to one's attorney. Finally, Choice **D** is incorrect because documents do not become an attorney's work product or confidential communications simply because they are delivered to, or reviewed by, legal counsel.

2. **D**   Only relevant evidence may be admitted. Evidence is relevant if it has any tendency to make the existence of a material fact more probable or less probable than it would be without the evidence. Joe's statement is relevant since it arguably links John to the crime. (*See* ELO Ch.2-I(B).) For this reason, Choice **A** is incorrect. A patient has a privilege to refuse to disclose, and to prevent any other person from disclosing, confidential communications for the purpose of diagnosis or treatment of a physical condition or injury. Choice **B** is incorrect because Joe's statement did not pertain to the treatment of his injury. Finally, Choice **C** is incorrect because a paramedic is ordinarily considered a "physician" for purposes of this privilege.

3. **B**   An expert may be cross-examined with respect to learned treatises. Out-of-court statements made in writings which are contained in a learned treatise and called to the attention of an expert witness constitute an exception to the hearsay rule. Such evidence may be read into the record; FRE 803(18). Since an exception to the hearsay rule exists with respect to the out-of-court statements in question, they may be considered as substantive evidence (as well as for impeachment). (*See* ELO Ch.6-VIII(B)(2)(d).) Choice **A** is incorrect because under this exception to the hearsay rule the statements are admissible as evidence. Choice **C** is incorrect because, while the statements in question are hearsay, an exception to the hearsay rule exists in this instance. Finally, Choice **D** is incorrect because Cox's belief that the passages in question were not applicable to Post's condition would probably ***not*** be determinative. Since Dr. Freed

testified that there is no difference between the two types of arthritis, the court could conclude that the passages of the textbook were relevant. The court should probably let the jury decide which expert they considered more credible.

4. **B** Tangible evidence must ordinarily be authenticated or identified prior to its admissibility; FRE 901(a). This requirement may be satisfied by evidence sufficient to support a finding that the matter in question is what its proponent claims. If the court determines there is adequate evidence of the letter's authenticity, it is admissible. (*See* ELO Ch.9-II(B)(4).) Choice **A** is incorrect because corroboration of Harry's signature is only one means of authentication (*i.e.*, a writing can also be authenticated by a witness with knowledge or a distinctive characteristic). Choice **C** is incorrect because the letter does tend to suggest that Harry was a co-conspirator. Finally, Choice **D** is incorrect because, although probably intended to be confidential in nature, the letter does not come within the purview of any recognized privilege.

5. **D** A hearsay statement is one made by an out-of-court declarant, which is offered into evidence to prove the truth of the matter asserted; FRE 801(c). Since the insurance adjuster is testifying as to an out-of-court statement by Martha to prove the truth of the matter asserted therein, it is hearsay (and therefore inadmissible). (*See* ELO Ch.5-II(C).) Choice **C** is incorrect because, whether Martha is unavailable or not, her statement to the insurance adjuster is still hearsay. There is no rule permitting a hearsay statement simply because the out-of-court declarant is unavailable. (FRE 804 describes the particular situations where an unavailable out-of-court declarant is pertinent.) Choice **A** is incorrect because Martha is not a party to the action. Finally, Choice **B** is incorrect, since Martha's statement was not an excited utterance (*i.e.*, a statement relating to a startling event while under the stress of excitement caused by the event); FRE 803(2). Martha's statement to the insurance adjuster was made three days after the incident had occurred.

6. **A** A hearsay statement is one, other than one made by the declarant while testifying at the trial or hearing, which is offered into evidence to prove the truth of the matter asserted therein; FRE 801(c). Pete's testimony as to how Jack had described Michael is not offered for the truth of the matter asserted (*i.e.*, that Michael really was a "sissy" or "scaredy cat"), but rather to show that Michael had a motive to murder Jack. (*See* ELO Ch.5-II(C)(5).) Choice **B** is incorrect because Pete's testimony is admissible whether or not Michael asserts his Fifth Amendment right against self-incrimination. Choice **C** is incorrect because Pete's testimony is, as

explained above, not hearsay. Finally, Choice **D** is incorrect because the statement is not offered to show that Michael acted in conformity with the character Jack had described on the occasion in question.

7. **A**   Under the doctrine of present recollection refreshed, a witness may consult a document before giving testimony as part of pretrial preparation; FRE 612(2). Since that is what Mike is doing here, his testimony is admissible. (*See* ELO Ch.4-IV(B)(3).) Choice **B** is incorrect because past recollection recorded pertains to a writing about a matter which the witness now has insufficient recollection to testify; FRE 803(5). The facts do not indicate that Mike, after taking the stand, had no recollection of the incident. Choice **C** is incorrect because Mike is testifying from his personal knowledge (rather than reading from the report in question). Finally, Choice **D** is incorrect because the report, not having been admitted into evidence, need not have been authenticated.

8. **C**   Where evidence of the content of a writing, recording or photograph is sought, the original writing, recording or photograph is ordinarily required; FRE 1002. This is especially true in transactions involving a contract, where the role played by the contract is so key that the contract really embodies the transaction. Since Deborah sought to testify about aspects of her performance which were actually set forth in the contract, the contract must be produced. (*See* ELO Ch.9-IV(C)(3).) Choice **A** is incorrect because the contract is not a writing kept in the course of a regularly conducted business activity. Choice **B** is inapplicable because when a document embodies a transaction, such as the contract here which sets forth the requirements of performance, its contents cannot be proved by oral testimony. Finally, Choice **D** is incorrect because Deborah's testimony does not pertain to an alleged understanding which occurred prior to execution of the written agreement.

9. **C**   Evidence of furnishing, or offering or promising to pay, medical expenses occasioned by an injury is not admissible to prove liability for that injury; FRE 409. Since a promise to pay another's medical bills is inadmissible, George's testimony about Paul's statement to Dora cannot be introduced. (*See* ELO Ch.3-XIV(I).) Choice **D** is incorrect because Paul's intent in making the statement is irrelevant. It is inadmissible because his statement is expressly prohibited under the FRE. Choice **A** is incorrect because, although George's testimony is a party-opponent admission, the statement is inadmissible for reasons other than hearsay. Finally, Choice **B** is incorrect because, even though Paul's statement may be relevant, it is inadmissible.

10. **A**   Relevant evidence is evidence having any tendency to make the existence of any fact of consequence more or less probable than it would be without that evidence; FRE 401. Since contributory negligence is not a defense to a products liability action, evidence of Paul's failure to act reasonably is irrelevant. (*See* ELO Ch.2-I(B)(3).) Choice **B** is incorrect because Paul's testimony would not be hearsay. Choice **C** is incorrect because, as discussed above, the evidence is not relevant. Finally, Choice **D** is incorrect because evidence of Paul's exceeding the speed limit to a minor degree is irrelevant, whether or not there is rebuttal evidence that his injuries would have occurred anyway.

11. **B**   While evidence that a person was or was not insured against liability is inadmissible upon the issue of whether he acted negligently or wrongfully, it is admissible when offered for any other relevant purpose (*i.e.*, proof of agency, ownership, control, bias, prejudice of a witness, etc.); FRE 411. If Dan had purchased liability insurance pertaining to the vehicle, such fact would suggest that he was a person "in control" of Amy's automobile. (*See* ELO Ch.3-XIII(A)(1).) Choice **A** is incorrect because Dan's purchase of insurance does not tend to show that it was more likely that Amy was at fault. Choice **C** is factually correct (*i.e.*, the existence of insurance is irrelevant to fault), but this evidence does suggest that Dan was "in control" of the vehicle. Finally, Choice **D** is incorrect because, although possibly factually accurate (*i.e.*, the availability of insurance tends to bias a factfinder against the insured party), the pertinence of this information with respect to the issue of whether Dan was "in control" of the vehicle probably justifies its admission into evidence.

12. **A**   Evidence of offering, or promising, a valuable consideration to compromise (or attempting to compromise) a claim which is disputed, is not admissible to prove liability; FRE 408. Since Mr. Jamison, on behalf of Frank's Market, made a compromise offer, the evidence is not admissible. (*See* ELO Ch.3-XIV(B).) Choice **B** is incorrect because Mr. Jamison's statement is not hearsay (it is a party-opponent admission), and would arguably be relevant to show that the defendant knew that it was at fault; FRE 801(d)(2). Choice **C** is arguably correct (*i.e.*, Mr. Jamison's statement tends to show that Frank's Market is liable), but is specifically made inadmissible by the FRE. Finally, Choice **D** is incorrect because Mr. Jamison's statement was not made in the course of formal settlement negotiations. It was an almost spontaneous offer by a party seeking to avoid legal action against it.

13. **A** When, after an event, measures are taken which, if taken previously, would have made the event less likely to occur, evidence of the subsequent measures are not admissible to prove culpable conduct in connection with such event; FRE 407. However, this rule does not exclude evidence of subsequent remedial measures offered for any other purpose (*i.e.*, proving proof of ownership, control, feasibility of precautionary measures, or impeachment). Since merely painting a vehicle is not the type of measure which would have made the incident less likely to occur, the objection should be overruled. (*See* ELO Ch.3-XII(A)(4), (B)(1) and (B)(2)(b).) Choice **B** is incorrect, since evidence of remedial measures is not ordinarily admissible. Choice **C** is correct as a general statement of law, but the measure (*i.e.*, the painting of the vehicle) undertaken in this instance is not remedial in nature. Finally, Choice **D** is incorrect since, as discussed above, the evidence is admissible in this particular situation.

14. **D** Evidence of subsequent remedial measures is not admissible to show negligence or culpable conduct in connection with such an event; FRE 407. Evidence of subsequent remedial measures is admissible, however, to prove ***ownership or control*** over the property that caused the accident. Evidence that Moneybags had the capability to order Cosgrove to install a retaining screen is relevant to determining whether Moneybags had control over the construction. Moneybags would, however, be entitled to a limiting instruction (*i.e.*, that the judge advise the jurors that this evidence should not be used in their determination of whether Cosgrove or Moneybags was negligent; but should be considered only for the purpose of deciding whether or not Moneybags had retained control over the construction). (*See* ELO Ch.3-XII(A)(4), (B)(1) and (B)(2)(b).) Choice **C** is factually incorrect. In fact, this evidence shows that Moneybags (rather than Cosgrove) had penultimate control of the construction. Choice **A** is incorrect because, while generally a correct proposition of law, evidence of remedial measures is admissible for the purpose of proving control over a particular activity. Finally, Choice **B** is incorrect because, while factually true, the evidence is admissible for the purpose of showing Moneybags' control over the construction.

15. **B** Generally, evidence of a party's character, or a trait of his/her character, is not admissible for the purpose of proving action in conformity therewith on a particular occasion; FRE 404(a). Since Marla is merely attempting to introduce general character evidence about Ripoff, the objection should be sustained. (*See* ELO Ch.3-III(A)(1)(a).) Choice **A** is incorrect because Ripoff's character is, to some extent, in issue. However, the majority view is that character evidence ordinarily entails too great of a potential to prejudice the factfinder (and is therefore inadmis-

sible). Choice **C** is arguably factually correct. But, as discussed above, character evidence of Ripoff's unethical reputation is inadmissible. Finally, Choice **D** is incorrect for the reasons described above. Additionally, Ripoff cannot introduce positive character evidence about himself.

16. A   Generally, evidence of a party's character, or a trait of his/her character, is not admissible for the purpose of proving action in conformity therewith on a particular occasion; FRE 404(a). Here, however, since the evidence is presumably offered to show that Paul's parents knew (or should have known) about his negligent or reckless tendencies, it is admissible. In this situation, it is not offered to show that Paul acted in conformity with these tendencies. (*See* ELO Ch.3-V(D)(1).) Choice **B** is incorrect because the evidence would not be admissible to show that Paul acted negligently or recklessly. Choice **C** is incorrect because, as explained above, the evidence is offered to show that Paul's parents were knowledgeable about his negligent or reckless tendencies. Finally, Choice **D** is incorrect because prior conduct might arguably tend to prove that the subject acted in conformity with those tendencies on the occasion in question. However, evidence is not admissible for that purpose. It might be mentioned that counsel for Paul's parents could probably request a limiting instruction (*i.e.*, that the jury be advised that it should only consider the evidence of Paul's prior conduct with respect to whether his parents knew, or should have known, that Paul's driving might result in an accident).

17. C   Evidence of prior crimes, wrongs or acts are admissible for any purpose, other than to show the character of a person for the purpose of showing that he acted in conformity therewith on the occasion in question; FRE 404(b). Theresa's prior convictions are pertinent to undermine her contention that she was coerced into the crime in question. (Of course, the jury could still believe her assertion, if they chose to do so.) (*See* ELO Ch.3-V(B)(1) and (J).) Choice **D** is incorrect because Theresa's identity is not in issue. She was arrested at the scene and has admitted committing the crime. Choice **A** is incorrect because, as discussed above, prior convictions are admissible in certain situations (such as the present one). Finally, Choice **B** is incorrect since Theresa's prior convictions are relevant to rebut her assertion that she was coerced into the crime in question.

18. A   While evidence of other crimes, wrongs, or acts is not admissible to prove character in order to show that a person acted in conformity therewith on the occasion in question, it may be admissible for any other relevant purpose (such as proof of motive, opportunity, intent, preparation, plan, knowledge, identity, or absence of mistake or accident); FRE 404(b). Since Magda had experienced a similar incident in which she had exited a store with an item that she had "tried on," the evidence should be admissible to rebut her assertion that an innocent mistake had been made. (Her attorney probably could obtain a limiting instruction - that the evidence be considered by the jury only upon the issue of whether Magda had made a good faith mistake or not.) The fact that no criminal charges were filed in the previous incident is of no significance. (*See* ELO Ch.3-V(B)(1) and (L).) Choice **B** is incorrect because it misstates the general proposition of law (*i.e.*, prior conduct is not ordinarily admissible to prove conduct in conformity therewith). Choice **C** is incorrect because the evidence is pertinent to Magda's assertion that she had made an innocent mistake. Finally, Choice **D** is incorrect because prior conduct, as explained above, is admissible in this situation.

19. **D**   One who consults an attorney for the purpose of obtaining legal assistance is privileged to refuse to disclose, and to prevent the attorney (and his essential personnel) from disclosing, communications made for the purpose of facilitating the rendition of advice. The letter which Adams sent to Ladd was for the purpose of obtaining assistance with respect to the preparation of the deed. It would therefore be within the attorney-client privilege. The fact that Evans saw the letter would not result in forfeiture of the privilege, since a legal secretary would presumably be considered "essential personnel" of her attorney-employer.(*See* ELO Ch.8-II(C) and (D)(3)(a).) Choice **A** is incorrect because the document is clearly relevant on the issue of Adams' intent. Choice **B** is incorrect because under the Federal and most state rules a photocopy is acceptable in lieu of the original. Choice **C** is incorrect because regularly-kept photocopy duplicates of an original document are ordinarily admissible; FRE 1003.

20. **D**   Evidence is relevant if it has any tendency to make the existence of any fact of consequence to the determination of the matter more or less probable; FRE 401. The fact that there was a call from Bungler's telephone number to Harvey's store on the day upon which a demand might have been made would permit an inference that Bungler was the extortionist. (*See* ELO Ch.2-II(A) and Ch.9-II(C)(7)(b)(ii).) Choice **A** is incorrect because directories which are generally used and relied upon by the public constitute an exception to the hearsay rule; FRE 803(17). Choice **C** is incorrect because there is no better document to prove a telephone number than the public directory; FRE 1003. Finally, Choice **B** is incorrect because, while it is entirely possible that Bungler called

Harvey's store for a business reason, it is also possible that he telephoned Harvey for the purpose of extorting money from him. Since the evidence has a tendency to prove that Bungler was the extortionist, it is relevant.

21. **C**   Out-of-court statements which are offered into evidence to prove that the statement was, in fact, made, or to show its effect on the listener, for example, to show that the listener had a certain emotion, had certain knowledge or was put on notice (as opposed to proving the truth of any matter asserted therein or inferable thereby) are not hearsay. The note in question is admissible for the purpose of showing that Harvey was being threatened with harm unless he complied with the demand to pay $50,000. It is ***not*** being offered to show that any statement in the note was, in fact, true and is, therefore, not hearsay. (*See* ELO Ch.5-II(C)(5).) Choice **D** is incorrect because the note is not being offered into evidence for the purpose of proving that Bungler wrote it. The party-opponent exclusion to the hearsay rule is not applicable. Choice **B** is incorrect because the note is not being offered into evidence to prove the truth of the matter asserted therein but only that it was received and caused fear. Finally, Choice **A** is incorrect because the prosecution has offered the note into evidence only to show that the victim was in imminent fear of harm, not to show that it was written by Bungler. (Evidence may be admissible for one purpose, but inadmissible for another; FRE 105.) Bungler could ask for a limiting instruction (*i.e.*, that the jury be instructed to limit the evidence to the element of Harvey's imminent fear of harm).

22. **A**   A witness who has testified with respect to the character of a person may be cross-examined with respect to relevant specific instances of conduct by that person; FRE 405(a). Because Blow testified as to Barker's character after the latter had testified, it was proper to cross-examine Blow with respect to prior acts of misconduct (although not resulting in prosecution) of Barker which are probative of the latter's truthfulness or untruthfulness. Since taking money from a cash register while working at an establishment (conduct probably constituting embezzlement or larceny) appears to be probative of truthfulness or untruthfulness, the question was proper. (*See* ELO Ch.3-VI(C)(2).) Choice **B** is incorrect because Blow has been asked about prior acts of misconduct not of himself but of ***another*** (*i.e.*, the defendant, Barker). Choice **C** is incorrect because embezzlement or larceny are crimes having similar ingredients as burglary and would probably be viewed as bearing upon truthfulness or untruthfulness. Therefore, the fact that Barker's prior conduct is somewhat different from that with which he is now charged is not perti-

nent. Finally, Choice **D** is incorrect because there is no requirement that *Barker* be asked about his prior misconduct to make Blow's testimony proper or relevant.

23. **C**   Out-of-court statements about an event or condition made while the declarant was observing that event or condition, or immediately thereafter, are admissible as an exception to the hearsay rule. Since Brown made his comment to Jock while he smelled the gas, his statement would be admissible; FRE 803(1). (*See* ELO Ch.6-IV(E).) Choice **B** is incorrect because there is no indication from the facts that Brown believed that his death was imminent. Choice **D** is incorrect because there is nothing to indicate that the gas was viewed by Brown as a "startling" event or condition. In fact, since Brown apparently continued to perform his work, there is no indication that he felt unusual stress. Finally, Choice **A** is incorrect because the evidence is offered on Brown's own behalf. The FRE's party-opponent exclusion to the hearsay rule is not applicable.

24. **C**   Evidence of a person's habit, or of the routine practice of an organization, is relevant to prove that person's conduct on a particular occasion was in conformity with such habit or routine practice; FRE 406. Since Arlene's testimony is basically "habit" evidence, it should be admissible. (*See* ELO Ch.3-X(D).) Choice **D** is incorrect because it sets forth an incorrect proposition of law (*i.e.,* prior conduct is not generally admissible to prove conduct in conformity therewith on a particular occasion). Choice **A** is incorrect because Arlene seeks to testify about a habit, rather than specific prior conduct. Finally, Choice **B** is incorrect, since Arlene's claim against the manufacturer does not preclude her from contesting Clyde's action against her.

25. **D**   Evidence of a person's character, or trait of character, is ordinarily inadmissible for the purpose of proving conduct in conformity therewith on a particular occasion; FRE 404(a). Although Matthew's character is in issue, he may not introduce evidence of even a pertinent character trait in a civil action. (The evidence is not being offered to offset Matthew's impeachment.) (*See* ELO Ch.3-IV(A).) Choice **C** is incorrect because reputation of a person's character constitutes an exception to the hearsay rule; FRE 803(21). Choice **B** is incorrect because, although Matthew's character is in issue, the evidence is not admissible. Finally, Choice **A** is incorrect because it sets forth an erroneous rule of law (*i.e.,* character evidence is not generally admissible in civil cases).

26. A   Evidence of other acts is not admissible to prove the character of a person to show that he/she acted in conformity therewith. However, it may be admissible for any other relevant purpose; FRE 404(b). Since Carlyle's character is directly in issue, the evidence is admissible to show that he lacked the mental competence necessary to modify a will. Testimony about Carlyle's actions, which is non-verbal conduct not intended as an assertion, does not constitute hearsay; FRE 801(a). (*See* ELO Ch.3-II(A).) Choice **B** is incorrect because character evidence is not ordinarily admissible. Choice **D** is generally a correct statement of law, but specific acts of Carlyle are nevertheless admissible in this situation. Finally, Choice **C** is incorrect because, as discussed above, the evidence of Carlyle's prior acts is admissible in this instance.

27. B   While evidence of a person's character is ordinarily not admissible for the purpose of showing that he acted in conformity therewith on a particular occasion, an accused may offer evidence of a pertinent trait of his character; FRE 404(a)(1). Since honesty and fair dealing are not pertinent to the crime for which Bill has been charged (*i.e.*, murder), the evidence is not admissible. In this situation, only evidence of a peaceable character would be pertinent. (*See* ELO Ch.3-VI(A)(3).) Choice **A** is incorrect because Bill may introduce evidence of his pertinent character traits. Choice **C** is incorrect because, even in a homicide case, the character trait in question must pertain to the crime for which the defendant has been charged. Finally, Choice **D** is incorrect, since evidence of his own character, when offered by an accused, must relate to the criminal activity involved.

28. A   While evidence of a person's character is ordinarily not admissible for the purpose of showing that he acted in conformity therewith on a particular occasion, an accused may offer evidence of a pertinent trait; FRE 404(a)(1). Since Sharon is charged with a crime which pertains to honesty, her reputation pertaining to truthfulness is pertinent. (*See* ELO Ch.3-VI(A)(3).) Choice **B** is incorrect because Sharon could not introduce evidence of any positive character trait. Choice **D** is a misstatement of the law (in a criminal case, an accused may introduce evidence of a pertinent trait of his character). Finally, Choice **C** is also an incorrect statement of law. Proof of reputation is admissible; FRE 405(a).

29. A   Evidence of a person's character is not admissible for the purpose of proving that he/she acted in conformity therewith on a particular occasion; FRE 404(a). Since the evidence offered is merely to show that Shawna acted in conformity with her aggressive bully-type tendencies, it is inadmissible. (*See* ELO Ch.3-IV(C)(2).) Choice **B** is incorrect because

Shawna's aggressiveness would arguably be relevant to the torts asserted by Kellie (*i.e.*, it would suggest that it was more likely than not that Shawna had aggressively accosted her). Choice **C** is incorrect because Shawna has not been charged with a crime. Kellie instituted a civil action against her. Finally, Choice **D** is incorrect because, while arguably pertinent, as discussed above, the evidence is inadmissible in this situation.

30. C Evidence of a pertinent character trait offered by a criminally accused is admissible; FRE 404(a)(1). In all cases in which character evidence is admissible, proof may be made by testimony as to reputation; FRE 405(a). Since the evidence offered by Jimmy is directly pertinent to the crime for which he is charged, it is admissible. (*See* ELO Ch.3-VI(A)(3) and (B)(1.).) Choice **D** is an incorrect statement of law (reputation evidence is admissible). Choice **B** is incorrect because opinion evidence as to Jimmy's character is admissible in this situation; FRE 405(a). Finally, Choice **A** is an incorrect statement of law. As discussed above, character evidence is admissible in this instance.

31. A Evidence of the victim's character for peacefulness may be offered by the prosecution in a homicide case to rebut an assertion that the deceased victim was the initial aggressor; FRE 404(a)(2). Since Tanya contends that Rita attacked her first and is charged with homicide, the prosecution may introduce evidence of Rita's peaceable character. (*See* ELO Ch.3-VII(B)(4).) Choice **B** is incorrect because it constitutes an overly broad statement of law (*i.e.*, evidence of the victim's character for peaceableness can often be introduced by the prosecution in a homicide case). Choice **C** is incorrect because there is no pre-condition that the prosecution have introduced evidence of Tanya's character during its case-in-chief. Finally, Choice **D** is incorrect because, in this situation, the prosecution may initiate evidence pertaining to the victim's peaceable character.

32. A Except in the case of a homicide, evidence of a pertinent character trait of the victim of a crime can be offered by the prosecution only to rebut similar evidence to the contrary offered by an accused; FRE 404(a)(2). Since the prosecution, as part of its case-in-chief, is offering character evidence pertaining to the victim, and the particular crime is not a homicide, the evidence is not admissible. (*See* ELO Ch.3-VII(B)(4).) Choice **B** is incorrect because "any type" of character evidence cannot be offered by Mark. While the accused may introduce evidence of the victim's character, such evidence must pertain to a pertinent trait. Choice **C** is incorrect because, as explained above, the prosecution cannot (except in the case of a homicide) initially offer evidence of the victim's character. Finally, Choice **D** is incorrect because, in this situation, no type of character evidence pertaining to the victim is admissible by the prosecution in its case-in-chief.

33. A   In a criminal case in which a person is accused of rape, reputation or opinion evidence of the past sexual behavior of the victim is not admissible; FRE 412(a). Choice **A** conforms to the applicable principle of law. (*See* ELO Ch.3-VII(C)(4)(d)(i).) Choice **B** is incorrect because the statement is too broad. Past instances of the victim's sexual behavior is admissible only upon the issue of whether the accused was or was not the source of semen or the victim's injury; FRE 412(b)(2)(A). In our case, there is no question that a sexual act occurred between Alan and Betty. Choice **C** is incorrect because such evidence, though arguably relevant, is not admissible. Finally, Choice **D** is incorrect because the fact that Betty had voluntarily gone into Alan's room does not establish that she consented to the sexual act.

34. D   In a criminal case in which a person is accused of rape, evidence of a victim's past sexual behavior is not admissible, unless it pertains to past relations with persons other than the accused and is offered by the accused upon the issue of whether he was the source of semen or the victim's injury; FRE 412(b)(2)(A). Since past sexual behavior with persons other than the accused is admissible with respect to the issue of whether the latter was the source of semen, Cindy's specific sexual behavior with other men is admissible; provided these relationships occurred approximately at the time during which she could have become pregnant. (*See* ELO Ch.3-VII(C)(4)(e)(i).) Choice **C** is incorrect because, as discussed above, past sexual behavior is admissible if it bears upon the source of semen. Choice **A** is incorrect because it states the applicable legal principle too broadly. Cindy's prior sexual behavior with men other than Steve must encompass the time period during which she could have been impregnated. Finally, Choice **B** is incorrect, since evidence of prior sexual behavior with other men would not be pertinent to whether Cindy consented to the sexual act which produced her child.

35. B   Hearsay is a statement, other than one made by the declarant while testifying at the trial or hearing, which is offered to prove the truth of the matter asserted therein; FRE 801(c). Since Terry is testifying as to what Bud told him, Terry's testimony is hearsay. Thus, it is not admissible. (*See* ELO Ch.5-II(C)(1).) Choice **A** is incorrect because the testimony is relevant. If the glasses were in perfect condition when shipped, it would arguably tend to prove that Brenda's assertion of minute cracks is erroneous. Choice **C** is incorrect because the party-opponent admission is a statement by the other side in the litigation. Here, the attorney for Bill is seeking the testimony of one of his client's employees as to a statement by another of his employees. Thus, the party-opponent exclusion from the hearsay rule is inapplicable. Finally, Choice **D** is incorrect because Bud's statement to Terry is offered to prove the truth of the matter asserted.

36. **C**   A statement which, by itself, gives rise to legal consequences (sometimes called an "operative fact" or a "verbal act") is not hearsay, since it is offered for the fact that it was said, rather than for the truth of the matter asserted therein. The statement in question was offered simply to show Jack's state of mind. Additionally, Jack's statement might also constitute a "statement against interest;" FRE 804(b)(3). Conveying one's farm to another would be "contrary to the declarant's pecuniary or proprietary interest." Of course, due to his death, Jack is an unavailable declarant. (*See* ELO Ch.5-II(C)(3) and (C)(6).) Choice **D** is incorrect because a dying declaration is one made by a declarant who believes death is imminent. Additionally, a dying declaration must concern the cause or circumstances of death; FRE 804(b)(2). Choice **A** is incorrect because, as discussed above, Lou's statement would not constitute hearsay (or would be admissible under the statement against interest rule). Finally, Choice **B** is incorrect, since Jack's statement would be relevant, whether or not the executor had contended that Jack was incompetent.

37. **A**   A statement which, by itself, gives rise to legal consequences (sometimes called an "operative fact" or a "verbal act") is not hearsay, since it is offered for the fact that it was said, rather than for the truth of the matter asserted therein. If Carol's testimony is offered simply to prove that the words were said, rather than their truth, her testimony is not hearsay. (*See* ELO Ch5-I(B) and II(C)(3).) Choice **B** is incorrect because Carol's testimony is not hearsay. Additionally, the "present state of mind" exception to the hearsay rule does not include statements of belief to prove the fact believed; FRE 803(3). Choice **C** is incorrect because Miss Gribbins' statement was in the nature of a fact, rather than mere opinion. Finally, Choice **D** is incorrect because proof of Miss Gribbins' competency is not a pre-condition to introduction of the testimony in question.

38. **A**   Hearsay is a statement, other than one made by the declarant while testifying at the trial or hearing, offered to prove the truth of the matter asserted therein; FRE 801(c). Jane's testimony is arguably not offered to prove the truth of the matter asserted (*i.e.*, that Susan slapped Amy across the face for no apparent reason). It is relevant in showing Claire's motivation in going to Susan's home. This evidence would also arguably

tend to show that Claire was not the initial aggressor in the fight/wrestling match. (*See* ELO Ch.5-II(C)(6).) Choice **B** is incorrect because Claire's motivation for being at Susan's home is relevant (*i.e.*, it shows that she did not necessarily go to Susan's house for the purpose of attacking the latter). Choice **C** is incorrect because evidence is rarely precluded due to the possibility of prejudicing the jury. Finally, Choice **D** is incorrect because Jane's testimony is, for the reasons described above, not hearsay.

39. B A statement which, by itself, gives rise to legal consequences (sometimes called an "operative fact" or a "verbal act") is not hearsay, since it is offered for the fact that it was said, rather than for the truth of the matter asserted therein. Since Conrad's testimony is not hearsay because it is not offered to prove the truth of the matter asserted (*i.e.*, that MegaBank actually had a large amount of money in its vault on Friday). Rather, the testimony is sought to show that Peter had a motivation to rob Mega-Bank on that day. (*See* ELO Ch.5-II(C)(6).) Choice **A** is incorrect because the evidence is admissible whether or not Donald is deemed "unavailable." Choice **C** is incorrect because Conrad's testimony is not hearsay. Finally, Choice **D** is incorrect because, as explained above, Conrad's testimony is relevant to whether or not Peter robbed MegaBank.

40. C The marital communications privilege ordinarily only pertains to communications (*i.e.*, oral or written statements, or non-verbal assertions). It ordinarily does not cover testimony about physical appearances. (*See* ELO Ch.8-V(C)(3).) Choice **D** is incorrect because, in most jurisdictions, either spouse may assert the marital privilege. Choice **A** is incorrect because Winona and Harry are no longer married. Therefore, the spousal privilege is inapplicable. Finally, Choice **B** is incorrect because Winona is not testifying as to a communication made by Harry.

41. D Where the out-of-court declarant testifies at the trial and is subject to cross-examination concerning the statement, and the statement is consistent with his testimony and offered to rebut an assertion of improper influence, the statement is not hearsay; FRE 801(d)(1). Thus, Morgan's testimony about what Bob told him is not hearsay. Morgan's testimony both rehabilitates Bob and can also be used as substantive evidence (since it helps establish that Tina was the party at fault). (*See* ELO Ch.4-XV(C)(3)(b).) Choice **C** is incorrect because Morgan's testimony can be used as substantive evidence, in addition to mere rehabilitation. Choice **A** is incorrect because the testimony, as discussed above, is not hearsay. Finally, Choice **B** is incorrect because the testimony is a proper means of rehabilitation.

42. B Evidence is relevant if it has a tendency to make the existence of any fact of consequence more or less probable; FRE 401. Vic's testimony tends to prove that Dan was acting negligently on the occasion in question. (*See* ELO Ch.2-II(A).) Choice **A** is incorrect because under the FRE one may always impeach his witness (including situations where the party was surprised by his witness' testimony); FRE 607. Choice **D** is incorrect because a party is *not* bound by the testimony of his witness. Finally, Choice **C** is incorrect because a party may impeach his own witness.

43. D While contradiction of prior testimony is ordinarily a proper means of impeachment, it cannot be achieved by extrinsic evidence where it pertains to a collateral matter (*i.e.*, one which is not related to the substantive issues of the litigation). In this instance, Vic is being contradicted over the statement that he has never been drunk in his life. Since whether or not Vic was intoxicated two years ago does not pertain to the issues of the case, a court would probably rule that Yank's testimony (which would constitute extrinsic evidence) is inadmissible. (*See* ELO Ch.4-XIII(D)(1)(a) and (D)(2).) Choice **C** is incorrect because it incorrectly states the law. A witness can be impeached *intrinsically* by specific acts of misconduct which bear upon his truthfulness or veracity; FRE 608(b). Additionally, a witness may ordinarily be impeached extrinsically with respect to prior criminal convictions; FRE 609(a). A witness may be impeached intrinsically (*i.e.*, out of his own mouth) with respect to specific, prior acts of misconduct bearing upon his truthfulness or veracity. Choice **A** is incorrect because Yank's impeaching testimony does *not* pertain to Vic's recollection of a recent event. Finally, Choice **B** is incorrect because the impeachment involved in this instance does not establish whether Vic was being truthful about his condition at the time of the accident.

44. C A witness may be impeached by evidence of his reputation or character for truthfulness or veracity, even if the evidence is an opinion; FRE 608(a). Zemo is apparently about to testify that Vic's reputation for veracity in his community is poor. Since this is a proper ground for impeachment, the question was proper. (*See* ELO Ch.4-IX(B) and (C)(1)(a)-(d).) Choice **D** is incorrect because it is not necessary that an impeaching witness personally know the party about whom he is testifying (it is only necessary that the witness know of that person's reputation in the community). Choice **A** is incorrect because Vic's veracity was not collateral to the issues since his testimony was on a critical issue. Finally, Choice **B** is incorrect because a witness' reputation for lack of truthfulness or veracity does prove that his testimony may not be truthful and therefore subject to impeachment.

45. B Evidence is relevant if it has a tendency to make the existence of any fact of consequence more or less probable; FRE 401. Conduct not intended as an assertion is not hearsay under the FRE; 801(a)(2). Assuming that the persons who were on the bus entered the hospital as a consequence of the accident, the doctor's testimony would be relevant in showing that Pat's neck injury was also caused by the collision. Additionally, there is no hearsay problem since the statements made by the other passengers about their neck pains would be admissible under the "then existing physical condition" or "medical diagnosis or treatment" exceptions to the hearsay rule; FRE 803(3) and (4), respectively. (*See* ELO Ch.2-II(A); Ch.5-II(A)(3)(a)(1); Ch.6-IV(B)(5).) Choice **A** is incorrect because the doctor's testimony does not pertain to a medical matter. He is testifying only as to the fact that three persons requested medical assistance for back pains at City Hospital. Choice **D** is incorrect because the Best Evidence Rule is not applicable in this instance (*i.e.*, Pat is not attempting to introduce testimony about the contents of a document). Finally, Choice **C** is incorrect because, as explained above, the statements of the three persons who were admitted to the hospital probably come within exceptions to the hearsay rule; FRE 803(3) and (4).

46. A A prior inconsistent statement of a witness, who is subject to cross-examination, is not hearsay, if that statement was (1) made under oath, and (2) made at a prior trial, hearing, or other proceeding, or in a deposition; FRE 801(d)(1). Since Beth's prior inconsistent testimony was made in a deposition (which statements are made under oath), it is not hearsay. It is admissible as substantive evidence against Samantha (*i.e.*, the jury may consider this evidence in determining if Tim has satisfied his burden of proof). (*See* ELO Ch.6-XIV(B)(6)(a).) Choice **B** is incorrect because Beth's deposition testimony can be used as substantive evidence (see the Advisory Committee's Note to FRE 801). Choice **C** is incorrect because admissibility of the deposition testimony is not dependent upon whether Samantha's attorney was present and had the opportunity to question Beth (which he presumably did). It's at least possible that Samantha's attorney decided to not attend Beth's deposition. Finally, Choice **D** is incorrect because, as discussed above, Beth's prior deposition testimony is not hearsay.

47. A If called to the attention of an expert witness upon cross-examination..., statements contained in a published treatise,...on the subject of history, medicine, or other science or art, established as a reliable authority by the testimony or admission of the witness...are not excluded by the hearsay rule. If admitted, the statements may be read into evidence (but may not be received as exhibits); FRE 803(18). Since Dr. Frank was acknowledged as an expert by Dr. Evans, the portion of the former's book pertaining to sterility occasioned by toxic emissions may be read into evidence. (*See* ELO Ch.6-VIII(B)(2).) Choice **B** is incorrect because the portion of Dr. Frank's book read into evidence can be considered for substantive (as well as impeachment) purposes. Choice **C** is incorrect because an exclusion from the hearsay rule exists in this situation. Finally, Choice **D** is incorrect because the portion of Dr. Frank's book described above may be read into evidence, whether or not he is available to testify.

48. A Evidence of a final judgment entered after a trial or upon a plea of guilty...adjudging a person guilty of a crime punishable by death or imprisonment in excess of one year, to prove any fact essential to sustain a judgment is not excluded by the hearsay rule; FRE 803(22). Since the crime in question was punishable by a term of up to five years, Justin's prior guilty plea is admissible to prove negligence with respect to his collision with William. (*See* ELO Ch.6-VIII(E)(5)(b)(iii).) Choice **B** is incorrect because there is no express requirement that a guilty plea be made under oath to constitute an exclusion from the hearsay rule. Choice **C** is incorrect because proper authentication of the guilty plea is not a basis for upholding the objection to its admissibility. Finally, Choice **D** is incorrect because, as explained above, the guilty plea in this situation constitutes an exclusion from the hearsay rule.

49. B Evidence of a final judgment, entered after a trial..., adjudging a person guilty of a crime punishable by death or imprisonment in excess of one year, which is offered to prove an essential fact in a subsequent proceeding, is ordinarily excluded from the hearsay rule. However, when such evidence is "offered by the government, in a criminal prosecution for purposes other than impeachment, judgments against persons other than the accused" are not within this exclusion; FRE 803(22). Since the prosecution is offering Mel's conviction of conspiracy for other than impeachment purposes, the evidence is excluded by the hearsay rule. (*See* ELO Ch.6-VIII(E)(5)(b)(iii).) Choice **A** is incorrect because the judgment against Mel for conspiracy to rob the Abco Bank with Duane would arguably make it "more probable" that Duane had committed the crime for which he has been charged; FRE 401. Choice **C** is incorrect because there is no general rule that prior criminal convictions constitute an exception to the hearsay rule (the conviction must ordinarily involve a crime punishable by death or more than one year in prison). Finally, Choice **D** is incorrect because the prior criminal conviction is being offered by the prosecution during its case-in-chief (not as impeachment).

50. C   A statement which was, at the time of its making, so contrary to the
declarant's pecuniary...interest...that a reasonable man in his position
would not have made the statement, unless he believed it to be true, is
(assuming the declarant is unavailable as a witness) not excluded by the
hearsay rule; FRE 804(b)(3). Since Alvin has died and admitted owing
Jim $1,000, his statement to Carl is admissible. (Additionally, it might
also constitute an admission, since the executor probably "stands in the
shoes" of Alvin.) (*See* ELO Ch.6-XII(B)(2).) Choice **B** is incorrect
because the dying declaration exception requires that the statement pertain to the cause or circumstances of the declarant's death. Choice **D** is
incorrect because the statement in question constitutes a factual conclusion. Finally, Choice **A** is incorrect because, as discussed above, Alvin's
statement constitutes an exclusion from the hearsay rule.

51. A   Out-of-court statements made by an unavailable declarant which would
tend to subject him to civil or criminal liability are excluded from the
hearsay rule; FRE 804(b)(3). Since Tim's statement exposed himself to
criminal liability and he is no longer available (he has relocated to
India), his statement to Jeff is not excluded by the hearsay rule. (*See* ELO
Ch.6-XII(B)(3).) Choice **B** is incorrect because Tim is not being sued by
Mary. Thus, he is not a party to this action. Choice **C** is incorrect because
the statement is not inadmissible simply due to a lack of "direct proof."
There is no such prerequisite. Finally, Choice **D** is incorrect because, as
discussed above, Tim's comment to Jeff constitutes a "statement against
interest," and is therefore not excluded by the hearsay rule.

52. B   Hearsay is a statement, other than one made by the declarant while testifying at the trial or hearing, offered into evidence to prove the truth of
the matter asserted; FRE 801(c). Since Ben would be testifying about an
out-of-court statement by Kerry, his testimony is hearsay. (*See* ELO
Ch.5-II(A)(3) and Ch.6-XII(A).) Choice **A** is incorrect because this privilege must be asserted by either Kerry or Ben. The latter apparently has
chosen not to assert the privilege, and the former is not at the trial.
Choice **C** is incorrect because Kerry is not unavailable (a prerequisite for
the "statement against interest" exception to the hearsay rule). Finally,
Choice **D** is incorrect, since testimony pertaining to a criminal conspiracy is not per se inadmissible.

53. B   "Testimony given at another hearing...or a different proceeding, by an
unavailable declarant, is not excluded by the hearsay rule, if the party
against whom the testimony is now offered, or, in a civil action..., a predecessor in interest, had an opportunity and similar motive to develop
the testimony by direct, cross, or redirect examination;" FRE 804(b)(1).

Since Jane may be considered a predecessor in interest of Megan, that is, one with a like motive to develop the same testimony about the same material facts, the "former testimony" exclusion from the hearsay rule is applicable. Thus, the evidence is admissible. (*See* ELO Ch.6-X(E)(3)(d).) Choice **A** is incorrect because the evidence falls under the "former testimony" exclusion from the hearsay rule. Choice **C** is incorrect because the fact that Dr. Peters' transcript was authenticated does not overcome a hearsay objection. Finally, Choice **D** is incorrect because the fact that Dr. Peters was an expert is irrelevant to the hearsay problem.

54. **A**   If a witness is not testifying as an expert, his testimony in the form of opinion or inference is limited to those opinions or inferences which are (a) rationally based on his perception, and (b) helpful to a clear understanding of his testimony or the determination of a fact in issue; FRE 701. Martin's testimony that Trish was "clearly speeding" is certainly helpful to a determination of who was at fault. (*See* ELO Ch.10-I(C)(6).) Choice **B** is incorrect because Trish's non-verbal conduct was not intended as an assertion, and is therefore not hearsay; FRE 801(a)-(c). Choice **C** is incorrect because layperson opinion is admissible in many circumstances, as explained above. Finally, Choice **D** is incorrect because no independent means of verifying Martin's opinion is necessary for it to be admissible.

55. **A**   Facts or data in a particular case upon which an expert bases an opinion may be those perceived by, or made known to, him at or before the hearing. If such facts are of the type reasonably relied upon by experts in that particular field in forming opinions, the facts or data need not be admissible in evidence; FRE 703. Since Dr. Martin presumably qualifies as an expert with respect to the extent of Angie's injuries, his opinion can be based upon the lab technician's evaluation of the X-rays, if this is the type of information reasonably relied upon by experts in the field. (*See* ELO Ch.10-II(C)(4)(b)(i).) Choice **B** is incorrect because there is no requirement that Dr. Martin must have personally examined Angie to render an opinion with respect to the permanency of her injuries. Choice **C** is incorrect because, as described above, an expert may render an opinion upon facts or data not otherwise admissible in evidence. Finally, Choice **D** is incorrect because, as discussed above, the applicable FRE rule permits Dr. Martin's opinion to be based upon the lab technician's analysis of Angie's X-rays.

56. **C**   The credibility of a witness may be attacked by any party, including the one calling him; FRE 607. Extrinsic evidence of a prior inconsistent statement by a witness is not admissible, unless (1) he is afforded an

opportunity to explain or deny the same, and (2) the opposing party is afforded an opportunity to interrogate him thereon, or, the interests of justice otherwise require; FRE 613(b). Assuming Jim was given the opportunity to explain his statement to Jason and was available for redirect examination (*i.e.*, had not left the courtroom), Jason's testimony is admissible. (*See* ELO Ch.4-X(C) and(D).) Choice **D** is incorrect because, as explained above, William must be available for redirect examination pursuant to FRE 613(b). Choice **A** is incorrect because impeachment testimony is not offered to prove the truth of the matter asserted therein. It is being introduced into evidence only to impugn a witness's credibility. Finally, Choice **B** is incorrect because under the FRE a party may impeach his own witness.

57. **B**   The credibility of a witness may be attacked by opinion or reputation evidence, but the evidence must refer to his character for truthfulness or untruthfulness; FRE 608(a). Since evidence that Tom had a reputation for having an "aggressive, impetuous nature" does not pertain to credibility, the testimony is not admissible. (*See* ELO Ch.4-IX(C).) Choice **A** is incorrect because impeachment evidence does not have to be relevant (*i.e.*, it only has to have a tendency to impugn the truthfulness of a witness). Choice **C** is incorrect because there is no requirement that a character witness initially state that he believes that he is personally familiar with the former witness's character. Finally, Choice **D** is incorrect because having an "aggressive, impetuous nature" probably does not impair a witness's credibility.

58. **B**   Questions leading to impeachment must have a tendency to discredit the witness' credibility. The fact that a witness is an alcoholic would arguably not tend to indicate that he would have a tendency to lie on the witness stand. (*See* ELO Ch.4-VIII(B)(1)(b).) Choice **A** is incorrect because bias in favor of the party for whom the witness is testifying is a proper basis for impeachment. Choice **C** is incorrect because prior misconduct (not resulting in a criminal conviction) is a proper ground of intrinsic impeachment where it pertains to truthfulness or veracity. Deliberately failing to report income would show a tendency to be untruthful, and therefore would be a proper ground for intrinsic impeachment. Finally, Choice **D** is incorrect because one may be impeached by prior criminal convictions which involve dishonesty or false statements; FRE 609.

59. **D**   One may claim the privilege against self-incrimination whenever there is a reasonable possibility that her testimony will incriminate her. Bystander is entitled to remain silent if there is a reasonable possibility that her answer could incriminate her. (*See* ELO Ch.8-IV(C)(2)(b).)

Choices **C** and **B** are incorrect because it is not necessary that there be (1) a preponderance of evidence, or (2) clear and convincing evidence that the testimony will be self-incriminating to assert the Fifth Amendment. Finally, Choice **A** is incorrect because it is not necessary that the judge be convinced; he must only believe that there is a reasonable possibility that the testimony by the witness will incriminate her.

60. **A**   An expert may base his opinion on information gained about the case by listening to other witnesses who testify before he does. This is usually done by use of a hypothetical question: the questioner asks the expert to assume that the prior testimony is true, and then to give an inference or opinion. Because Dr. Jones, an expert in this area, was asked to give his opinion based on listening to the prior testimony of Phillips and to assume that the testimony was true, his opinion is admissible. (*See* ELO Ch.10-II(C)(2).) Choice **B** is incorrect because the jury determines issues of credibility. Choice **D** is incorrect because an expert's testimony may be based upon facts or data perceived by him even as a result of lay testimony at the trial. Finally, Choice **C** is incorrect because a hypothetical question may be based upon prior testimony at the trial.

61. **B**   The facts or data upon which an expert bases an opinion may be those perceived or made known to her at or before the hearing. If of a type reasonably relied upon by experts in that particular field in forming an opinion, the facts or data upon which an expert bases her opinion need not have been admitted into evidence; FRE 703. Since the reports in question are (presumably) reasonably relied upon in medical practice, Dr. Black could render an opinion that Phillip's injuries were permanent. (*See* ELO Ch.10-II(C)(4)(b).) Choice **A** is incorrect because, while the laboratory reports probably come within the "business records" exception to the hearsay rule, these items are not themselves being offered as evidence. Choice **C** is incorrect because there is no requirement that an expert be qualified to conduct the tests upon which she is basing her opinion. Finally, Choice **D** is incorrect because there is no requirement that an expert's opinions be based upon tests which were done under her supervision. The data considered must only be of the type which is reasonably relied upon by experts in that field in forming their opinions.

62. **D**   Impeachment by contradiction as to a collateral matter may ordinarily not be accomplished by extrinsic evidence. It can only be achieved by intrinsic evidence — statements made from the witness's own mouth while on the stand. Since the question of why (not if) Walter was standing on Second and Maple is a collateral matter, contradicting Walter on this point cannot be accomplished by extrinsic evidence (*i.e.*, calling

another witness to dispute his testimony). (*See* ELO Ch.4-X(D)(1)(b).) Choice **C** is incorrect because Shirley's testimony has nothing to do with substantive evidence. The only question presented by this factual pattern is whether her testimony constitutes a proper mode of impeachment. Choice **A** is incorrect because, even though Shirley's testimony impeaches Walter's veracity, it is inadmissible because it pertains to a collateral matter. Finally, Choice **B** is incorrect because, despite arguably undermining Walter's moral character, for the reasons described above Shirley's testimony is not admissible.

63. **C**   A witness's personal partiality or bias constitutes a proper basis for impeachment. The fact that Desmond worked for Peggy suggests he would be partial to her. Additionally, the possibility that he hated attorneys is also a proper question, since Daniel is a member of that group. Presumably, Daniel's attorney had a good faith basis for the second question. (It might be noted that Peggy's attorney could have objected to this inquiry on the ground that it was a compound question, since Daniel's attorney, in effect, asked two questions.) (*See* ELO Ch.4-XI(B)(1) and (2).) Choice **D** is incorrect because a witness's state of mind is not per se a proper basis for impeachment. Choice **A** is incorrect because leading questions are ordinarily permissible upon cross-examination. Finally, Choice **B** is incorrect because the potential for prejudicing the jury is not outweighed by Daniel's attorney's right to cross-examine Desmond.

64. **B**   Impeachment with respect to prior bad acts not resulting in a conviction ordinarily cannot be accomplished by extrinsic evidence. Since Dahlia's testimony constitutes extrinsic evidence, the objection should be sustained. (*See* ELO Ch.4-VIII(B)(1)(a).) Choice **A** is incorrect because the impeachment in this situation goes to improper conduct which has not resulted in a conviction and is sought to be accomplished by extrinsic evidence — Dahlia's testimony. Choice **C** is incorrect because Clara's veracity is a proper basis for impeachment. Finally, Choice **D** is incorrect because, while the prior negative act in question pertains to veracity, it cannot be proven by extrinsic evidence in this situation.

65. **A**   Where a witness testifies with respect to the character for truthfulness or untruthfulness of another witness, the former may be cross-examined with respect to specific instances of conduct by the latter which pertain to truthfulness or untruthfulness; FRE 608(b). Since Jeanine testified as to Winifred's lack of trustworthiness, Olivia's attorney had the right to ask her if she was aware that Winifred had recently returned a lost wallet (with cash inside of it) to the police.(*See* ELO Ch.4-VIII(B).) Choice **B** is incorrect, since it does not constitute a basis for determining whether

Jeanine could be asked about Winifred's recent act of exceptional honesty. Choice **C** is incorrect because this type of rehabilitation is expressly authorized by the FRE. Finally, Choice **D** is incorrect because, while the jury can still decide whether to believe Jeanine or not, the rehabilitation described in this situation is expressly authorized by the FRE.

66. B A court is entitled to exercise reasonable control over the mode and order of interrogating witnesses and the presentation of evidence; FRE 611. Ordinarily, however, a court will not permit evidence which is irrelevant to the issues. Once the evidence is in, however, the court may permit the other side to show that the evidence is not true to discredit the party offering the evidence. (*See* ELO Ch.4-II(C)(1)(b).) Choice **D** is incorrect because the determination whether to permit Don to impeach Peter by extrinsic evidence (*i.e.*, Don's testimony) is discretionary with the court. Choice **A** is incorrect because it was not necessary for Don to object to Peter's testimony to preserve the right to impeach and the court had discretion not to permit Don to testify further on a collateral issue. Choice **C** is incorrect because Don did not have to object.

67. A For purposes of establishing its content, execution and delivery, recitals contained in a deed which has been recorded in a public office pursuant to a statute authorizing such recordation are admissible as an exception to the hearsay rule; FRE 803(14,15). Although the statement of Paula's relationship is hearsay, because it comes contained in the deed it is hearsay within this exception. (*See* ELO Ch.6-VIII(C)(2).) Choice **B** is incorrect because the "past recollection recorded" exception to the hearsay rule is applicable only where a witness testifies that she has no present recollection about a writing made or adopted by her when the document was fresh in her mind. Choice **C** is incorrect because the testimony comes within an exception to the hearsay rule is present in this instance. Finally, Choice **D** is incorrect because authenticated duplicates of a deed are ordinarily admissible in place of the original; FRE 1003.

68. A Out-of-court statements pertaining to a startling event, made by a declarant while under the stress of the excitement caused by the event, are admissible as an exception to the hearsay rule; FRE 803(2). The imminent collision between Driver's car and Walker would constitute a "startling" situation and Paul's exclamation would be an "excited utterance". (*See* ELO Ch.6-IV(D).) Choice **C** is incorrect because the "excited utterance" exception to the hearsay rule does not require that the declarant be unavailable as a witness. Choice **D** is incorrect because the startling event was the imminent collision with Walker. The fact that the statement preceded the accident strengthens the sense of excitement which must have prompted Paul. Choice **B** is incorrect because Ralph's statement was not a declaration against his interest, which must be either pecuniary or proprietary, (FRE 804(b)(3)). The facts fail to indicate any reason why Driver's negligent operation of his car would result in liability to Ralph.

69. B   The Federal rules treat admissions as non-hearsay. Out-of-court statements made by another in the presence of a party-opponent, who fails to object to or deny the statements, are deemed to be adopted as admissions by the party-opponent and do not constitute hearsay; FRE 801(d)(2)(B). Driver's failure to object to or deny Paul's statement that Walker was hit while in the crosswalk would probably constitute an adoptive admission. Paul's statement would, in effect, be attributed to Driver. Under the FRE, admissions of a party-opponent are not hearsay. (*See* ELO Ch.6-II(D)(3)(a).) Choice **A** is incorrect because Driver's silence would not, in itself, make Paul his agent. Choice **C** is incorrect because adoptive admissions are treated in the same way as admissions of a party; they are not hearsay. Finally, Choice **D** is incorrect because there is no necessity that a party-opponent be given an opportunity to admit or deny a statement before he may be deemed to have adopted or admitted it.

70. A   Out-of-court statements made by a declarant pertaining to his contemporaneous state of mind, physical condition or pain are admissible as an exception to the hearsay rule; FRE 803(3). Walker's statements described a simultaneous physical sensation or condition. Joe's testimony about Walker's statement would be admissible as an exception to the hearsay rule. Choice **B** is incorrect because whether Walker's elbow was permanently injured or not would require expert medical testimony and is not established by Walker's statement to Joe. Choice **D** is incorrect because Walker's description of the severe pain which he is experiencing does ***not*** require confirmation by expert testimony. Finally, Choice **C** is incorrect because, while Joe's testimony is hearsay, it comes within an exception to the hearsay rule.

71. D   An oral or written statement, made to the witness out-of-court which is offered into evidence at trial to prove the truth of the statement, is hearsay. Hearsay evidence is inadmissible unless some exception to the hearsay rule exists; FRE 801(c). Since Sheriff is testifying as to what Passerby stated to him, his statement is not admissible unless some exception to the hearsay rule exists. (*See* ELO Ch.5-II(A)(3).) Choice **C** is incorrect because Sheriff is not trying to prove the contents of a document. Choice **A** is incorrect because Passerby was not "under the stress of excitement" caused by the accident (Passerby made his statement half an hour after the accident.) Finally, Choice **B** is incorrect because the statement involved was made by Passerby who did not record his recollection. Sheriff was not recording his own recollection but Passerby's.

72. **C**   Hearsay evidence is inadmissible unless some exception to the hearsay rule exists; FRE 801(c). Since Sheriff is testifying as to what Ralph told him out-of-court, the latter's statement is hearsay. It would therefore be inadmissible unless some exception to the hearsay rule exists. (*See* ELO Ch.5-II(A)(3).) Choice **D** is incorrect because Ralph's remark that each of the persons in Driver's car had "downed" at least four cans of beer is a statement of fact, rather than opinion. Choice **A** is incorrect because Ralph is not a party to the lawsuit. Finally, Choice **B** is incorrect because there is no relationship between Ralph and Driver which would make Ralph liable for Driver's operation of the vehicle; Ralph's statement would not appear to be against his pecuniary or proprietary interests.

73. **A**   Where a witness testifies that he has no present recollection about a matter about which he had prior personal knowledge, his recollection may be refreshed by virtually any means (including writings). Where a witness does not recall a detail or fact, an adverse party is entitled to introduce a prior writing by him, to cross-examine the witness with respect to it, and to introduce into evidence those portions of the writing which relate to the witness' testimony; FRE 612. Since Walker's attorney is merely attempting to refresh Ralph's recollection, the judge should rule that Ralph may be shown the letter which he wrote to his sister. (*See* ELO Ch.4-IV.) Choice **B** is incorrect because the doctrine of past recollection recorded is *not* applicable until the witness testifies that he has no present recollection with respect to the statements made in the writing. Walker's attorney is not attempting to prove the contents of the letter but to refresh Ralph's recollection about some of its details. Choice **C** is incorrect because there is no requirement that opposing counsel must be shown the "refreshing" writing prior to the time it is utilized. He is, however, entitled to inspect it after the witness' memory is refreshed by the document. Finally, Choice **D** is incorrect because there is no requirement that an item which refreshes a witness' memory (if, in fact, Ralph's letter to his sister had this effect) must be read into evidence. If the doctrine of past recollection recorded were made applicable, Walker's attorney would *then* be entitled to have the letter read into evidence (*if* the court determined that the accident was still fresh in Ralph's mind during the evening of the day on which it had occurred).

74. B Under the Best Evidence Rule, to prove the contents of a writing the original document is ordinarily required; FRE 1002. Since Bellman is testifying as to the contents of a writing (his contract with Owner), he would be required to introduce the original agreement or show that it is not obtainable before his testimony would be allowed. (*See* ELO Ch.9-IV(A)(4).) Choice **C** is incorrect because the parol evidence rule applies when an effort is made to introduce evidence pertaining to prior or contemporaneous understandings which vary or modify the terms of an integrated writing. In this instance, Bellman is seeking only to establish the existence of a contract with Owner (not to modify or vary it). Choice **A** is incorrect because there is a written contract as required by the Statute of Frauds, which is not violated. Finally, Choice **D** is incorrect because the testimony would be relevant (tend to prove or disprove a fact or consequence) because Waiter (as Owner's assignee) would be bound by the agreement to retain Bellman for 10 years.

75. A Preliminary questions concerning the admissibility of evidence are ordinarily determined by the court. However, where the relevancy of evidence defends upon the proof of a fact, the court will admit it subject to the introduction of evidence sufficient to support a finding of that fact; FRE 104(a) and (b). Assignment depends upon the authenticity of the Owner's signature. Absent such signature, the document would not be relevant. Thus, the court could admit the Assignment subject to the introduction of adequate evidence by Waiter that the signature was actually that of Owner. If the proof introduced by Waiter on this point were inadequate (*i.e.*, a reasonable fact-finder would not conclude that the Assignment was signed by Owner), the court would be obliged to instruct the jury to disregard the Assignment. (*See* ELO Ch.11-III(C)(3)(b)(iv).) Choice **D** is incorrect because the fact-finder (rather than the judge) would determine whether Owner's signature is genuine or not (assuming, of course, sufficient evidence to permit this conclusion is introduced). Choice **C** is incorrect because the judge is not obliged to conclude that the signature is genuine as a matter of law. Rather, the fact-finder would decide by a preponderance of the evidence, whether the signature was genuine. Finally, Choice **B** is incorrect because the authenticity of a signature is not determined by the trial judge's opinion whether the signature on the document bears a reasonable facsimile to another signature by the Owner.

76. C One who consults an attorney for the purpose of obtaining professional assistance is privileged to refuse to disclose, and to prevent the attorney (and his essential personnel) from disclosing, communications made for the purpose of facilitating such services (whether or not the attorney is actually retained). Since Lyons approached Lawyer for the purpose of obtaining his services, the fact that Lawyer declined to represent Lyons is irrelevant and does not destroy the latter's attorney-client privilege. (*See* ELO Ch.8-II(C)(1).) Choice **A** is incorrect because, as long as Lawyer was a party to statements by Lyons, the attorney-client privilege is applicable. Choice **B** is incorrect because Lyons is privileged to prevent Lawyer from disclosing his admission that he committed the crime for which he is charged. A defendant must be permitted to disclose his involvement in a crime to enable the attorney to represent him adequately and to prepare his plea. (Disclosures with respect to *prospective* illegal conduct are, however, *not* within the attorney-client privilege.) Finally, Choice **D** is incorrect because Lawyer's testimony with respect to Lyon's statement comes within the party-opponent exclusion to the hearsay rule; FRE 801(d)(2)(A).

77. **A** A witness may be impeached intrinsically or *extrinsically* by proving an outstanding conviction for a crime which involves dishonesty or false statements; FRE 609(a)(2). Prior convictions for perjury are a proper means of impeachment and may be proven by extrinsic evidence (*i.e.*, a properly authenticated copy of the court record of the conviction). (*See* ELO Ch.4-VII(D).) Choice **D** is incorrect because, impeachment through specific instances of misconduct relating to perjury *which have resulted in a conviction* may be shown by extrinsic evidence. Choice **B** is incorrect because it states the wrong reason for admitting the testimony. While evidence of other crimes is ordinarily not admissible to prove that one acted in conformity therewith on a particular occasion, a prior conviction for perjury does not tend to prove the crime of murder; it goes to defendant's credibility; FRE 404(b). Finally, Choice **C** is incorrect because public records are ordinarily admissible in lieu of the original writing (FRE 1003); and they are an exception to the hearsay rule; FRE 803(8).

78. **C** Under the parol evidence rule, where the parties intended a writing to be the final and complete expression of their contract, the document is a total integration; and evidence of any prior or contemporaneous oral or written understandings which vary, contradict or add to the terms of the document are not admissible. Since the agreement in question was made *after* the written contract, the parol evidence rule would not be applicable. Choice **D** is incorrect because the fact that a particular subject was not dealt with in the written agreement would *not* preclude subsequent modification of the original contract. Finally, Choices **A** and **B** are incor-

rect because the parol evidence rule does not apply to agreements made *subsequent* to the integration; subsequent agreements may vary the original and may add to it.

79. **A**   Under the parol evidence rule, if the parties intended a writing to be the final and complete expression of their understandings with respect to those items recited (but not their entire agreement) the document is a partial integration; and evidence of any prior or contemporaneous oral or written understandings which do not contradict the terms of such writing is admissible. If the court can be persuaded that the writing was merely a partial (as opposed to a total) integration, evidence of collateral agreements which do not contradict the writing are ordinarily admissible. Since the "overtime" provision would not necessarily conflict with the term calling for a fixed number of hours and for regular monthly installments, evidence of the collateral agreement would probably be admissible. Choice **B** is incorrect because prior negotiations are not ordinarily admissible unless there has not been a total integration. Choice **C** is incorrect because, while stating a truism in the law (parol evidence is ordinarily admissible to show an oral condition precedent to the existence of a contract), ABC is not offering to prove a condition precedent to the existence of the written agreement. Finally, Choice **D** is incorrect because there is no suggestion of fraud in the facts upon by the parties.

80. **C**   Specific instances of misconduct (other than those resulting in the conviction of a crime) by a witness other than the defendant for the purpose of impeaching the witness may *not* be proved by extrinsic evidence; FRE 608(b). Since Joanna's cheating at the card game has not apparently resulted in a criminal conviction, she may *not* be impeached by extrinsic evidence (*i.e.*, by means other than out of her own mouth). The prosecution's offer to have Bill testify is inadmissible. (*See* ELO Ch.4-VIII(B)(5).) Choice **D** is incorrect because it is irrelevant whether gambling is a federal crime. Bill's testimony is inadmissible because Joanna's conduct has not resulted in a conviction. Choice **A** is incorrect because, while the card-cheating incident might impugn Joanna's credibility, the evidence is nevertheless inadmissible. Finally, Choice **B** is incorrect because the fact that Joanna had given her opinion of Alfred's character did *not* make her misconduct admissible, since the conduct did not result in conviction.

81. **A**   A statement is not hearsay (1) if the declarant testifies at the trial or hearing, (2) he is subject to cross-examination concerning the statement, and (3) the statement is one of identification of a person made after perceiv-

ing him; FRE 801(d)(1)(C). Since Jones passed away prior to John's trial, he obviously was not available to testify. Melvin's testimony is hearsay and therefore inadmissible. (*See* ELO Ch.6-XIV(D)(2).) Choice **B** is incorrect because Jones' identification of John was a statement of fact, rather than opinion (*i.e.*, John was the person who had attacked him with a tire iron). Choice **C** is incorrect because the fact that a witness is unavailable does not make his out-of-court statement admissible. Finally, Choice **D** is incorrect because, while Jones' statement is probative of John's motive, it is nevertheless hearsay.

82. **C** A statement is not hearsay if (1) declarant testifies at the trial or hearing, (2) the statement is the subject of cross-examination, and (3) the statement is inconsistent with the testimony and was given under oath at a trial, hearing, or other proceeding, or in a deposition; FRE 801(d)(1)(A). However, since the facts indicate that Sue's statement was simply delivered to the prosecution (*i.e.*, it was **not** made under oath at a prior proceeding or deposition), it is hearsay and may not be admitted as substantive evidence. (*See* ELO Ch.6-XIV(A)(4)(b).) Choices **D** and **B** are incorrect because Sue's statement is hearsay and not admissible as substantive evidence. However, her statement, inconsistent with her testimony at trial, may be used to impeach her. Choice **A** is incorrect because, since Sue's statement is hearsay, it is not admissible except for impeachment. The statement is not being introduced to prove the truth of its contents. It is being utilized to discredit Sue's credibility by showing that, at a different time, she made conflicting statements. It should be noted that under the FRE no foundation need be laid prior to impeaching a witness via a prior inconsistent statement. It is only necessary that the witness be afforded an opportunity to explain or deny the prior inconsistent statement.

83. **B** An oral or written statement, other than one made by the declarant thereof while testifying at the trial or hearing, which is offered into evidence at trial to prove the truth of the contents, is hearsay. Hearsay evidence is inadmissible unless some exception to the hearsay rule exists; FRE 801(c)(d). Officer Bones' report is hearsay (the report embodies Officer Bones' description of Josephina's speech at the time of the arrest). The mere fact that Officer Smith can authenticate the report because of his familiarity with Bones' signature does not cure the hearsay objection. (*See* ELO Ch.5-II(A)(3).) Choice **C** is incorrect because proper authentication of Bones' report does not cure the hearsay problem. Choice **D** is incorrect because the fact that Officer Bones is unavailable does not constitute a reason for overcoming the hearsay objection. Finally, Choice **A** is incorrect because it states the wrong reason for

excluding the report: Bones' statement that Josephina's speech was slurred is probably a statement of fact, rather than opinion, because it describes an objective symptom of Josephina's condition.

84. B   A statement is not hearsay if offered against a party and it is his own statement; FRE 801(d)(2)(A). Although Warren is testifying as to what Driver said out-of-court, the statement is not hearsay because it was made by Driver, the party against whom the evidence is being offered. (*See* ELO Ch.6-II(C).) Choice **A** is incorrect because Driver's statement is not intrinsically a statement against interest and Driver is available to testify. Choice **D** is incorrect because an inference may be drawn that a party who attempts to induce false testimony was culpable with respect to the incident in question. Finally, Choice **C** is incorrect because Driver's statement is *not* hearsay.

85. C   Evidence of a person's character is *not* admissible in a civil lawsuit for the purpose of proving that his actions on a particular occasion were consistent with his reputation; FRE 404(a). Since this is a civil action, Driver cannot introduce evidence of his reputation for being a safe and prudent driver. (*See* ELO Ch.3-IV(B).) Choice **D** is incorrect because character evidence is admissible in civil litigation where a person's character is directly in issue (*e.g.*, in a negligent entrustment case or defamation action). Choice **A** is incorrect because evidence of one's reputation to prove conduct in conformity therewith on a particular occasion is inadmissible in a civil lawsuit. Finally, Choice **B** is incorrect because the character evidence would be inadmissible whether or not a foundation had been laid by the testifying witness.

86. B   Under the parol evidence rule, where the parties intended a writing to be the final and complete expression of their contract, the document is a total integration, and evidence of any prior or contemporaneous oral or written understanding which varies, contradicts or adds to the terms of the writing is not admissible. The "most effective argument" of HDS is that the writing was not intended by the parties to be the complete expression of their agreement. If this argument prevailed, the memorandum would not preclude evidence of additional, consistent terms. Choice **A** is incorrect because, while stating a valid rule of law, the understanding which CP desires to introduce does *not* appear to be necessary in interpreting any of the provisions of the writing. Choice **C** is incorrect because detrimental reliance does *not* vitiate the parol evidence rule. Finally, Choice **D** is incorrect because it would be inconsistent with HDS's position (HDS would argue that the memorandum was a partial integration, a finding which would permit evidence of additional terms agreed upon orally).

87. **A**   Evidence of a person's prior habitual conduct is relevant to prove that his conduct on a particular occasion was in conformity with his habits; FRE 406. Since Dever "always" came around that ***particular*** corner at an excessive rate of speed, his conduct probably rises to the level of a "habit." Thus, the evidence is admissible to prove that Dever acted in conformity with his habits (a habit is a person's regular response to a particular type of situation) on the occasion in question. A witness who is not an expert may render an opinion (*i.e.*, that Dever's driving exceeded the speed limit) where it is (1) rationally based on his perception, and (2) helpful to the determination of a fact in issue; FRE 701. (*See* ELO Ch.3-X(D) and Ch.10-I(C)(6)(a)-(b).) Choice **B** is incorrect because (1) Dever's conduct is not hearsay since it was ***not*** intended as an assertion, FRE 801(a)(2); and (2) statements of the opponent in the litigation are not treated as hearsay; FRE 801(d)(2)(A). Choice **D** is incorrect because James' statement is ***not*** character evidence (rather it describes particular acts of the defendant on earlier occasions). Finally, Choice **C** is incorrect because, as described above, the evidence is neither hearsay nor inadmissible opinion. While prior conduct to prove the same conduct on a later occasion is ordinarily ***not*** admissible, evidence of conduct conforming to a habit is usually admitted; FRE 404(b) and 406.

88. **A**   A statement is not hearsay and may be admitted as substantive evidence if (1) the declarant testifies at the trial or hearing, (2) the declarant is subject to cross-examination and (3) the statement is inconsistent with his testimony and was given under oath at a trial, hearing, other proceeding, or in a deposition; FRE 801(d)(1)(A). Prior inconsistent statements of the witness are always a proper means of impeachment whether or not hearsay. (*See* ELO Ch.6-XIV(A)(4).) Choice **B** is incorrect because the report is double hearsay (the investigator is stating what Malcolm said) There is no indication that Malcolm's statement to the investigator for the insurance company was made under oath. Thus, it is hearsay, and therefore not admissible as substantive evidence. The investigator's statement might come within the "business records" exception to the hearsay rule, if it is deemed to be trustworthy. However, since ***all*** levels of hearsay within a statement must qualify as exceptions, the report is inadmissible. Choice **C** is incorrect because, while the written report of the investigator is hearsay, it is nevertheless admissible for the purpose of impeachment. In that context, the evidence is being offered

to discredit the witness, rather than for the purpose of proving whether the prior statement was true or not. Choice **D** is incorrect because it is not necessary that a witness first be asked to explain a prior inconsistent statement. Extrinsic evidence of a prior inconsistent statement is admissible if the witness is afforded an opportunity (before or after his testimony) to explain or deny the statement; FRE 613(b). Since Malcolm was on the stand, he would have an opportunity to explain or deny the statement purportedly given to the insurance company's investigator.

89. **A**   Statements are not hearsay if (1) the declarant testifies at the trial or hearing, (2) the declarant is subject to cross-examination concerning the statement, (3) the statement is consistent with his testimony, and (4) the statement is offered to rebut an express or implied charge of recent fabrication by, or improper influence upon, the declarant; FRE 801(d)(1)(B). Although Officer Oates is testifying as to what Walter said out-of-court, his testimony is not hearsay under this provision of the FRE. (*See* ELO Ch.6-XIV(C)(2).) Choice **B** is incorrect because the "business records" exception to the hearsay rule is applicable only to data compilations (*i.e.*, something written or, possibly, tape-recorded). Choice **C** is incorrect because the statement is not considered hearsay under the FRE. Finally, Choice **D** is incorrect because, while proof of a prior consistent statement by a witness is ordinarily **not** admissible, an exception to that rule exists under the FRE where the statement is offered to rebut an assertion of recent (*i.e.*, the threat to murder Walter one week ago) fabrication or improper influence; FRE 801(d)(1)(B).

90. **A**   Statements made by a decedent pertaining to his belief with respect to the execution, revocation, identification or terms of his will, for the purpose of proving the fact believed, are admissible as an exception to the hearsay rule; FRE 803(3). Although Ray's statement with respect to what Decker told him is hearsay, it proves Decker's belief that he had revoked a portion of his will. Since the evidence is being introduced to prove that Decker deleted the clause in question with the intention of preventing Otto from inheriting the sports car, an exception to the hearsay rule exists. (*See* ELO Ch.6-IV(C)(4)(e).) Choice **B** is incorrect because the statement in question does not pertain to the declarant's "then existing" state of mind, but to his intent in deleting the clause. Choice **D** is incorrect because "Dead Man" statutes apply to litigation about a transaction between the deceased and a survivor and limit testimony by the survivor. Finally, Choice **C** is incorrect because while Ray's statement of what Decker said out-of-court is hearsay, it is within an exception recognized by the FRE.

91. D A party's words or acts may be offered as evidence against him. This rule, for an admission by a party-opponent, applies only where the out-of-court statement is made by a party to the present proceeding, and where the statement is offered against, not for, the party who made it. There is no requirement that the party who made the statement be available to testify. Since Susan's statement meets these requirements, her statement is admissible as an admission by a party-opponent; FRE 801(d)(2)(A). (*See* ELO Ch.6-II(B) and (C).) Choice **A** is incorrect because the physician-patient privilege usually pertains only to statements made for the purpose of diagnosis or medical treatment and is limited to statements made to a physician. Thus, Susan's statement to a paramedic as to how the accident occurred would *not* appear to be within the purview of this privilege. However, it could be argued that the fact that Phil was a paramedic (as opposed to a doctor) would *not* preclude assertion of the privilege because (1) the paramedic might be considered essential personnel of the doctor who ultimately assisted Susan, or (2) Susan may have believed that Phil was a doctor. Choice **B** is incorrect because Susan's statement, the admission of a party-opponent, would not constitute hearsay FRE 801(d)(2)(A). Finally, Choice **C** is incorrect because the dying declaration exception to the hearsay rule is only available where the out-of-court declarant is unavailable; FRE 804(b)(2). (Note, however, that the federal rule does not require that the declarant have died.) Since Susan has now regained her health and counter-claimed, she is presumably capable of being called as a witness.

92. C Milton's statement was made outside of the present courtroom, and is therefore hearsay. But prior statements made under oath by an unavailable declarant constitute an exception to the hearsay rule if the party against whom the statements are offered had an opportunity and similar motive to question the declarant at the time the statements were made; FRE 804(b)(1). Choice **A** is incorrect because Jones did not have the opportunity to cross-examine Milton in the criminal case. Choice **B** is incorrect because Milton is not the party-opponent of Alex (Jones is the litigant in the present lawsuit). Finally, Choice **D** is incorrect because the fact that Milton was acquitted in the prior criminal case is not material in deciding whether or not his statement is admissible in the present litigation.

93. A An out-of-court statement which is offered into evidence not to prove the truth of the contents of the statement but simply to show that the statement was made, is not hearsay. Sally's statement is being offered into evidence not to prove that Mitchell ordinarily carried a switchblade knife, but that Karl reasonably believed that Mitchell might be reaching for a weapon when he struck him. (*See* ELO Ch.5-II(C)(5)(b).) Choice **B** is incorrect because a defendant in a criminal case may introduce evidence of specific acts of misconduct by the victim only where the victim's character trait is an essential element of the charge, claim or defense; FRE 405(b). Choice **C** is incorrect because Sally's statement was not hearsay, as explained above. Finally, Choice **D** is incorrect because the victim's character may be shown by evidence of acts of misconduct in crimes not involving homicide, if the character is an essential element of the charge, claim or defense (see above).

94. A   When an ambiguous physical act is accompanied by words that resolve the ambiguity, the accompanying words are called the "verbal part of the act," and are not hearsay since they are not offered into evidence to prove the truth of the matter asserted. Since the words in question tend to show that John did not intend the gift to Milt to be immediately operative, the words clarify the ambiguous physical act of John's handing the deed over to Milt. These words are the verbal part of the act, and are not hearsay. (*See* ELO Ch.5-II(C)(4).) Choice **B** is incorrect because the "statement against interest" exception to the hearsay rule is not applicable (Milt's statement is not hearsay at all and there is no showing that the statement is against John's interest). Choice **C** is incorrect because evidence pertaining to a condition precedent to the effectiveness of a document which appears to be complete on its face constitutes a recognized exception to the parol evidence rule. In such a case, the evidence is not being offered to modify or supplement the writing but to show only that the document was not to become effective until the occurrence of a particular condition. Finally, Choice **D** is incorrect because John's statement is not hearsay.

95. B   If a witness uses a writing to refresh his memory before testifying, the court, in its discretion and if it determines that it is necessary in the interests of justice, may permit an adverse party to (1) have the writing produced at the hearing, (2) inspect it, (3) cross-examine the witness thereon, and (4) introduce into evidence those portions of the writing which relate to the testimony of the witness; FRE 612. Since Garland used the Accident Report to refresh his memory prior to the trial, counsel for Banes may, with the court's permission, introduce into evidence the portion of the report dealing with Garland's testimony. (*See* ELO Ch.4-IV(B)(3).) Choice **C** is incorrect because the cross-examining party may introduce that portion of the writing which was used to refresh the witness's memory into evidence. Choice **D** is incorrect because Banes may be permitted to introduce into evidence the portion of the writing which related to Garland's testimony, whether or not it was consistent with Garland's testimony. Finally, Choice **A** is incorrect because only that part of the report introduced by Banes' attorney may be used on redirect. The entire report may not be introduced.

96. **A** Out-of-court statements made by a party-opponent are not hearsay; they are considered admissions; FRE 801(d)(2)(A). Mrs. Boone's testimony may seem to be double hearsay (she is testifying as to what her husband told her Dr. Fine said), but her testimony is admissible and is not deemed hearsay under the Federal Rules. Dr. Fine's statement would constitute a party-opponent admission. (*See* ELO CH.6-II(C).) Choice **B** is incorrect because the statements are not hearsay, and the "statement against interest" exception to the hearsay rule is not operative unless the declarant is unavailable. The facts do not state that Dr. Fine, who initiated the lawsuit, cannot be called as a witness. Choice **C** is incorrect because the right to assert or waive the physician-patient privilege would be held by Mrs. Boone (as the executrix of her husband's estate), rather than the physician. Finally, Choice **D** is incorrect because, even if Mr. Boone related Dr. Fine's statement to his wife in confidence, the privilege against testifying belonged to the husband or the wife, not to Dr. Fine.

97. **C** In cases in which character, or a trait of character, of a person is an essential element of a charge, claim or defense, proof may be made of specific instances of prior conduct showing that trait; FRE 405(b). Since an individual's character is very much in issue in determining whether he should have custody of a child, proof of specific instances of prior misconduct is admissible. (*See* ELO Ch.3-VIII(A)(4).) Choice **D** is incorrect because the Best Evidence Rule is only applicable where the witness is attempting to prove the contents of a document. Damien is testifying about what personally occurred to him (not about the contents of a document). Choice **A** is incorrect because character evidence may be admissible in non-criminal proceedings based on the character of a party. Finally, Choice **B** is incorrect because specific instances of conduct are admissible where an individual's character is an essential element of the case. Otherwise, a party's general reputation would exclude testimony as to specific acts contradicting or belying his reputation.

98. **C** Where specialized knowledge will assist the factfinder to understand the evidence or to determine a factual issue, a person qualified as an expert by her knowledge, skill, experience, training or education may testify with respect thereto; FRE 702. The determination whether a particular dog was an Australian Blue Hound probably requires an expert opinion. Since Wally was not apparently an expert about rare dog breeds his opinion as to the type of dog which attacked Paul (formed only from looking

at a photo in the library) was impermissible opinion. Additionally, since Wally is testifying about the contents of a writing, the Best Evidence Rule would also be applicable (*i.e.*, counsel for Paul would be obliged to introduce into evidence the pages of the book which Wally had reviewed). Wally's testimony is subject also to the objection that violates of the hearsay rule because he is testifying about the contents of a writing (*i.e.*, the pictures and "Australian Blue Hound" designation contained in the book). The book was not authenticated (*i.e.*, there was no proof that it was genuine). (*See* ELO Ch.10-II(B)(2).) Choice **D** is incorrect because, while bias is a proper form of impeachment, it would not constitute a basis for striking Wally's testimony which has no apparent element of bias. Choice **A** is incorrect because Wally, having witnessed the attack upon Paul, does have personal knowledge of the incident and of his conduct at the library. Finally, Choice **B** is incorrect because 100 feet is not such a great distance as to preclude Wally from being capable of identifying the type of dog which attacked Paul. The possible defect in Wally's perception caused by the distance, is a proper point to raise on cross-examination; but it is not a basis for excluding Wally's entire testimony.

99. C   A witness may be impeached via extrinsic evidence as to his ability to have observed the matter about which he testified. Since Sharon's testimony goes directly to William's ability to have perceived the incident in question, the objection to her testimony should be overruled.(*See* ELO Ch.4-XIII(A)(1)(d).) Choice **D** is incorrect because Sharon's testimony does not pertain to a collateral matter. Choice **A** is incorrect because marital infidelity is usually not considered a proper basis for impeachment. Many jurisdictions view such conduct as unrelated to truthfulness. In any case, even if it is viewed as a prior negative act bearing upon veracity, extrinsic evidence is not permissible (since no conviction resulted). Finally, Choice **B** is incorrect because impeachment evidence need not bear upon any substantive issue.

100. B   The federal psychotherapist-patient privilege applies to confidential communications made to psychiatrists, psychologists and to licensed social workers in the course of psychotherapy. FRE 501: *Jaffee v. Redmond*, 516 U.S. 1091 (1996). Since Jeffers received counseling from a licensed clinical social worker, the notes from these sessions are protected by the psychotherapist-patient privilege. Choice **A** is incorrect because the federal psychotherapist-patient privilege is an absolute, not a qualified, one, and therefore is not guided by a balancing test. Choice **C** is incorrect because Jeffers consulted with Karen for the purpose of receiving counseling, not to permit her to serve as an expert in the case.

Choice **D** is incorrect because the comments contained in the notes were not made immediately after Jeffers shot Roland but were made during the course of 50 counseling sessions.

101. **C** In a criminal case in which the defendant is accused of a sexual assault, evidence of the defendant's commission of another sexual assault is admissible, and may be considered for its bearing on any matter to which it is relevant; FRE 413(a). So the fact that Darby raped Maria is admissible to show that "If he did it before, he probably did it again." This is true, even if the circumstances surrounding the two crimes are quite different, and even though the prior crime took place a long time ago. It's also true even though Darby was never charged with, or convicted of, the prior crime. (*See* ELO Ch.3-IX(A) and (B).) Choice **A** is incorrect because while the rape of Maria is separate from and unrelated to the rape of Wanda, evidence of the defendant's commission of another rape is admissible. Choice **B** is incorrect because in a criminal case involving sexual assault, evidence that the defendant committed a prior sexual assault is admissible and may be considered on any matter to which it is relevant. Choice **D** is incorrect because the right to have this evidence admitted is absolute and does not depend on a balancing test.

102. **D** In a criminal case in which the defendant is accused of child molestation, evidence of a previous commission of child molestation by the defendant is admissible, and may be considered for its bearing on any matter to which it is relevant; FRE 414(a). So evidence of the previous child molestation may be admitted to show that "if he did it before, he probably did it again." (*See* ELO Ch.3-IX(A) and (B).) Choice **A** is incorrect because evidence of a previous child molestation is admissible even if there was no conviction. Choice **B** is incorrect because FRE 414 imposes no time limit on the other-crimes evidence. Choice **C** is incorrect because no balancing test is required to be used to admit this evidence.

103. **A** When an expert's testimony concerns a scientific test or principle, it must be shown that the scientific test or principle is "scientifically valid" and that it is relevant to an issue in the case; FRE 702. Some of the factors used in determining whether evidence is scientifically valid are: (1) whether the test can be reliably tested; (2) whether it's been subject to peer review and publication; (3) its error rate; and (4) whether it's generally accepted in the field. Since Dr. Jacobs' testimony meets these criteria and the testimony is relevant to a determination as to whose teeth marks are on the cheese, the testimony should be admissible. (*See* ELO Ch.10-

III(A)(2)(d)-(f).) Choice **B** is incorrect because in determining whether scientific evidence is admissible, the standard of whether the evidence is "generally accepted" was replaced by the standard of whether the evidence is "scientifically valid." General acceptance is still a factor, although no longer the sole factor to be considered. Choice **C** is incorrect because the evidence is in fact relevant to an issue in the case, that being, whose teeth marks are on the cheese. Choice **D** is incorrect because Dr. Jacobs, with his knowledge and skill in bite mark identification, is qualified to be treated as an expert.

Table of References to the Federal Rules of Evidence

Index

References are to the number of the question raising the issue.
"E" indicates an Essay Question; "M" indicates a Multiple-Choice Question

Products for 2000-01 Academic Year

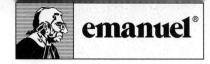 emanuel®

Emanuel Law Outlines

Steve Emanuel's Outlines have been the most popular in the country for years. Twenty years of graduates swear by them. In the 1999–00 school year, law students bought an average of 3.0 Emanuels each – that's 130,000 Emanuels.

Civil Procedure ◆	$19.95
Constitutional Law	23.95
Contracts ◆	19.95
Corporations	19.95
Criminal Law ◆	17.95
Criminal Procedure	17.95
Evidence	19.95
Property ◆	19.95
Secured Transactions	15.95
Torts (General Ed.) ◆	19.95
Torts (Casebook Ed.)	19.95
Keyed to '94 Ed. Prosser, Wade & Schwartz	
Also, Steve Emanuel's First Year Q&A's (see below)	$19.95

First Year Set

All outlines marked ◆ *plus* Steve Emanuel's First Year Q & A's *plus* Strategies & Tactics for First Year Law. Everything you need to make it through your first year.

Complete Set	*$105.50*

Question & Answer Collections

Siegel's Essay & Multiple–Choice Q & A's

Each book contains 20–25 essay questions with model answers, plus 90–120 Multistate-style multiple-choice Q & A's.

Civil Procedure ◆	$15.95
Constitutional Law	15.95
Contracts ◆	15.95
Corporations	15.95
Criminal Law ◆	15.95
Criminal Procedure	15.95
Evidence	15.95
Professional Responsibility	15.95
Real Property ◆	15.95
Torts ◆	15.95
Wills & Trusts	15.95

Siegel's First Year Set

All titles marked ◆ included in the this set.

Complete Set	*$64.95*

CrunchTime Series (New)

Designed to get you through the final days before exams. Each title contains: a Capsule Summary; Exam Tips; Flowcharts; Short-Answer Q&A's; and Essay Q&A's. All in a small, easy-to-carry format with less than 300 pages. And they come with a *30-day money-back guarantee* (see www.emanuel.com for details).

Civil Procedure*	$15.95
Constitutional Law*	15.95
Contracts*	15.95
Corporations**	15.95
Criminal Law*	15.95
Criminal Procedure**	15.95
Evidence**	15.95
Property**	15.95
Torts*	15.95

* Available Sept. 2000
** Available by late '00 or early '01

Emanuel Law Tapes - Constitutional Law

Includes mnemonics, skits, a special night-before-the-exam review tape, and a printed supplement.

11 Cassette Set, '98-99 Ed.	*$37.95*

Steve Finz's Multistate Method

967 MBE (Multistate Bar Exam) – style multiple choice questions and answers for all six Multistate subjects, each with detailed answers – *Plus* a complete 200 question practice exam modeled on the MBE – perfect for law school and **bar exam** review.

	$35.95

Steve Emanuel's First Year Q&A's

1,144 Objective–style short-answers question with detailed answers, in first year subjects. A single volume covers Contracts, Torts, Civil Procedure, Property, Criminal Law & Criminal Procedure.

	$19.95

For any titles not available at your local bookstore, call us at 1-800-EMANUEL or order on-line at **http://www.emanuel.com**. Visa, MasterCard, American Express, and Discover accepted.

Law in a Flash®

Law In A Flash

Flashcards or Software

Civil Procedure 1 ◆	$19.95
Civil Procedure 2 ◆	19.95
Constitutional Law ▲	19.95
Contracts ◆▲	19.95
Corporations	19.95
Criminal Law ◆▲	19.95
Criminal Procedure ▲	19.95
Evidence ▲	19.95
Federal Income Taxation	19.95
Future Interests ▲	19.95
Professional Responsibility (950 cards)	37.95
Real Property ◆▲	19.95
Sales (UCC Art.2) ▲	19.95
Torts ◆▲	19.95
Wills & Trusts	19.95

Law In A Flash Sets

First Year Law Set — 115.00
(includes all sets marked ◆ *plus* the book
Strategies & Tactics for First Year Law.)

Multistate Bar Review Set — 195.00
(includes all sets marked ▲ *plus* the book
Strategies & Tactics for MBE)

Professional Responsibility Set — 57.95
(includes the *Professional Responsibility* flashcards
plus the book Strategies & Tactics for the MPRE Exam.)

Professor Series

All titles in this series are written by leading law professors. Each follows the Emanuel style and format. Each has big, easy-to-read type, extensive citations and notes, and clear, crisp writing. Most have capsule summaries and sample exam Q & A's.

Agency & Partnership	$17.95
Bankruptcy	17.95
Environmental Law	17.95
Family Law	17.95
Federal Income Taxation	17.95
Intellectual Property	19.95
International Law	17.95
Labor Law	17.95
Neg. Instruments & Payment Systems	17.95
Professional Responsibility	18.95
Property	18.95
Torts	17.95
Wills & Trusts	17.95

Lazar Emanuel's Latin for Lawyers

This book defines every word and phrase derived from the Latin in common use by lawyers. Each listing gives the Latin derivation and meaning. Many of these will help you to understand how the law developed from its earliest days.

$15.95

Strategies & Tactics Series

Strategies & Tactics for the MBE

Packed with the most valuable advice you can find on how to successfully attack the MBE. Each MBE subject is covered, including Criminal Procedure (part of Criminal Law), Future Interests (part of Real Property), and Sales (part of Contracts). The book contains 350 actual past MBE questions broken down by subject, plus a full-length 200-question practice MBE. Each question has an answer which describes in detail not only why the correct answer is correct, but why each of the wrong answer choices is wrong.

Covers all the new MBE specifications on and after July, 1997.

$35.95

Strategies & Tactics for the First Year Law Student

A complete guide to your first year of law school, from the first day of class to studying for exams. Packed with the inside information that will help you survive what most consider the worst year of law school and come out on top.

$13.95

Strategies & Tactics for the MPRE

Packed with exam tactics that help lead you to the right answers and expert advice on spotting and avoiding the traps set by the Bar Examiners. Contains actual questions from past MPRE's with detailed answers.

$21.95

Prices effective 8/1/2000 through 7/31/2001.
Visit our website at **http://www.emanuel.com** for the latest product information.

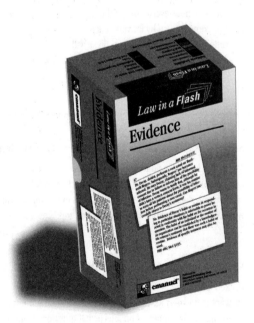

We'd like to know . . . .
Siegel's Evidence (3rd ed.)

We value your opinions on our study aids. After all, we design them for *your* use, and if you think we could do something better, we want to know about it. Please take a moment to fill out this survey and feedback form and return it to us. We'll enter you in our monthly drawing where 5 people will win the study aid of their choice! If you don't want to identify yourself, that's OK, but you'll be ineligible for the drawing.

Name: _____ Address: _____

City: _____ State: _____ Zip: _____ E-mail: _____

Law school attended: _____ Graduation year: _____

Please rate this product on a scale of 1 to 5:

General readability (style, format, etc.)........................... *Poor*	①	②	③	④	⑤	*Excellent*
Length of book (number of pages)................................. *Too short*	①	②	③	④	⑤	*Too long*
Essay questions... *Poorly written*	①	②	③	④	⑤	*Well written*
Multiple-choice questions .... *Poorly written*	①	②	③	④	⑤	*Well written*
End-of-book aids (tables & index) .... *Not useful*	①	②	③	④	⑤	*Useful*
Book's coverage of material presented in class .... *Incomplete*	①	②	③	④	⑤	*Complete*
OVERALL RATING...*Poor*	①	②	③	④	⑤	*Excellent*

Suggestions for improvement: _____
_____
_____

☛ **What other study aids did you use in this course?** _____
_____

☛ **If you liked any features of these other study aids, describe them:** _____
_____
_____

☛ **What casebook(s) did you use in this course?** _____

☛ **What study aids other than Emanuel do you use, and what features do you like about them?** _____
_____
_____

☛ **Please list the items you would like us to add to our product line:**

Outline subjects: _____

Flashcard subjects: _____

Other products (e.g., software, multimedia, etc.): _____

☛ **If you win our drawing, what one study aid would you like?** _____

Send to: *Emanuel Law* **Survey**   OR   Fax to: *(914) 834-5186*
         1328 Boston Post Road
         Larchmont, NY 10538

Please
complete & return
the Survey Form
on the other side